S0-BAE-135

Lewis Carroll
Interviews and Recollections

Charles Lutwidge Dodgson
(by kind permission of the Mansell Collection)

LEWIS CARROLL

Interviews and Recollections

Edited by

Morton N. Cohen

University of Iowa Press ᴪ Iowa City

First edition 1989
University of Iowa Press, Iowa City 52242

Printed in Hong Kong

International Standard Book Number 0–87745–231–8
Library of Congress Catalog Card Number 88–51149

Contents

PART IV　ARTISTS, WRITERS, OTHER OBSERVERS

Acknowledgements

I wish to thank Philip Dodgson Jaques for permission, given on behalf of the Dodgson Estate, to use the excerpts from transcripts of my conversations with his mother, Irene Dodgson Jaques, Lewis Carroll's last surviving niece; excerpts from her letters to me; and extracts of the reminiscences by F. Menella and Violet Dodgson in *The Diaries of Lewis Carroll*.

Special thanks must also go to Christina Colvin for the right to publish the extracts from the unpublished diary of Catherine Lucy Pollard and to Rosemary Olivier for permission to publish extracts from Edith Olivier's *Without Knowing Mr Walkley*, originally published by Faber and Faber.

In addition, the publishers and I wish to acknowledge the kindness of the following for granting us permission to use copyright material:

Allen & Unwin Ltd, for the extracts from Greville MacDonald's *George MacDonald and His Wife* and *Reminiscences of a Specialist*;

The Bodley Head Ltd, for the extract from Kate Terry Gielgud's *Autobiography*, published by Max Reinhardt Ltd;

Chapman & Hall Ltd, for the extract from Alan Mackinnon's *The Oxford Amateurs*;

Constable Publishers, for the extracts from Michael Sadleir's biography of his father, Michael Ernest Sadler, and for the extracts from Derek Hudson's *Lewis Carroll*;

J. M. Dent & Son Ltd, Publishers, for the extract from Isa Bowman's *The Story of Lewis Carroll*;

Grafton Books Ltd, for the extract from Laurence Irving's *The Successors*;

Hodder & Stoughton Ltd, for the extracts from Claude M. Blagden's *Well Remembered*;

Macmillan Publishers Ltd, for extracts from Evelyn M. Hatch's *A Selection from the Letters of Lewis Carroll . . . to His Child-Friends* and Charles Morgan's *The House of Macmillan*;

Muller, Blond and White Ltd, for the extract from Sydney Fairbrother's *Through a Stage Door*;

the Editors of *Notes and Queries*, for the extract from Stanley Godman's 'Lewis Carroll's Sister: Henrietta Dodgson', which appeared in volume 203, January 1958;

the Editor of the *Observer*, for the extract from Mrs Shawyer's 'Letter to the Editor';

Oxford University Press, for the extract from H. A. L. Fisher's *An Unfinished Autobiography*;

the Editor of *The Times*, for the extract from T. B. Strong's article.

I have tried to trace all the copyright-holders of the material in this volume, but I have not always succeeded in finding them. If I have infringed upon or inadvertently overlooked any copyright, I apologize in advance and will be happy to make an acknowledgement in a future reprinting of this volume.

As always, I am deeply indebted to Richard N. Swift for his careful surveillance of my work.

New York   M. N. C.

Short Titles

Diaries Entries from C. L. Dodgson's diaries that appeared in *The Diaries of Lewis Carroll*, ed. Roger Lancelyn Green, 2 vols (1953)

Diaries Passages from Dodgson's diaries that do not appear in the published *Diaries* (above)

Gernsheim Helmut Gernsheim, *Lewis Carroll Photographer*, rev. edn (1969)

Handbook Sidney Herbert Williams and Falconer Madan, *The Lewis Carroll Handbook*, rev. Roger Lancelyn Green, further rev. Denis Crutch (1979)

Hatch *A Selection from the Letters of Lewis Carroll to His Child-Friends*, ed. Evelyn M. Hatch (1933)

Hudson Derek Hudson, *Lewis Carroll* (1954)

Jabberwocky *Jabberwocky*: the Journal of the Lewis Carroll Society

Letters *The Letters of Lewis Carroll*, ed. Morton N. Cohen with the assistance of Roger Lancelyn Green, 2 vols (1979)

Life and Letters Stuart Dodgson Collingwood, *The Life and Letters of Lewis Carroll* (1898)

Picture Book *The Lewis Carroll Picture Book*, ed. Stuart Dodgson Collingwood (1899)

Reed Langford Reed, *The Life of Lewis Carroll* (1932)

Introduction

Lewis Carroll spells paradox. Not literally, of course, but in everything connected with the name. Indeed, if we could somehow make *paradox* an anagram of *Lewis Carroll*, we should do full justice to the author's spirit and might even hear him chuckling neath the eaves. The name *Lewis Carroll* is all air anyway; the man himself was Charles Lutwidge Dodgson, a hard-working, devout, conservative Victorian who by chance wrote two unusual children's books that changed for all time the course of storytelling and of children's literature.

The first obvious paradox is that a staid, unobtrusive mathematics don and clergyman could provide the unbridled laughter, whimsy, and wit that transcend time, place, nationality, even political, social, and language differences, and catapult the *Alice* books into the firmament of world classics. The facts are all the more amazing when we recall that Mr Dodgson was one of the shyest, most reserved, least public figures of all time. The limelight was anathema to him; any personal reference to him in the press saddened him, thrust him into deep gloom, even sickened him.

But Charles Dodgson has been dead for almost a century now, and he himself recognized that, in death, one loses the right to withhold facts. He knew that history has its way, voices speak out, memory is enshrined. It is certainly high time for a collection of reminiscences of this paradoxical gentleman to appear.

The only fit introduction to Charles Dodgson is through that inspired pair of children's stories that he wrote and that show how thin and fragile the thread is that sometimes leads to artistry. Indeed, the remarkable story of what happened when a girl named Alice fell down a rabbit hole might never have been preserved for posterity had one of the children who first heard it not pestered the teller of the tale to write it down.

The persistent young girl, Alice Pleasance Liddell, aged ten, daughter of the Dean of Christ Church, Oxford, was the model for the story's heroine. The storyteller was thirty years old, also of Christ Church, when, on 4 July 1862, he took Alice and her two sisters on a river picnic. As they glided over the water, the children demanded a story. They had grown accustomed to having stories from their friend Mr Dodgson, and today they wanted another. This time he made up a new one, on the spot, just for them. They liked it most particularly and made him continue the tale when they met later on. And then the middle sister, Alice herself, insisted that Mr Dodgson commit it to paper for her.

By her own admission, she kept nagging him about it. Finally, he bought a small notebook, wrote out his tale in a careful script and illustrated it with his own drawings. In the front he inscribed it, 'A Christmas Gift to a Dear Child in Memory of a Summer Day', and he gave the booklet to Alice in 1864, more than two years after he invented the first instalment. It was probably the most valuable gift a child has ever received. The following year, he published an enlarged version under his *nom de plume*. It transformed his life, and Alice's too: that casually created tale made both Lewis Carroll and Alice Liddell world famous.

What is more, today, well over a century after the publication of *Alice's Adventures in Wonderland* and the sequel that followed seven years later, Lewis Carroll remains one of the most popular writers of all time. Along with the Bible and Shakespeare, he is most widely quoted by statesmen, literary figures, and just plain folks. Millions of copies of the *Alice* books have been printed, they have been translated into more than fifty languages (some thirty different translations into French alone have appeared), and they have been adapted for the stage, made into films, and remade several times for television. They have inspired poems, musical compositions, and monuments, apart from the constant avalanche of tea towels, children's pottery, decorative wall plates, and all manner of clothing and artefacts that fit well into jumble sales.

But, more important, they have revolutionized writing for children: children's books after Carroll are less serious, more entertaining, contain less the tone of the preacher and more the voice of a friend. Moreover, the influence of the *Alice* books upon children growing up and upon the minds and hearts of mature people has been considerable.

It is not surprising, then, that scholars and critics have tried to get at the heart of the books to analyse them, to understand the magic that makes them so universally popular and meaningful. Nor is it surprising that they have been curious about the man behind the books. Dodgson's life has indeed been scrutinized: editions of his diaries and letters have been published, a bibliography of his writings has been revised three times, and library shelves hold innumerable critiques of the *Alice* books. It is, in fact, difficult to think of a serious critic, poet or essayist who has not written something about Carroll. The list of those who have includes W. H. Auden, Kenneth Burke, G. K. Chesterton, John Ciardi, William Empson, Robert Graves, Harry Levin, Walter de la Mare, Vladimir Nabokov, Joyce Carol Oates, J. B. Priestley, Saki, Allen Tate, Edmund Wilson, Virginia Woolf, and Alexander Woolcott.

Part of the paradox is the 'ordinary' man behind the name. We find nothing remarkable about the life that Charles Dodgson led. He was born on 27 January 1832, in Daresbury, Cheshire, the eldest son (the third of eleven children) of an intelligent and sensitive cleric. He grew up in what appears to have been a pleasant domestic environment. The family was solid English stock on both sides, with a heavy sprinkling of clergy, an occasional bishop, and the odd military man on the family tree. With effort, a claim could even be made of a distant relationship to Queen Victoria. It was an upper-crust family, steeped in tradition, religious, devoted to serving God, country, and mankind. But it was not remarkably distinguished or in any way notorious. It was British to the core, even to the point of intermarrying: Charles Dodgson's mother and father were both grandchildren of Charles Dodgson, Bishop of Elphin (1722?–95).

Dodgson's father could be witty and whimsical at times, but, on the whole, he was occupied with his clerical duties and gives the impression of a strong, stolid, authoritarian, sometimes high and dry churchman. We know less about Dodgson's mother. She died before his nineteenth birthday. She was, it seems, a gentle creature, and, with eleven children, a busy one. In his few allusions to her, Dodgson is kind and affectionate. But his relationship with his father was more important. Father and son developed close sympathies early, in the years when the father was the boy's tutor. Dodgson adopted his father as his model: his principles, his character, his faith, and his ambitions mirrored the parent's. The father died in 1868, when the son was thirty-six, but even years later, when the son himself was greying, he called that loss 'the greatest sorrow of my life'.

The son had as good a childhood as Victorian times allowed. He had a gaggle of sisters and brothers to play with, and, because the family had moved to Yorkshire when the father took up a living at Croft, near Ripon, soon after the lad's birth, Dodgson enjoyed walks and outings in the country, in touch with nature. He was good at mechanical things and built a miniature railway in the back garden and a puppet theatre for which he wrote original plays. He was also an avid reader, had a good memory, liked to sketch and paint and write poetry and short stories. But most of all he learned to live a purposeful life: much of his energy was to be spent in the service of God and for the benefit of others.

When Charles Dodgson left home for the first time for school, he was twelve. He went to Richmond School, not far from home, but far enough to lodge there. When he enrolled at Richmond, he was already proficient in higher mathematics and could read Latin easily and write it well. He entered Richmond School, one might argue, with more in his head than most young people today have in theirs when they enter – perhaps even when they leave – college.

But, if life was so serious, whence came that whimsy that was to make Charles Dodgson, as Lewis Carroll, famous? In fact, it was there from childhood, or, at least, its roots were, as Dodgson's youthful jottings prove. His early compositions are not only inventive but also delightful, clever, spell-binding, and, indeed, whimsical. The moral tone is present, and the purposefulness, but they blend with the whimsy into a confection that we have come to recognize as characteristically Carrollian.

Like so many Victorian families, the Dodgsons produced a stack of home-made, hand-sewn family magazines. The earliest of these scrapbooks is appropriately entitled *Useful and Instructive Poetry*; it is entirely the work of Charles Dodgson, aged thirteen. It contains fifteen verses and some pencil and watercolour sketches. Three of the verses are entitled 'Punctuality', 'Charity' and 'Rules and Regulations'. They wear the cloak of seriousness, but in reality the sombre titles mask the whimsical contents. Here is the first verse of the collection, complete with moral tag:

My Fairy

I have a fairy by my side
   Which says I must not sleep,
When once in pain I loudly cried
   It said 'You must not weep.'

If, full of mirth, I smile and grin,
   It says 'You must not laugh,'
When once I wished to drink some gin,
   It said 'You must not quaff.'

When once a meal I wished to taste
   It said 'You must not bite,'
When to the wars I went in haste,
   It said 'You must not fight.'

'What *may* I do?' At length I cried,
   Tired of the painful task,
The fairy quietly replied,
   And said 'You must not ask.'

Moral: 'You mustn't.'

Charles Dodgson remained at Richmond School for only a year and a half, boarding with the headmaster and his huge family in what must have been a close replica of his own home.

He next went to Rugby, but his three years there were not his happiest. Bashful and contemplative, he did not fit well into the rough-and-ready atmosphere of the public schoolboys' world. His studies did not, however, suffer. If he felt no enthusiasm for Rugby, the school still left its mark on him. The strong, militant preaching of Dr Thomas Arnold still echoed in the school chapel, and Dodgson came away convinced, as Dr Arnold had been, that life was a struggle between good and evil, between God and the devil, and that one must defeat the devil by means of self-denial, strong discipline, and righteous, uncompromising thought and action. Given his family background and his school training, it is fitting that he was ordained deacon before his thirtieth birthday.

But, before then, he went from Rugby to Oxford, to the same college where his father had earned a double first, Christ Church. Here too he made a good academic record and in 1855 was made a Student (equivalent to Fellow) of the college and was appointed Mathematical Lecturer.

Dodgson had eclectic interests. He liked gadgets and invented a few himself. He dabbled in art and enjoyed drawing, especially from live models, sometimes nudes. He moved freely among artists and was acquainted with many, including the Pre-Raphaelites. He was himself an early art photographer, and his camera portraits of Tennyson, the Rossettis, Ellen Terry and her family, and many less famous people rank with those of Julia Margaret Cameron. He stands alone, in Helmut Gernsheim's words (p. 28), as 'the most outstanding photographer of children in the nineteenth century'. He courageously spoke out on behalf of the theatre as a wholesome means of education and entertainment. He spent much time in London visiting art galleries, theatres, friends; he went regularly to Guildford in Surrey, where his unmarried sisters and brothers lived after their father's death in 1868; and he spent summers at the seaside, usually Eastbourne, on writing holidays. He travelled abroad only once, in the summer of 1867, across Europe to Russia and back.

Dodgson was deeply and genuinely religious, withdrawn from and untroubled by the theological storms of the day. He never married. His natural reticence was intensified by his stammer and by deafness in his right ear.[1] He lived a highly regulated life, ate little, worked hard. He was a compulsive record-keeper: a letter-register he began half-way through his life recorded that in the last thirty-five years of his life he sent and received 98,721 letters.

Dodgson's self-control and stern determination helped him rack up a formidable record of accomplishment. Most people have read the *Alice* books, and some know that he wrote works on mathematics and logic. But not all realize that, by any standard, Dodgson's life was one of enormous productivity, that his bibliography contains some 300 separately published items.

For one thing, he was a prolific poet. Three volumes of his verse appeared in his lifetime and one posthumously: *Phantasmagoria and Other Poems* (1869), *The Hunting of the Snark* (1876), *Rhyme? and Reason?* (1883), and *The Three Sunsets and Other Poems* (1898). He wrote a considerable quantity of occasional verse, acrostics, and verse puzzles, some of which he used as inscriptions in copies of his books that he gave to child friends. *The Collected Verse of Lewis Carroll* (1932) contains the bulk of his output, but a fair amount of manuscript verse has come to light since and a new collection is badly needed.

Dodgson published mathematical treatises for the serious student and specialist. These include *A Syllabus of Plane Algebraical Geometry* (1860), *Euclid and his Modern Rivals* (1879), *Curiosa Mathematica, Part I* (1888) and *Part II* (1893), and *Symbolic Logic, Part I* (1896). Much of his *Symbolic Logic, Part II* was discovered after he died and appeared in print in 1977.[2] This last publication has led mathematicians and philosophers to reassess more favourably Dodgson's contributions to both mathematics and logic.

But not all of his mathematical works are awesome or even designed for the specialist. He actually wrote more mathematical books for the general reader than for mathematicians. Because his greatest interest centred on his child friendships, he spent much of his energy providing a mathematical education and supplying innocent recreations for children. He was good at playing games and at devising them. Many of his young friends illustrate in this volume how clever and amusing Mr Dodgson was. He taught Alfred Tennyson's children 'elephant-hunters' and showed two of Queen Victoria's grandchildren how to fold paper pistols and to blot their names in creased paper. One other child friend recalled that 'As time went on, and the children grew older, games such as Lanrick, which was played on a chess-board, or word-puzzles, such as Syzygies, Misch Masch, and Doublets took the place of toys.' These names, along with others that Dodgson invented, have entered our language. In time, they became the titles of books that he published in the hope of amusing and educating a larger circle of children than he could ever know personally.

Both layman and specialist take warmly to the added spice and whimsy in almost all his mathematical writings, however serious in purpose. The exercises he invented, the paradoxes he posed, the examples he supplied are all couched in drama and suspense and are infused with an intrinsic sense of fun, a quality of real life. For his students, in both tutorials and classes, mathematics and logic must have come alive as never before. No wonder, too, that professional mathematicians the world over smile irrepressibly when they refer to Dodgson's 'Barber-Shop Paradox' or to his 'Paradox of Achilles and the Tortoise'. For these inventions, too, bear the humour and the genius characteristic of the *Alice* books and, like those books, have become ingrained in our culture.

But Dodgson did more than write and teach. Though he never held a curacy, he frequently took Sunday service for others. On several occasions, in fact, a university congregation filled St Mary's, Oxford, to capacity to hear him preach. For more than nine years, he held the curatorship of Christ Church Senior Common Room, an arduous job requiring close attention to detail and keen business acumen. He also did a good amount of parochial work of one sort or another.

Dodgson lived his entire mature life simply, in college rooms. He allowed himself modest pleasures but nothing extravagant, he ate frugally when he ate at all, and he usually dressed in black. For much of his life, he helped support his sisters and brothers, and other people as well, relatives, friends, even strangers. He was always willing to take on new students, and he stood ready, albeit with genuine modesty, to try to help young and old with spiritual problems. When he realized that his children's books would yield a modest income for the rest of his life, he actually asked the University of Oxford to reduce his salary.[3]

These biographical details say much about Charles Dodgson, but they do not explain how this sheltered academic managed to encompass two disparate worlds within one being or how he succeeded in writing serious mathematical tomes on the one hand and in creating nonsensical flights into Wonderland on the other. Perhaps the most important clue to untangling the knot is his exceptional interest in children, particularly the female of the species, whom he generally preferred to adults and in whose company he often lost his stammer. He had more than a preference for associating with children – he also had an uncanny insight into their beings. But how could a bachelor living in an all-male college understand the child well enough to write two children's classics?

The answer reveals itself in the facts of his life. As a child, Dodgson was himself extremely sensitive and especially gifted – we have seen that. He learned the lessons of duty and responsibility early as well, and, as the eldest boy in a large family, he took it upon himself to instruct and amuse his brothers and sisters. The family magazines that he wrote and edited for them gave free rein to his imagination and marked his beginnings as a creative writer for children. Later, he always remembered his childhood, with the joys and glooms that punctuated it. Because of that vivid memory, he knew instinctively how, in his relationships with children, to avoid the unintentional callous remark, the rebuke, condescending baby talk or impatient explanations – the insensitive behaviour by which adults so often alienate the young. Dodgson concentrated on finding new ways of enlightening them, helping them, pleasing them, amusing them, and – perhaps where he performed his greatest service – making them shriek with laughter.

Was it unforgivably frivolous in a cleric to spin tales and make his impressionable friends, and later his readers, burst into laughter? In Dodgson's view, it was not. He believed that enjoying life neither diminished its seriousness nor violated the canons of the Church or the lessons of Scripture. For him nothing wrong inhered in fun and laughter at the right time and in the right place.

How could a professional mathematician, thinking customarily along strict, straight, disciplined lines, abandon all logic and create disjointed worlds where systems and order break down completely and where nonsense rules? But Dodgson, like the rest of us, liked to take a holiday once in a while and let his mind run outside the confining grooves of academic discipline. Besides, no one unskilled in logic could have created the special brand of illogic that so delights us in the *Alice* books, *The Hunting of the Snark* and other works.

We have, then, a man with an impressionable nature, a good memory of his own childhood, a deep sense of fun, and a turn for adventurous illogic: do these elements satisfactorily explain Charles Dodgson? Not entirely. We must consider at least one more important element – his genius. After all, he told the first *Alice* story spontaneously on a river picnic near Oxford. He knew that a story would amuse his three child companions, and so he simply made one up. In those few moments on the river, Charles Dodgson Oxford don became Lewis Carroll storyteller. He surely realized then, perhaps earlier, that he was gifted with an exceptional facility not given to all. He must also have realized that his gift was to be treasured and meant to be fanned into life again and again.

He must have realized too that his partiality for young female friends was connected with his exceptional gift, that these creatures ignited the spark, stimulated his creative faculties, fired his imagination. And, indeed, for them he composed not only the *Alice* books, but later ones as well. Fanciful work followed fanciful work, all stimulated by his friendships, all meant for his child friends, all dedicated to individual children.

Some analysts insist that ominous, deep-seated desires prompted Carroll's particular interest in female children, and they see a Mr Hyde lurking behind Dr Jekyll. But we have not yet found precise scientific tools and techniques for understanding subconscious promptings clearly or for interpreting them conclusively. Limited as we are by imperfect and often conflicting analytical readings, we are perhaps on sounder ground seeing Dodgson on the conscious plane, examining his attitudes and noting his behaviour. From the evidence we have in these collected reminiscences, Dodgson sought friendships untrammelled by sexual overtones. The better one comes to know the man, the clearer one sees that his associations with young females, while indeed romantic, achieved a quality nowhere base, but rather uplifting both for him and for his young friends.

Here is how, in a letter to a child friend, he wrote about love:

> Photographs are very pleasant things to have, but *love* is the best thing in the world. . . . Of course I don't mean it in the sense meant when people talk about 'falling in love': that's only *one* meaning of the word, and only applies to a few people. I mean in the sense in which we say that everybody in the world ought to 'love everybody else'. But we don't always do what we ought. I think you children do it more than we grown-up people do; *we* find so many faults in one another.[4]

Elsewhere he wrote to the mother of a young friend, '*many* thanks for again lending me Enid. She is one of the dearest children. It is *good* for one (I mean, for one's spiritual life, and in the same sense in which reading the Bible is good) to come into contact with such sweetness.'[5]

To another mother he wrote, 'you need not thank me for kindness to her! Who could help being kind to her? and where is the merit of doing what one cannot help? It is very sweet to me, to be loved by her as children love. . . .'[6]

Whatever was locked in Dodgson's subconscious being, he consciously worshipped innocence, purity, and beauty as he perceived them – and he knew full well the dangers and temptations that hovered over his world of romantic friendship. But, like other Victorians, he successfully suppressed his sexual promptings. He was a master at regulating his life, and superhuman, surely in our terms, in controlling his impulses. He lived a celibate life and so could court the delicate friendships he so enjoyed.

Dodgson's life was reasonably healthy and happy. Even in his sixties, one detects no decline in physical or mental agility. In reality, a quiet contentment overtakes him, as we see in a letter he wrote to one of his sisters when he was sixty-four:

> news [of other people's death] comes less and less of a shock: and more and more one realizes that it is an experience each of *us* must face, before long. That fact is getting *less* dreamlike to me, now: and I sometimes think what a grand thing it will be to be able to say to oneself 'Death is *over*, now: there is not *that* experience to be faced, again!' . . . I am beginning to realize that, if the *books* I am still hoping to write, are to be done *at all*, they must be done *now*, and that I am *meant* thus to utilize the splendid health I have had, unbroken, for the last year and a half, and the working-powers, that are fully as great as, if not greater than, what I have ever had.[7]

On 23 December 1897, he travelled from Oxford to Guildford to join his family for the Christmas holiday. On 5 January, he learned that his brother-in-law had suddenly died. Then Dodgson himself came down with a fever and chest cold. Today, his symptoms would have been dealt with routinely, with antibiotics. But, in 1898, bronchial infections were much more serious than they are today. Dodgson's condition worsened, and on 14 January, thirteen days before he would have turned sixty-six, he died of pneumonia. He was buried where he died, in Guildford, the only home he had away from Oxford.

We have no actual interviews with either Charles Dodgson or Lewis Carroll: Dodgson would have been appalled at the thought of giving one. Beatrice Hatch tells us (p. 103, below) what happened when a stranger managed to penetrate Dodgson's *sanctum sanctorum* seeking an interview, and one of Dodgson's obituaries records the incident of a reporter from the *Daily Chronicle* requesting some biographical facts and a photograph. The reply was 'in the negative with a half-brick. ... he could be almost insolent to such inquirers ...', the writer adds.[8]

A few interviews with members of his family and with close friends and associates survive, however; together with material gleaned from memoirs and reminiscences, they capture the man in sharp relief and help us grasp the subtle qualities of his character and personality.

NOTES

1. Although Dodgson's mother attributes his deafness to 'Infantile fever' (in a letter to her sister Lucy Lutwidge dated 11 Nov [?1846]: Dodgson Family Papers), Selwyn H. Goodacre suggests that deafness may have resulted from mumps – see 'The Illness of Lewis Carroll', *Practitioner*, 209 (Aug 1972) 230–9. In any event, Dodgson remained deaf in his right ear for the rest of his life.
2. See *Lewis Carroll's Symbolic Logic, Part I and Part II*, ed. W. W. Bartley III (1977).
3. *Diaries*, p. 386.
4. *Letters*, p. 869.
5. Ibid., p. 905.
6. Ibid., p. 441.
7. Ibid., p. 1100.
8. 'Death of the Author of *Alice in Wonderland*', *St James's Gazette*, 15 Jan 1898, p. 15.

Biographical Chronology

1832   Born 27 Jan, the eldest son (third of eleven children) of Charles Dodgson, Perpetual Curate of Daresbury, Cheshire, and Frances Jane (born Lutwidge).

1843   Father becomes Rector of Croft, Yorkshire, and family moves there.

1844–5   At Richmond School, Yorkshire (from 1 Aug 1844).

1846–9   At Rugby School (from 27 Jan 1846).

1850   Matriculates at Christ Church, Oxford (23 May).

1851   Takes up residence at Christ Church (24 Jan).
Mother dies (26 Jan).

1852   Student of Christ Church (Dec 1852 until his death).

1854   BA (first-class honours in Mathematics; second-class in Classics).

1855   Sub-Librarian, Christ Church (until 1857).
Mathematical Lecturer (until 1881).

1857   MA

1861   Ordained deacon (22 Dec).

1862   Tells the story of Alice's adventures to the Liddell sisters on a boat trip (4 July).

1865   *Alice's Adventures in Wonderland* published (July).

1867   Journey through Europe with H. P. Liddon (13 July–14 Sep).

1868   Father dies (21 June).
Moves his family to Guildford (1 Sep).

1869   *Phantasmagoria* published.

1871   *Through the Looking-Glass and What Alice Found There* published (Dec).

1876   *The Hunting of the Snark* published (Mar).

1877   First takes Eastbourne summer lodgings (31 July).

1879   *Euclid and his Modern Rivals* published.

1881   Resigns mathematical lectureship (but retains his studentship) to devote more time to writing.

1882   Curator of Senior Room, Christ Church (Dec 1882 to Feb 1892).

1885   *A Tangled Tale* published.

1886   *Alice's Adventures Under Ground* published.

1887   *The Game of Logic* published (Feb).

1888   *Curiosa Mathematica, Part I* published.
1889   *Sylvie and Bruno* published.
1890   *The Nursery 'Alice'* published.
1892   Resigns curatorship of Senior Common Room, Christ Church
        (Feb).
1893   *Curiosa Mathematica, Part II* published.
        Sylvie and Bruno Concluded published.
1896   *Symbolic Logic, Part I* published (21 Feb).
1898   Dies at Guildford (14 Jan) and is buried there.
        Three Sunsets and Other Poems published.

PART I

Childhood and Family

Beginning*

STUART DODGSON COLLINGWOOD[1]

On January 27, 1832, Charles Lutwidge Dodgson was born at Daresbury [Cheshire], of which parish his father was then incumbent. The village ... is about seven miles from Warrington; its name is supposed to be derived from a word meaning oak, and certainly oaks are very plentiful in the neighbourhood. A canal passes through an outlying part of the parish. ...

The parsonage is situated a mile and a half from the village, on the glebe-farm, having been erected by a former incumbent. ... Here it was that Charles spent the first eleven years of his life – years of complete seclusion from the world, for even the passing of a cart was a matter of great interest to the children.

In this quiet home the boy invented the strangest diversions for himself; he made pets of the most odd and unlikely animals, and numbered certain snails and toads among his intimate friends. He tried to encourage civilized warfare among earthworms, by supplying them with small pieces of pipe, with which they might fight if so disposed. His notions of charity at this early age were somewhat rudimentary; he used to peel rushes with the idea that the pith would afterwards 'be given to the poor', though what possible use they could put it to he never attempted to explain. Indeed he seems at this time to have actually lived in that charming 'Wonderland' which he afterwards described so vividly; but for all that he was a thorough boy, and loved to climb the trees and to scramble about in the old marl-pits. ...

Mr Dodgson from the first used to take an active part in his son's education, and the following anecdote will show that he had at least a pupil who was anxious to learn. One day, when Charles was a very small boy, he came up to his father and showed him a book of logarithms, with the request, 'Please explain.' Mr Dodgson told him that he was much too young to understand anything about such a difficult subject. The child listened to what his father said, and appeared to think it irrelevant, for he still insisted, '*But*, please, explain!'

* *Life and Letters*, pp. 9–21.

On one occasion Mr and Mrs Dodgson went to Hull, to pay a visit to the latter's father, who had been seriously ill. From Hull Mrs Dodgson wrote to Charles, and he set much store by this letter, which was probably one of the first he had received. He was afraid that some of his little sisters would mess it, or tear it up, so he wrote upon the back, 'No one is to touch this note, for it belongs to C. L. D.'; but, this warning appearing insufficient, he added, 'Covered with slimy pitch, so that they will wet their fingers.' . . .

In 1843 Sir Robert Peel presented . . . [Mr Dodgson] to the Crown living of Croft, a Yorkshire village about three miles south of Darlington. This preferment made a great change in the life of the family; it opened for them many more social opportunities, and put an end to that life of seclusion which, however beneficial it may be for a short time, is apt, if continued too long, to have a cramping and narrow influence. . . .

Charles was at this time very fond of inventing games for the amusement of his brothers and sisters; he constructed a rude train out of a wheelbarrow, a barrel and a small truck, which used to convey passengers from one 'station' in the Rectory garden to another. At each of these stations there was a refreshment-room, and the passengers had to purchase tickets from him before they could enjoy their ride.[2] The boy was also a clever conjuror, and, arrayed in a brown wig and a long white robe, used to cause no little wonder to his audience by his sleight-of-hand. With the assistance of various members of the family and the village carpenter, he made a troupe of marionettes and a small theatre for them to act in. He wrote all the plays himself – the most popular being 'The Tragedy of King John' – and he was very clever at manipulating the innumerable strings by which the movements of his puppets were regulated. One winter, when the snow lay thick upon the lawn, he traced upon it a maze of such hopeless intricacy as almost to put its famous rival at Hampton Court in the shade.

NOTES

1. Lewis Carroll's first nephew (the first child of his sister Mary) was born in January 1870. He later entered Christ Church and became a friend and sometime companion of his uncle. He took a BA in theology in 1892 and in time became Professor at St Edmund's Seminary, Ware, and Headmaster at St Gerard's School, Bray, Co. Wicklow, where he died in 1937. His biography of his uncle, which draws considerably on the memoirs of the surviving family members, appeared in the year of Carroll's death.

2. Living at Croft, the Dodgson family were keenly aware of the earliest passenger line, running as it did from nearby Darlington to Stockton; and, before Charles left Richmond School in 1846, both Croft and Richmond had their own railway stations. Charles clearly came under the spell of the railway mania of the time. He made up a timetable and rules for operating his railway, and wrote a three-act comic opera

entitled *Guida di Bragia*, burlesquing Bradshaw's Railway Guide, for his own marionette theatre. Manuscripts of both survive (the timetable and rules at Harvard; the opera in the Berol Collection, New York University).

The Young Poet–Artist*

STUART DODGSON COLLINGWOOD

When the boy was about eleven years old . . . [he] began to show great taste for drawing; he kept a little book in which he used to sketch roughly any humorous ideas that occurred to him, and these pictures were afterwards painted by his brothers and sisters, who all regarded him as a paragon of wit and cleverness. No wonder, for from the first he was always the leader in their amusements, and was continually inventing all sorts of games to please himself and them. . . .

It is a curious fact that though so many different sorts of animals figure in Lewis Carroll's books, and even play more or less important *rôles*, as the white rabbit in *Alice's Adventures*, yet he never seemed to care about animals himself. He hated, indeed, to see them ill-treated in any way, and would go out of his way to relieve their distress when he could, while the preface to *Sylvie and Bruno* contains an emphatic denunciation of 'sport' when it involves suffering to animals. But he never kept pets of any sort, and very much resented it if any of his friends kept that unpleasant species of dog which makes a point of barking at everyone who comes up to the house. Even as a child, he did not care much about the rabbits and chickens and other such creatures which his brothers and sisters were so fond of. It must be recorded, however, that in very early youth the charms of snails and earth-worms proved too much for him, and he used to try to add to their 'joy of living' by providing them with sticks to fight with 'if so dispoged!' But he soon overcame any such amiable weakness, and used, as we shall see, to make fun of the other members of the family about their pets.

Somewhere about the year 1845 he felt the first stirrings of literary ambition, and started a magazine called *Useful and Instructive Poetry*. Of this periodical . . . he was the editor and contributor-in-chief: its circulation was limited by the walls of Croft Rectory, and it died an untimely death after a life of only six months. It was followed by a

* From 'Before "Alice" – The Boyhood of Lewis Carroll', *Strand Magazine*, 16 (Dec 1898) 616–27.

host of equally short-lived ventures, in the following order: 'The Rectory Magazine', 'The Comet', 'The Rosebud', 'The Star', 'The Will-o'-the Wisp', and 'The Rectory Umbrella'. The last . . . was started on its career about 1849. Lewis Carroll wrote all the articles, and drew all the pictures himself, and I think everyone will agree that for a boy of seventeen to have produced them is a proof that he was already gifted with very remarkable talent. . . . Some years after the decease of the 'Umbrella', Lewis Carroll, now upon the verge of manhood, started his last family magazine, 'Misch-Masch'. . . . It consisted largely of printed stories and verses, which he had written for the *Oxonian Advertiser* and the *Whitby Gazette*, but a good part of it was then 'published' for the first time.[1]

NOTE

1. Four of the Dodgson family magazines survive: the first two, *Useful and Instructive Poetry* and *The Rectory Magazine*, and the last two, *The Rectory Umbrella* and *Misch-Masch*. All four have been published, *The Rectory Umbrella* in facsimile. The earliest, entirely the work of the thirteen-year-old Lewis Carroll, consists of fifteen verses, a number followed by moral tags, and twenty-eight pages of sketches, some unfinished, some embellished by watercolour paints. The handwriting is mature; the verses and sketches are precocious.

At Richmond School*

JAMES TATE[1]

Sufficient opportunities having been allowed me to draw from actual observation an estimate of your son's character and abilities, I do not hesitate to express my opinion that he possesses, along with other and excellent natural endowments, a very uncommon share of genius.

Gentle and cheerful in his intercourse with others, playful and ready in conversation, he is capable of acquirements and knowledge far beyond his years, while his reason is so clear and so jealous of error, that he will not rest satisfied without a most exact solution of whatever appears to him obscure.

He has passed an excellent examination now in mathematics, exhibiting at times an illustration of that love of precise argument which seems to him natural.

* From *Life and Letters*, pp. 24–6.

I must not omit to set off against these great advantages one or two faults, of which the removal as soon as possible is desirable, tho' I am prepared to find it a work of time.

As you are well aware, our young friend, while jealous of error, as I said above, where important faith or principles are concerned, is exceedingly lenient towards lesser frailties – and, whether in reading aloud or metrical composition, frequently sets at nought the notions of Virgil or Ovid as to syllabic quantity.

He is, moreover, marvellously ingenious in replacing the ordinary inflexions of nouns and verbs, as detailed in our grammars, by more exact analogies, or convenient forms of his own devising. This source of fault will in due time exhaust itself, though flowing freely at present. . . .

You may fairly anticipate for him a bright career. Allow me, before I close, one suggestion which assumes for itself the wisdom of experience and the sincerity of the best intention. You must not entrust your son with a full knowledge of his superiority over other boys. Let him discover this as he proceeds. The love of excellence is far beyond the love of excelling; and if he should once be bewitched into a mere ambition to surpass others I need not urge that the very quality of his knowledge would be materially injured, and that his character would receive a stain of a more serious description still. . . .

NOTE

1. James Tate (1801–63) was Headmaster of Richmond Grammar School. According to Tate's diary, Charles Dodgson entered on 1 August 1844, and lived with the Tates as a boarder; see Peter Wenham, 'Lewis Carroll – Schoolboy in Yorkshire', *Yorkshire Evening Press*, 1 Aug 1956, p. 28. When, in early 1846, Charles left Richmond School, Tate again wrote to his father: 'Be assured that I shall always feel a peculiar interest in the gentle, intelligent, and well-conducted boy who is now leaving us.' For Charles on his impressions of Richmond School soon after arriving there, see his letter home in *Letters*, pp. 5–6.

Prizes at Rugby*

FRANCES JANE DODGSON[1]

Croft Rectory, Darlington
June 25 [?1847]

My dearest Lucy,[2]

I too must write in dashing haste, but I *will* not leave it to *another's* pen to tell *you all* . . . what give *us much* pleasure: dearest Charlie came

* This letter is among the Dodgson Family Papers, which also include a list of Dodgson's six prizes earned at Rugby.

home safely yesterday bringing with him *two* handsome prize books! one gained last Christmas, Arnold's *Modern History*, the other Thierry's *Norman Conquest* just *now* gained for having been the best in Composition (Latin and English verse and prose) in his form during the Half. He is also 2nd in Marks – 53 boys in his Form – they have marks for *every*thing they do in their daily work and at the end of their Half they are added up. He is to go into a higher Form when he returns to School. Dearest Charlie is *thinner* than he was but looks well and is in the *highest* spirits, *delighted* with his success at School. He is going to write to you himself. He sends you his love and *humblest* apologies and says he *will* write very soon. . . .

NOTES

1. Lewis Carroll's mother (1803–51), born Lutwidge.
2. Lewis Carroll's aunt Lucy Lutwidge (1805–80) came to Croft to care for the Dodgson family when their mother died in January 1851.

Charlie's Hooping Cough*

FRANCES JANE DODGSON

[Croft Rectory, Yorkshire]
March 24 [?1849]

Dearest Lucy,
   You will I am sure be as much surprised as *we* are to hear that dearest Charlie *really has* got the Hooping cough, after having been so proof against the complaint during the whole of his last summer holiday, constantly nursing and playing with the little ones who had it so *decidedly*. I cannot of course *help* feeling anxious and fidgetty about him, but at this very *favourable* time of year for it, I trust the complaint will be of very *short* continuance and that with care he will get through it as well as our other darlings have done. He writes in excellent spirits and evidently feeling quite well. For this I am indeed *most thankful*. Again, I must treat you shabbily, as I have been writing to dearest Charlie and have no time for more. . . .

---

* These extracts from two letters written by Lewis Carroll's mother to her sister appear as typewritten copies among the Dodgson Family Papers.

[Croft Rectory, Yorkshire]
July 5 [?1849]

... I think I may now say that dearest Charlie's Hooping cough has quite gone. He rarely coughs and never really hoops so that he began last Sunday to go to church as usual. He is quite well and strong – and his appetite and spirits never fail at the *Railroad* games, which the darlings *all delight* in. He *tries* and *proves* his strength in the most *persevering* way, *Edwin*[1] *always* being glad to accept any number of tickets. *Your capital Horse* is most useful on the occasion. ...

NOTE

1. Edwin Heron Dodgson (1846–1918), youngest of the eleven Dodgson children, was from 1881 to 1889 missionary and schoolmaster on the outpost island of Tristan da Cunha, where he was much admired and loved by the inhabitants. In 1981 the islanders issued a block of stamps to honour his memory and mark the centenary of his arrival there.

Unhappy at Rugby*

STUART DODGSON COLLINGWOOD

Although his father had been a Westminster boy, Charles was, for some reason or other, sent to Rugby. The great Arnold who had, one might almost say, created Rugby School ... had gone to his rest, and for four years the reins ... had been in the firm hands of Dr [Archibald Campbell] Tait [1811–82], afterwards Archbishop of Canterbury. ... Charles ... must have found his new life a great change from his quiet experiences at Richmond. Football was in full swing ... his abilities [however] did not lie much in the field of athletics. But he got on capitally with his work, and seldom returned home without one or more prizes. ...

[Robert Bickersteth Mayor (1820–98), mathematics master at Rugby,] formed a very high opinion of his pupil's ability, for in 1848 he wrote to Archdeacon Dodgson: 'I have not had a more promising boy at his age since I came to Rugby.'

Dr Tait speaks no less warmly:

* From *Life and Letters*, pp. 26–31.

My Dear Sir, – I must not allow your son to leave school without expressing to you the very high opinion I entertain of him. I fully coincide in Mr Cotton's estimate both of his abilities and upright conduct. His mathematical knowledge is great for his age, and I doubt not he will do himself credit in classics. As I believe I mentioned to you before, his examination for the Divinity prize was one of the most creditable exhibitions I have ever seen.

During the whole time of his being in my house, his conduct has been excellent. . . .

. . . Charles kept no diary during his time at Rugby; but looking back upon it, he writes in 1855:

During my stay I made I suppose some progress in learning of various kinds, but none of it was done *con amore*, and I spent an incalculable time in writing out impositions – this last I consider one of the chief faults of Rugby School. I made some friends there . . . but I cannot say that I look back upon my life at a Public School with any sensations of pleasure, or that any earthly considerations would induce me to go through my three years again.

When, some years afterwards, he visited Radley School, he was much struck by the cubicle system . . . and wrote in his Diary, 'I can say that if I had been thus secure from annoyance at night, the hardships of the daily life would have been comparative trifles to bear.'

An Interview with Lewis Carroll's Nephew– Biographer*

[O]ne of my 'finds' is, I think, the discovery that the Princess Alice of Albany was actually taught to read out of *Alice in Wonderland*. I have a letter from the Duchess of Albany attesting the fact.[1]. . .

* From 'Lewis Carroll: An Interview with his Biographer', *Westminster Budget*, 12 (9 Dec 1898) 23. Italicized passages belong to the anonymous interviewer.

[Writing the *Life and Letters of Lewis Carroll* was 'intensely' interesting.] The material to be gone through was enormous. . . . First, there is a diary which he began in his tenth year, and kept to the end of his life, with only a single hiatus. There is nothing in it about my uncle's life at Rugby under Tait. Rugby almost crushed him; his shy and sensitive nature could not stand the ways of public school, and he said afterwards that he did not think he could endure the horrors of his school life again. But save for Rugby, his diary is complete.[2]

'*He was very methodical.*'

In proof, take the fact that later in life he kept a numbered register of every letter, telegram, or parcel received or sent by him. It nearly fills twenty-four volumes. I have had to go through nearly 100,000 entries. There are cross-references, too, all perfectly adjusted. Then he left many thousands of letters sent to him; and, besides, he kept copies of many of the letters he despatched. They were not arranged until I took them in hand. Moreover, there were some MSS. I may say that we have lost, I fear for ever, one unpublished chapter of *Alice*. Its existence is shown by a letter from Sir John Tenniel objecting to draw a wasp in a wig, and saying that the chapter was not so good as the others, and he should advise its omission if it were thought desirable to shorten the book. It was omitted, and has, perhaps, been destroyed.[3] But one of the funniest MSS. cannot be published (except privately). It is too personal. It relates to the time when Mr Dodgson was Curator in 'the House'. And he criticizes in his best manner everybody and everything, even the grammar of the rules which were supposed to guide him.

There was one rule which ran something like this: 'There shall be a committee of five members, including the Curator, whose duty it shall be to assist the Curator in the care of the cellars.' Lewis Carroll's remark is: 'I will not say whether on some dark night I may not have been seen emerging from the common room cellars with two mysterious-looking bottles sticking out of my coat-tail pockets, as I muttered to myself, Assist thyself! Assist thyself!'[4]

[Mr Collingwood went on to speak of the distinguished correspondents of his uncle.] There are records of conversations with Tennyson about Tennyson's own poems. And there is evidence that *Sylvie and Bruno* took shape in the giving of New Year's Day recitals to the annual children's party assembled at Hatfield by the Marchioness of Salisbury.[5]

'*Most of the MSS.*', I hazarded, '*are, I suppose, comic?*'

By no means. A great many are controversial. Shy as he was, hating – almost loathing – self-advertisement, my uncle dearly loved a little discussion with his friends on religious, ethical, and practical questions. He could then be very solemn.

'*What side did he take on religious matters?*'

He was very Broad Church, with perhaps a tendency of sympathy towards Evangelicalism. He disliked Ritualism. He would not, for example, stand up in church when the choir entered, because he feared it made the choristers self-conscious and proud. You may guess his position when I say that he was preparing a work against the dogma of endless torture when his design was frustrated by his death. But he was not always absorbed in abstract questions. He watched the stage, for example, with solicitude, and having strong views against such pieces as *The Second Mrs Tanqueray*, if he found any of his friends playing in them or going to see them, he would invite a debate by a remonstrance.

'*He had many interests – and some fads – may I say it?*'

He was greatly interested in art, and knew a great number of artists. He enjoyed coming to London, going to their studios, criticizing their pictures, suggesting changes in them, and tendering titles.

'*I have seen some of his humorous sketches.*'

. . . Ah, but he intended to be a serious artist. He had, competent critics tell me, a fine feeling for line, but an imperfect idea even as a critic of the more delicate tones of colour. It was Mr John Ruskin who dissuaded him from an artistic career, for which he was not fitted. But he made lots of marginal sketches, some in letters, but most of all in the *Rectory Umbrella*, the sort of magazine he began as a youth and continued as a young man for the delight of his younger brothers and sisters. He was no mean photographer, and I am publishing some of his photographs. To name his other interests, he was a great student of certain sides of medicine, and left a very good library of medical works to his nephew, my brother, who is a doctor.[6] Once he was taken by homœopathy, but he presently saw the error of his ways. His particular concern was with what is called . . . psycho-physiology. . . . That pursuit made him a member of the Psychical Research Society, but he abandoned the movement, dissatisfied either with its methods or their results. He was an anti-vivisectionist, though he kept no pets. No, not also an anti-vaccinationist.

'*And all this time he was doing very remarkable mathematical work?*'

He was, in my belief, a very profound mathematician, with an exceptional capacity for carrying the most intricate problems in his head.

'*Does not your experience make it singular that a profound mathematician should be a humorist?*'

His mathematical mind had a great deal to do with the form of his humour. It was the exactitude of a mind mathematically trained which dealt with words with such delicately absurd preciseness. You'll find that true if you consider it.

I don't think I've told you, have I [Mr Collingwood continued], that as it was Ruskin who dissuaded my uncle from being an artist, so it was Dr George MacDonald who induced him to publish *Alice in Wonderland*.[7] Edmund Yates chose the pen-name of Lewis Carroll.[8] For Yates in 1860 he wrote some comic poems, which appeared in the *Comic Times*.

'*Alice is immortal*', I exclaimed.'

I am convinced that that work has perennial qualities. It has popular qualities, too: witness the sixpenny edition of *Alice* just issued. You have not seen the letters and other materials which I have been arranging. Some of them are quite as good as *Alice's Adventures*.

NOTES

1. Elsewhere, Collingwood records that Dodgson 'received a note of thanks from [Princess Alice for a copy of *The Nursery 'Alice'*] . . . , and also a letter from her mother, in which she said that the book taught the Princess to like reading, and to do it out of lesson-time' (*Life and Letters*, pp. 297–8). For more on Dodgson and the Albanys, see *Letters*, pp. 748–50.

2. Complete when Collingwood was working with his uncle's effects, the diaries have not, apparently, survived entire. Four volumes have been lost or destroyed. Almost three-quarters of the surviving text appears in Roger Lancelyn Green's two-volume edition of 1953. The surviving nine manuscript volumes, accompanied by a comprehensive index, are now housed in the British Library. Dodgson's letter register has also been lost.

3. The rejected 'Wasp in a Wig' chapter surfaced, in the form of a printer's proof with corrections in Dodgson's hand, when it came up for auction at Sotheby's in 1974 and has since been published. See *The Wasp in a Wig*, ed. Martin Gardner (1977); Morton Cohen, 'Alice: The Lost Chapter Revealed', *Telegraph Sunday Magazine*, 4 Sep 1977, pp. 17–18; 'A Suppressed Adventure of "Alice" Surfaces after 107 Years', *Smithsonian*, 8 (Dec 1977), 50–[7].

4. Dodgson did in fact publish these passages, in *Twelve Months in a Curatorship* (1884) ch. 5.

5. For Dodgson and the Tennysons, see *Letters*, esp. pp. 34–9, 150–3. For Dodgson and the Cecils, see ibid., esp. pp. 211–12. For Dodgson and Ruskin (below), see ibid., esp. p. 326.

6. Bertram James Collingwood (1871–1934), BA, Caius College, Cambridge (1893), did research on administering chloroform, took the Rogers Prize at the University of London (1905), earned the degree of MD (1906), did research on poisonous gases during the First World War, was a major in the Medical Corps, and was awarded the Order of the British Empire. He was, by one account, 'a brilliant lecturer and a stimulating teacher and administrator. . . . It was also due to . . . [his] initiative and drive that funds were collected for the establishment in the Hospital of the Lewis Carroll ward for Children' – Zachary Cope, *The History of St Mary's Hospital Medical School* (1954) p. 83.

7. See pp. 149–50 below.

8. But Yates did not invent it. On 11 February 1856, Dodgson wrote in his *Diaries* (p. 77): 'Wrote to Mr Yates sending him a choice of names. . . .' Dodgson lists four choices, the last one *Lewis Carroll*, 'derived from Lutwidge=Ludovi=Louis [Lewis], and Charles [Carolus]'. On 1 March, Dodgson adds a note that '*Lewis Carroll* was chosen.'

'Do you believe in fairies?'*

F. MENELLA DODGSON[1]

Never, I suppose, has an author talked less about his writings in the family circle. In our eyes 'Lewis Carroll' was just 'Uncle Charles', one of the large family of uncles and aunts. . . .

Our meetings with our uncle during childhood generally took place at 'The Chestnuts', Guildford, the family home after Archdeacon Dodgson died. 'The Chestnuts' was looked upon as a second home by all the nieces and nephews, so much so that we read again and again in his Diary that Lewis Carroll had to 'put up at the White Lion', his home being over full of the younger generation. . . .

My sister Violet[2] and I must have stayed there at the same time as my uncle when we were 9 and 10 years old, as, although we don't remember it, he seems to have made pencil drawings of us. . . . But we do remember our uncle superintending a sketch of us together drawn in crayon by Lucy Walters,[3] his Guildford artist friend. The picture has vanished, but I fancy we were perched on the two arms of a big chair and I remember it was an irksome task for us, and I expect for the artist too, as Lewis Carroll walked about the room during the sittings making suggestions.

During the years that followed we met him fairly often at 'The Chestnuts'. We were shy children and I cannot remember him taking much notice of us. One walk, when I was about eight, stands out clearly. He took me Newlands Corner way, and when we came to the 'fairy rings' among the may trees there, he asked me, 'Do you believe in fairies?' I answered that I didn't know, to which he replied: 'Ah, that is because you have never seen one.' The rest of the conversation is a blank in my memory.

Later on, when we were in our teens, we were introduced to 'Symbolic Logic' in the little room which was always looked upon as his and in which he spent most of his time, working on one book or another. We enjoyed the lessons, but, personally, I have forgotten all I learnt. For one great thrill I shall always feel indebted to my uncle. He took me to my first real theatre – *Liberty Hall*. George Alexander, Marion Terry, Maude Millett, and Ben Webster were acting in it, and

---

* From Introduction to *Diaries*, pp. xix-xxii.

I came away dazed with the glamour of it all.[4] Although I have tried to harden my heart and throw away the brochure my uncle gave me on leaving, I just cannot do it. Later he took me to other plays, but never again did I experience the same exhilaration.

Although Lewis Carroll's personality seems to have been somewhat unique, his family shared his characteristics. No one but my father seems to have had the gift of story-telling and, except for contributions to the home magazines of his youth, and to those we produced in our childhood, his stories were never written down. They were told to us when we were tiny and illustrated as he went along. Several members of the family stammered slightly; nearly all shared Lewis Carroll's love of detail, and one especially his passion for inventing small devices. One sister, Louisa,[5] was as good a mathematician as he was, and he often consulted her when confronted with a difficult problem. They were doubtless an eccentric family, but their eccentricities were as bubbles on the surface of a deep sincerity and large-heartedness. During the last years of his life Lewis Carroll was much interested in his nieces' careers. He did his best to persuade our parents to let one of my sisters try her vocation on the stage, which she was longing to do – but without success. And he was quite determined that I should become a governess, a prospect which filled me with horror as I detested teaching. I was taken very unwillingly to see several of his friends with small children, but to my joy I never proved acceptable, either 'too young' or 'not strong enough'.

NOTES

1. Frances Menella Dodgson (1877–1963) was fifth of Lewis Carroll's brother Wilfred's nine children. She enters the *Diaries* frequently, and Lewis Carroll wrote her at least one amusing letter (see *Letters*, p. 704). In fact she did teach for a time, and then joined her sisters in running a small nursing home in Guildford. On the death of her older brother, Major C. H. W. Dodgson, in 1941, she took over the management of the Lewis Carroll Estate. She was instrumental in having Dodgson's *Diaries* edited and published. She spent the last years of her life with her sisters Violet and Gladys at St Katherine's House, Wantage, Berkshire.
2. See p. 17n, below.
3. Lucy (b. 1856?) was the daughter of Henry Littlejohn Master Walters (1821?–98), a graduate of Christ Church, Oxford, sometime Curate of Aust, Gloucestershire, and his wife, Harriet, born Mitchell. The Walters were Guildford friends of the Dodgsons. Lucy first enters Lewis Carroll's *Diaries* on 14 January 1878, when she comes up to London with two of Carroll's sisters to join him for a recitation of *Macbeth* and an exhibition of old masters at Burlington House. Later he took her on similar outings, and on one occasion called on her at the Slade School, where he observed her draw and paint in a life class (*Diaries*, p. 423). Carroll frequently called on the Walters family when he was in Guildford.
4. On 3 April 1893, Dodgson 'took Nella and Violet to town. We visited the British Artists, and . . . then to *Liberty Hall* [by R. C. Carton]' (*Diaries*, p. 498).
5. Louisa Fletcher (1840–1930) was eighth of the eleven Dodgson children.

A Rebuke from Him*

VIOLET DODGSON[1]

Sifting my childhood memories for glimpses of my uncle Charles, I recall a quiet, precise, and very kindly figure, an occasional and welcome addition to the comfortable household at 'The Chestnuts'. I remember him, with one or two of us small things on his knee, telling stories, propounding puzzles, teaching games; or again pacing the dining-room while the rest of the party lunched, sipping his sherry and helping himself to a dry biscuit from the biscuit-barrel on the sideboard; or setting out on one of his long solitary walks.

I came to know him better when, at the age of about thirteen, I was honoured but slightly alarmed by an invitation to spend ten days with him in his rooms at Eastbourne – ten days so crowded with good things that I had no time to feel lost or homesick (as one usually did when separated from one's family). We did 'lessons' in the morning – Bible-reading, a few sums, a little symbolic logic, some poetry-reading – all of an unexpectedly spicy quality which raised them above ordinary 'lessons'. They included an exciting attack on the first few propositions of Euclid, hitherto only a name to me. I shall never forget my bewilderment when paper, pencil, ruler, and compasses were laid before me with the smiling request that I should, unaided, draw an equilateral triangle on the line *A–B* ruled for me. I had learned no geometry. It got done, but I need scarcely say *not* 'unaided'! He made it quite fascinating, as also the symbolic logic. The rest of the day went on a variety of amusements, expeditions to here, there, and everywhere, concerts, theatres (five plays in the ten days), talks on the beach, every day ending with games of backgammon, &c., which removed my bed-time almost into the small hours and sent me home finally a somewhat washed-out little person. I probably bored him: he liked children to talk and we were rather dumb. But he never let me see it and was the most thoughtful, courteous, and unwearying of hosts. Moreover, he made one feel that one was of interest to him as an individual – a novel experience to a child picked out of the middle of a large family. He invited opinions and discussed them with respect and understanding. His face lighted up with appreciation of my feeble

* From Introduction to *Diaries*, pp. xxii–xxiv.

little jokes or my admiration of something he was showing or explaining. He was always a cheerful, keen, and sympathetic companion, and I had not a dull moment.

A few years later, about a year and a half before his death, two of my younger sisters and I went to live in Oxford, at his suggestion, to attend the High School. He showed himself then to be the Perfect Uncle. From the moment when he met us at the station he took us under his wing and ran round after us like a hen fussing over her chicks. He showed us Oxford, introduced us to his friends, children and grown-ups, made us free of his rooms at Christ Church, saw to it that we had everything we needed, friends, amusements, books, and so on, and kept an eye on us generally. We used to find little notes awaiting us after school, with suggestions or invitations for the afternoon, some little plan which meant that he was thinking of us and wishing us to be happy. We spent hours in his rooms, exploring his cupboards, browsing among his books, and playing games. He was, I remember, very particular about neatness and care of books and toys. The sternest rebuke I ever received from him (well-deserved and never forgotten!) was for leaving an open book face downwards on a chair.

My uncle had undoubtedly his foibles. For instance, though invariably welcoming and courteous to guests both at 'The Chestnuts' and in his rooms, he had a disconcerting way (on becoming aware that the informal tea which he was settling down to enjoy was a real *party*, with people invited to meet him) of rising and departing with polite but abrupt excuses, leaving an embarrassed hostess and a niece murmuring scared apologies. It is undeniable also that there were many who found him difficult, exacting, and uncompromising in business matters and in college life. But I write of him as 'Uncle Charles', and his care for us and the trouble he took for us made just *all* the difference to our life in Oxford. I fear we took it all very much for granted! but, though I cannot remember our making more than the usual little speeches of thanks after a tea-party or outing, I hope he realized somehow our deep gratitude for the kindness with which he encompassed us and the feeling of security he gave us.

NOTE

1. Violet Eleanor Dodgson (1878–1966) was Wilfred Dodgson's sixth child. She became one of Dodgson's favourite nieces. From the Oxford High School, Violet went on to study modern languages as a Home Student, earned a *Diplôme d'Etudes Françaises (Ier degré)*, and went into private teaching. She became Assistant Secretary to the Southwark Diocesan Moral Welfare Association and later Treasurer of the St Michael's, Camberwell, Relief Committee (both posts in south London).

An 'uninspiring lecturer'*

VIOLET DODGSON

I first remember Lewis Carroll at 'The Chestnuts', my aunts' home at Guildford. I was very small, and we were playing a delightful game. He carried me from one room to another. I ran back and had to be discovered and carried back again. This simple game might have gone on indefinitely as far as I was concerned had not some interfering elder rescued my playmate. But I think he enjoyed it. He wrote about it to one of my sisters: 'There seemed no end to the violets I had to carry across – a perfect bed of violets.' . . .

[A]t Rugby, Charles worked hard and avoided games as far as possible. His favourite form of exercise was always walking. I remember so well seeing him set off on one of his long rounds – anything from ten to twenty-seven miles – with top hat already slipping to the back of his head, grey cotton gloves, and a neat umbrella.

The year 1851 saw him settled down to forty-seven years of residence at Christ Church. At the age of twenty-five he was appointed Lecturer in Mathematics and held the post for twenty-six years, disliking it all the time. After two or three terms of it he writes in his diary: 'I am weary of lecturing, and discouraged. . . . It is thankless, uphill work, goading unwilling men to learning they have no taste for.'

The fact was that the 'unwilling men' found him a very uninspiring lecturer – 'dull as ditchwater' they said. He was shy, and stiff, and ill at ease with his pupils. He did not understand young men. It has been said that he disliked them but that was not so. His diary records: 'Dined with Baynes to meet six undergraduates – a very pleasant evening', and again: 'Invited Dr Hook's son to dinner and liked him extremely.' And in 1881 he defends the undergraduates vigorously in a letter to the *Observer*, answering a charge of bad manners and general disorder at Christ Church. I hope his pupils read that letter, and forgave him hours of boredom.

Getting mathematics into other people's heads was a very different matter from dabbling in it by himself, which he loved – though I

---

* 'From Lewis Carroll – as I Knew Him', *London Calling*, 28 June 1851, pp. 6–7.

understand that he was not a first-rate mathematician. At any rate, after twenty-six years he wanted more leisure for writing and thankfully resigned the lectureship; and one supposes that his pupils were equally thankful.

From undergraduate days up to his last illness my uncle kept a diary. We still have the greater part of it, in many volumes, bound neatly in grey, written also neatly, partly in black and partly in his favourite purple ink. It was often written in the small hours after a night of work, which accounts for its being for the most part a dry record of events. There is a disappointing absense of Carrollian flavour and imagination; and he dismisses in a few words happenings which must surely have been very interesting without comment, like this: 'Fell in with Charles Kingsley at Macmillan's and was glad, as I had never met him before.' 'Breakfasted with Fowler of Lincoln to meet Thackeray . . . was much pleased with what I saw of him; his manner is simple and unaffected; he shews no anxiety to shine in conversation though full of fun and anecdote when drawn out.' He met a great many interesting people, writers, artists, and others but he says extraordinarily little about them.

But the diary was also used for working out mathematical problems and inventions: pages are covered with figures and diagrams. There is a long description, with illustrations, of the velociman, a kind of tricycle, which was constructed for him, but which he used very little. He sent it to us and we had some exciting rides on it. The steering wheel was behind, and you guided it by means of a curved rail at your back. If you leaned forward at all the tricycle tipped up and shot you into the road. It reminded one of the White Knight.

Then there was the nyctograph, an apparatus of wood and wire, for writing on in the dark; and a round billiard table with no pockets, which he also sent to us but which appealed to us very little. Much of the diary was for years given to his photographic activities. But of this side of him I need say nothing. Mr Gernsheim has dealt fully and delightfully with it in his book, *Lewis Carroll, Photographer*.

My uncle's love of the theatre produced longer and more revealing entries. Here is one written after seeing *Henry VIII* for the first time: 'The evening began with a capital farce . . . and then came the great play *Henry VIII*, the greatest theatrical treat I ever had or ever expect to have. I had no idea that anything so superb as the scenery and dresses was ever to be seen on the stage. Kean was magnificent as Cardinal Wolsey, Mrs Kean a worthy successor to Mrs Siddons as Queen Catherine. . . . I never enjoyed anything so much in my life before and never felt so inclined to shed tears at anything fictitious.' There are two or three pages in this vein. Well, he was twenty-four when he wrote that. His later notices of plays are more critical, but he always breaks into superlatives over Ellen Terry and her sisters, whose careers he follows with deep admiration and affection.

He also loved wandering round picture galleries and the studios of his many artist friends, and would fill pages of his diary with descriptions of his favourite pictures, written apparently just for the pleasure of dwelling on them. He was intensely susceptible to beauty in any form.

Dr Liddon related that when on a tour of the Continent with him he left him to look round Cologne Cathedral, he returned to find him in tears, overcome by the loveliness of the building.[1] And I remember his breaking down entirely over a poem he was reading to me as a child.

My uncle's child-friendships made up a large part of his life and were a source of great joy to him. There were literally hundreds of them. At the seaside during the Long Vacation he was on the beach most days, with sketch-book and pencil, also safety-pins and sticking-plaster for emergencies; and there he made many friends. The diaries contain all their names and ages and very often their birthdays. . . .

He loved the companionship of children, and I think they always felt safe and at home with him: he was so gentle and understanding. He talked to us as equals and listened to us with respect. This was a new and agreeable, experience to me as a child.

It was at my aunts' house at Guildford that we got to know him. The seven sisters moved south when Archdeacon Dodgson died. Five of them remained together and made The Chestnuts a second home to their fourteen nephews and nieces; and there was always a room ready for Uncle Charles. . . .

My uncle shared . . . his sisters' indifference to the conventions. He wore, and did, what seemed good to him. We used to stay with my aunts in batches and for weeks together, and when he was there he devoted much of his time to us, producing games, puzzles, and stories, and making sketches of us. Later, when he was writing his *Symbolic Logic*, we became his pupils in that fascinating subject, and certainly had no cause to complain that those lessons were dull. I for one enjoyed them enormously. He was anxious, he said, to be considered a watchful uncle, in token whereof he gave several of his nieces a gold watch. They were good watches, and I believe they are all going still.

He expresses so often in his diary his wish to be of some use in the world, and I think the wish was realized. The memory of that gentle face with its mild blue eyes and slow smile recalls many happy and stimulating hours in the study at Christ Church and a hundred little (and big) acts of kindness to one niece alone. Surely he must have brought as much happiness and beauty and comfort into the lives of others as it is given to most men to do.

NOTE

1. See pp. 243–6, below.

His Kindness to Animals*

HENRIETTA DODGSON[1]

Mention has been made of Lewis Carroll's consideration for animals. I send some instances of this I heard of from himself. When away from home he saw a kitten in the street with a fish-hook in its mouth. Knowing what suffering this would cause, he carried the kitten to the house of a medical man for relief. 'Your own cat, I suppose?' said the doctor, but any knowledge of it was disclaimed. Happily the removal of the hook was no difficult matter. Lewis Carroll held the kitten, and I think the doctor was able to snip off the barbed end, so that the hook came easily out. Payment having been declined, Lewis Carroll took the kitten back to where he had found it.

On another occasion, compassionating some horses which were being worked with bearing-reins on, he spoke to the man with them, and put the case against bearing-reins so convincingly that they were then and there taken off, and the man had the satisfaction of seeing his animals work all the better for being allowed the natural use of their necks.

With regard to some papers he enclosed he wrote to me: 'It is greatly to be hoped that the suggestions for a painless death for the animals used as food may do good. I quite believe that the time will come when, in England at any rate, such death will be painless.'

To get rid of mice in his rooms a square live trap was used, and he had a wood and wire compartment made which fitted on to the trap whose door could then be opened for the mice to run into the compartment, a sliding door shut them in, and the compartment could then be taken from the trap and put under water; thus all chance of the mice having an agonized struggle on the surface of the water was removed.

[After the death of a pet dog he wrote,] 'I am very sorry to hear of your sad loss. Well, you have certainly given to *one* of God's creatures a *very* happy life through a good many years – a pleasant thing to remember.'

H. H. D.
Brighton

* From *Picture Book*, pp. 357–8.

NOTE

1. Henrietta Harington Dodgson (1843–1922) was Lewis Carroll's youngest sister and tenth of the eleven children. 'She had come to Brighton in 1885', writes Stanley Godman, '"in pursuance", as Lewis Carroll wrote in his Diary (2 Jan 1885) "of her new plan of living by herself." [Her remaining friends'] . . . chief memory of her is her devotion to cats. She lived "surrounded by them". [One friend] . . . "often had tea with the tall, gaunt Miss Dodgson and inspected and played with the many cats which she housed beneath wire netting in the little front garden". . . . For one [nearby] resident . . . who was a boy at the time Henrietta was "a rather starchy person who did not like us to play too close to her house" ' – 'Lewis Carroll's Sister: Henrietta Dodgson', *Notes and Queries*, 203 (Jan 1958) 38–9.

Two False Stories about Him*

STANLEY GODMAN[1]

Henrietta Dodgson . . . wrote to the local press after her brother's death to refute two stories about him that had appeared in obituary notices. . . . As related in the *Sussex Daily News* . . . [one] story was that having been invited to a children's party it occurred to . . . [Charles Dodgson] that a pleasant sensation might be produced if he entered the rooms on all fours. Unfortunately he mistook the number of the house but did not discover his error until, warned by a strange silence, he looked up from the floor and was horrified to find himself in the midst of a party of adult strangers. According to Langford Reed, that 'party' was 'a conference of serious females in connection with some reform movement or other'. Henrietta's denial was remarkably swift for the following appeared the next day in the column headed 'Society, Fashion and Gossip':

'One of his mourning relatives' writing with reference to the Lewis Carroll anecdote mentioned yesterday, says:
    'The incident actually occurred, but not to Lewis Carroll himself. It was one of the good stories he used to tell.'

. . . The story that had appeared in that paper on 22 Jan was that

* From 'Lewis Carroll's Sister: Henrietta Dodgson', *Notes and Queries*, 203 (Jan 1958) 38–9.

an undergraduate who had driven the late Khedive of Egypt through Oxford on his tandem had the misfortune to 'spill' his Highness. The following day, the young man, on the same tandem, overtook Mr Dodgson who looked rather tired. 'May I give you a lift?' he enquired jauntily. To which Dodgson replied: 'Wilt thou slay me as thou didst the Egyptian yesterday?' Henrietta's letter, published on 29 Jan, was as follows:

> Sir – Will you kindly disclaim the joke about the Khedive as having been made by Lewis Carroll. . . . he could not have made it as he most strongly objected to any witticisms connected with words of Scripture. . . .

NOTE

1. In the 1950s, Stanley Godman wrote a number of articles on Lewis Carroll (in the *Listener*, *The Times*, and *The Times Literary Supplement* as well as *Notes and Queries*), all listed in *Handbook*, pp. 295–6.

'He shaved in cold water'*

'WYEFARER'

[The anonymous author here tells of a 'chat' he had with a nephew of Charles Dodgson, Major C. H. W. Dodgson,[1] during the centenary celebration of his uncle's birth. Major Dodgson reports that he sought to correct the legend of a hopeless love affair and other myths in a letter to the *Daily Mail*, a copy of which he supplies:]

I have read with interest Mr Falk's article on my uncle, Lewis Carroll, but I fear in some ways he will have given those who did not know Mr Dodgson personally a totally wrong impression of him. I gather Mr Falk did not know him, otherwise he would not have alluded to his tall figure. He certainly was spare, but shortish.

I do not know where the quotation, 'A solitary, broken-hearted, hopeless old bachelor' is from, but assuredly it was written more in

* From 'Lewis Carroll Centenary: A Talk with the Famous Author's Herefordshire Nephew . . .', *Hereford Times*, 30 Jan 1932, p. 9. Passages in italics belong to the anonymous interviewer.

humour than pathos. He was always a bachelor, sometimes (from choice) solitary, but broken-hearted or hopeless, never.

His diaries . . . are open before me as I write. They contain a full and detailed account of his life, but there is no trace of hopelessness or broken heart. Curiously, as he grew older it would appear that his enjoyment of life increased, while his love of solitude lessened. I was myself a guest at the Chestnuts, Guildford, on the occasion of his last visit, which terminated with his death. I can personally vouch for the vigour of his mind and, until he caught the fatal chill, his body, during that time.

Referring to his diary of 1897, I find that on July 29th he walked 20 miles, and a similar distance on July 31st. These are only two of many such walks which he took about that time. Yet Mr Falk says, 'As I picture him, in the last years, wondering whether a day would find him too feeble to creep into the sunlight. . . .' At all events, on August 10th, 1897, about five months before his death, his diary shows that he 'crept' 17 miles in 5½ hours.

Lewis Carroll's admirers will be grateful to Mr Falk for his article, but let me assure them that there is no occasion to wax maudlin over his latter years. How he would have hated it!

As a matter of fact, the diary shows that, as some friends were not at home, Lewis Carroll had to extend the jaunt: he covered 20 miles, and 'I was hardly at all tired, and not at all footsore.'

As for the statement that he was a 'solitary, broken-hearted, hopeless old bachelor' – . . . the famous author *did* use those words of himself, but only in genial chaff. He was writing to a young lady . . . engaged to be married. . . . This is the part [of the letter] that matters:

Accept the very heartiest congratulations of an old friend, and his sincerest wishes for the happiness of yourself and your future husband.

My old friends are all marrying off now terribly quick, but for a solitary, broken-hearted, hopeless old bachelor it is certainly soothing to find that some of them, even when engaged, continue to write as 'yours affectionately'.[2]

The letter was written when Lewis Carroll was in his forties and, to the general knowledge, anything but solitary, broken-hearted, or hopeless. His phraseology – can it be doubted? – was merely a little genial extravagance.

There's another little legend to the effect that Lewis Carroll died in poverty. 'Any truth in it?' . . . 'Well,' [the Major . . . replied] 'if I leave as much as did my uncle, my legatees will be very surprised.'

Legend-laying over, the Major and I talked over his reminiscences of his uncle, who visited his father's place at Moor Hall, Ludlow, several times.

'I have vivid recollections of him in frock coat, top hat, and white tie. When I was a little boy of about six he would give me pick-a-back rides – and I remember that as I hung on with my arms, round his neck, his chin and his cheeks were rough. You see, he shaved in cold water with a blunt razor.'

NOTES

1. Charles Hassard Wilfrid Dodgson (1876–1941) was the eldest son of Lewis Carroll's younger brother Wilfred Longley (1838–1914), who, after taking his BA at Christ Church, Oxford, studied land surveying and later became the estate agent for Lord Boyne's Shropshire estates. In time he became a magistrate for Shropshire (see *Letters*, p. 32). Major Dodgson was, at the time of this chat with the anonymous author, Executor for the Lewis Carroll Estate.

2. To Maud Standen, dated 17 Sep 1891 (see *Letters*, p. 862).

My Uncle, Lewis Carroll*

IRENE DODGSON JAQUES[1]

I remember very clearly walking hand in hand with Uncle Charles (Lewis Carroll) to the village shop when he was staying with us in Worcestershire to choose a present for me to give to my mother. I chose a white china milk jug in the shape of a bag with a frill top drawn in with china cord. There were wild roses painted on it. Uncle Charles carried it home very carefully for me to present.

On another visit he took me again to the little shop to buy my mother's present. On this occasion my choice was in appalling taste as one thinks of it now. It was a large, opaque glass vase, decorated with *violent* strawberries! But I was allowed my choice, and my mother, the sweetest person on earth, was of course, very pleased with it and thanked me!

* Mrs Jaques' account of her uncle helping her select a gift for her mother appeared in *Jabberwocky*, Mar 1970, p. 2; the excerpts that follow come from letters she wrote to the editor of this book.

Little Croft
Canford Cliffs, Dorset
December 5, 1966

. . . You asked me to tell you about my little metal pig. One day when I was very small I saw in a shop window a beautifully modelled little bee. I remember I quite fell in love with it, and at once thought that Uncle Charles would love it too, so I sent it to him. He replied with the tiny pig with a curly tail, and a note, explaining how clever it was compared with my bee!

[April 27, 1975]

. . . Yes, I have the book Böhm on the Flute. It is inscribed SHD from CLD, in what looks like Uncle Charles's hand. On the next page it says 'An Essay on the Construction of Flutes . . . Originally written in 1847 by Theobald Böhm . . . published 1882. . . .

Uncle Charles gave Father a *silver* flute. This was stolen from him and makes quite an interesting story. Father was on a train journey and had it in his Gladstone bag', I think they called it. He had to wait at Charing Cross for his train and placed his two bits of luggage on the waiting room table while he walked up and down the platform, keeping a watchful eye on them through the window. But one disappeared – it was the bag with the flute in it. There was only one person sitting in the waiting room and it was a woman. She said a clergyman had just come in and taken the bag. Father went to the police, but no one could help. A fortnight later he read in the newspaper that a silver flute had been left in a hansom cab, and giving an address for the owner to come and claim it. So he took this to the police. It was an address in a fashionable square (the name I forget) but when the police saw it, they said 'You can't go alone, Sir, one of us must go with you.' When they arrived at the house a powdered footman answered the door and explained that someone else had just called for it and taken it away. Three months later, a friend of Uncle Charles had his bag stolen on Charing Cross Station, and in its place, a Gladstone bag was put! He opened it, and found it to contain a clergyman's robes, and a copy of *Alice in Wonderland* inscribed by the author to his brother Skeffington Hume! The result was, he sent it to Uncle Charles, who returned it to Father, minus the flute of course!

NOTE

1. Amy Irene Hume Dodgson (1884–1980) was the eldest child of Lewis Carroll's younger brother Skeffington Hume (1836–1919), parish priest, and his wife, Isabella Mary, born Cooper (1848–1937). Irene married John Jacques (1862–1937). When her Uncle Charles died, she was thirteen. On 13 May 1893, Dodgson visited his brother

Skeffington and family at Alfrick, Worcestershire. Skeffington 'met me at Knightwick Station', Dodgson wrote in his *Diaries* (pp. 498–9), 'from which it is 2 miles to his house. There we found Isa and the 3 children. . . . Irene is now quite free from shyness, and with perhaps some little tendency to become an *enfant terrible*.' On 10 October 1893, Dodgson wrote to his niece from his summer lodgings in Eastbourne:

My dear Irene,
    Thank you for the Bee.
    But a *bee* can only *buzz*.
    Now a *Pig* can *grunt*.
    Did you ever hear a Bee grunt?
    No never!
    And, besides, *this* pig can measure how tall you are!

Your affectionate Uncle,
C. L. D.

The letter and the pig are in the Dodgson Family collection. The pig is hollow and contains a tape measure. In February 1884, Dodgson wrote to his brother Skeffington,

I came across this book, and thought you might like to possess it. Also I thought Isa might like to see what may be *hoped* for, in your case, when you reach the age of 60, if only you persevere in flute-playing [the frontispiece shows Böhm, aged 60, leaning on a draped pillar, holding a flute diagonally across his chest, gazing into the distance]. Ask her (with my love) to look at the frontispiece and say candidly whether she does not feel really *exhilarated* at the thought 'and *my* husband, also, may come to be like this, if he takes pains!' . . .

This letter is also among the Dodgson Family Papers.

A Conversation with Dodgson's Niece*

IRENE DODGSON JAQUES

All the female Dodgsons and Charles stammered, although she believes the other men escaped. One 'aunt' repeated every initial consonant, k-k-k-k-kind of thing. Others 'hesitated', like Uncle Charles. She makes the distinction between stammering and stuttering and says that there were both of these in the family: stammering is

* From notes taken by the present editor on a visit to Little Croft, Canford Cliffs, Dorset, 9 Dec 1978.

getting caught on an internal sound, a case of hesitation; stuttering is repetition of initial consonants.

She has no recollection of any problem about Uncle Charles's deafness. She herself is slightly deaf in one ear, but she never remembers hearing anything about Uncle Charles's deafness.

Certainly his eyes were blue or gray – all the family had blue or gray eyes. The thought that they were brown is beyond belief.

In stature and general physical appearance, he and Skeffington (her father) were very much alike; in fact, she remembers her mother saying that when she came upon them next to each other, kneeling in church, she coming up from behind, she could not tell them apart. Both Charles and Skeffington were about six foot tall.

Uncle Charles was kind, and when he came to stay and took her into the village to buy a present for her mother, he always paid for what she bought (her weekly pocket money was something like a halfpenny). She remembers holding his hand as they walked along. . . .

Skeffington was once shocked by Charles's reaction to a beautiful landscape. They were on a long walk together when Charles was visiting Skeffington and his family, and Skeffington led him to Storridge Common, a beautiful sight by any measure. Charles could not care less apparently, and Skeffington was disappointed. Artistically, Charles was more interested in the human form and in architecture as embodiments of beauty than in landscapes or natural configurations.

She and her family visited Charles at Christ Church, but she did not stay the night. They usually stopped there on their way to Guildford. At Guildford, she and her family looked over all the Dodgson sisters' account books to make sure that the charges from the local merchants were correct, and then the bills were paid.

PART II

Oxford

'I figure as the "duck"'*

ROBINSON DUCKWORTH[1]

Five-and-thirty years ago, when I was an Oxford tutor, I received frequent notes from the Rev. C. L. Dodgson, But I am afraid that these have all been destroyed, and since I left Oxford in 1866 I have seldom had communication with him.

I was very closely associated with him in the production and publication of *Alice in Wonderland*. I rowed *stroke* and he rowed *bow* in the famous Long Vacation voyage to Godstow, when the three Miss Liddells were our passengers, and the story was actually composed and spoken *over my shoulder* for the benefit of Alice Liddell, who was acting as 'cox' of our gig. I remember turning round and saying, 'Dodgson, is this an extempore romance of yours?' And he replied, 'Yes, I'm inventing as we go along.' I also well remember how, when we had conducted the three children back to the Deanery, Alice said, as she bade us good-night, 'Oh, Mr Dodgson, I wish you would write out Alice's adventures for me.' He said he should try, and he afterwards told me that he sat up nearly the whole night, committing to a MS. book his recollections of the drolleries with which he had enlivened the afternoon. He added illustrations of his own, and presented the volume, which used often to be seen on the drawing-room table at the Deanery.

One day Henry Kingsley, when on a visit to the Dean, took up the MS., and read it through with the greatest delight, urging Mrs Liddell to persuade the author to publish it. On hearing this, Dodgson wrote and asked me if I would come and read *Alice's Adventures*, and give him my candid opinion whether it was worthy of publication or not, as he himself felt very doubtful, and could not afford to lose money over it. I assured him that, if only he could induce John Tenniel to illustrate it, the book would be perfectly certain of success, and at my instance he sent the MS. to Tenniel, who soon replied in terms of warm admiration, and said that he should feel it a pleasure to provide the illustrations for so delightful a story. Every time that a batch of Tenniel's drawings arrived, Dodgson sent me word inviting me to

* This appears as a letter from Canon Duckworth to S. D. Collingwood in *Picture Book*, pp. 358–60.

dine, and to feast after dinner on the pictures which the world now knows so well.

I figure as the 'duck' in the *Adventures*, Lorina Liddell (now Mrs Skene) is the 'lory' or parrot, Edith Liddell (now no more) is the 'eagle'.

I wish I had preserved some of the interesting notes which Dodgson had occasion to write to me before and after the publication of the book which has made him famous; but in those days one did not foresee the interest which was destined to attach to his name.

NOTE

1. Robinson Duckworth (1834–1911) was then Fellow of Trinity; he later became Chaplain in Ordinary to the Queen and Canon of Westminster. Not all the notes that Dodgson wrote Duckworth have vanished. One, dated 12 April 1864, asks Duckworth to dine at Christ Church, and adds, 'And should you be disposed any day soon for a row on the river, for which I could procure some Liddells as companions.' The note is pasted into a presentation copy of the 1866 *Alice* bearing the inscription, 'R. Duckworth with the sincere regards of the Author, in memory of our voyage' (Rosenbach Library, Philadelphia). The copy of *Alice's Adventures Under Ground* (the facsimile of the original Alice tale that Dodgson gave to Alice as a gift) presented to Duckworth bears the inscription, 'The Duck from the Dodo, 9 June 1887' (Rosenbach). For more on the Duck and the Dodo, see *Letters*, esp. p. 63; for a photograph of Duckworth, see *Letters*, facing p. 124.

He was of the Old Order at Oxford*

T. B. STRONG[1]

It is not easy to write of Lewis Carroll adequately. It is natural to expect that so exceptional a mind should have been developed in exceptional surroundings by means of exceptional experiences, and therefore any account of his life that is truthful must be, in some measure, disappointing: for he spent his time within the walls of Christ Church, and the life of an Oxford don is for the most part uneventful; at least, it is not rich in incidents that are likely to attract the general reader. Mr Dodgson was the product of the old order of things in Oxford. He belonged to the time when places on academic

* From 'Lewis Carroll', *Cornhill Magazine*, n. s. 4 (Mar 1898) 303–10.

foundations were held, under certain conditions, for life, and when the work required of those who held them was not precisely defined by statute, but was left largely to the discretion of the individual. Mr Dodgson came up to Christ Church from Rugby in 1850, as a Commoner, according to the old practice, and was made student in 1852 on the nomination of Dr Pusey. According to the constitution of the House then prevailing the dean and canons nominated by turns; and the person so nominated held his position for life, provided he remained unmarried and proceeded to Holy Orders. It was to a position of this sort that Mr Dodgson was nominated. This was shortly before the era of great university changes. It was Mr Dodgson's fate to live under a series of successive enactments which modified in many ways the old conditions; still, though the nature of his tenure was in some measure affected by them, he remained till his death on the Foundation of Christ Church to which he had been originally nominated by Dr Pusey.

He was not bound, as we have already said, to any special course of academic study or teaching, but he held from 1855 to 1881 the position of mathematical lecturer. This office was in no way an arduous one, and he had plenty of time left to him in which to pursue his own studies. He was a laborious worker, always disliking to break off from the pursuit of any subject which interested him; apt to forget his meals, and toil on for the best part of the night, rather than stop short of the object which he had in view. A person who works in this way is usually dependent on his moods; and if the mood for work rarely visits him, he gets very little done. Mr Dodgson's paroxysms, though frequent, were, fortunately for him, intermittent. No man could have held out for very long under such a *régime* as his when the fever of work came upon him. But though this passion for violent labour was irregular, he never seemed idle; his mind was original and perpetually busy; and the general average of his working time was high.

In 1860 Mr Dodgson took Holy Orders as a deacon; he was never ordained to the priesthood. It is difficult to speak of a side of his character in regard to which he was very reserved, but no one who knew him at all intimately could doubt that the old friend who has sketched his character in the *Oxford Magazine*[2] is right in finding the keynote of his life here. His ministry was seriously hindered by native shyness, and by an impediment in speech which greatly added to his nervousness. And the fact that he was never ordained priest restricted still further the already narrow limited opportunities of an academic cleric. It prevented, for instance, his being invited to preach before the University in regular course. But though his voice was rarely heard, there was no question as to the deeply religious bent of his life; there is nothing more curious to his friends than to see his name connected in some of the papers with stories turning on the light use of Biblical language. He held this and all such things in severe abhorrence, and he acted out his principles in his life.

A man who separates himself from what is called University business, who pursues a recondite subject at hours that differ widely from those of the majority, can be indeed solitary in Oxford. To a large extent, especially in his later years, Mr Dodgson did live as a recluse. There must be many people in Oxford who did not know him by sight, and still more who never spoke to him. To all these it must have been a marvel that such books as the 'Lewis Carroll Series' and the works on mathematics should have come from one retiring academic don. But those who knew him ceased to find it puzzling. There was always the same mind displayed in his talk. When he was playful or inclined to be paradoxical he could be as irresistibly funny as any of the characters in his books. The things he said in conversation do not lend themselves to description. He talked readily and naturally in connection with what was going on around him; and his power lay, as so often in the books, in suddenly revealing a new meaning in some ordinary expression, or in developing unexpected consequences from a very ordinary idea. Jokes like these require a long explanation of the circumstances to make them intelligible. They are not like the carefully elaborated impromptu which is easily handed about, being specially prepared for exportation. In the same way, Mr Dodgson was always ready to talk upon serious subjects; and then, though he restrained his sense of humour completely, he still presented you with unexpected and frequently perplexing points of view. If he argued, he was somewhat rigid and precise, carefully examining the terms used, relentless in pointing out the logical results of any position assumed by his opponent, and quick to devise a puzzling case when he wanted to bring objections against a rule of principle. But his skill lay rather in tracing consequences than in criticizing fundamental assumptions; and he was apt at times to exaggerate the value of side-issues.

When all this has been said of Mr Dodgson, and when we have noted his unfailing courtesy to those with whom he was brought in contact, we have given some account of the impression made by him upon his colleagues. . . . Oxford life is greatly the poorer by Mr Dodgson's death. . . .

It is impossible to do justice in a sketch like this to any mind of impressive originality, and the peculiar circumstances of Mr Dodgson's life, together with the very unusual character of his genius, do not make the task easier. Those who knew him and mourn his loss are able to read between the lines in his books, and see there the working of the mind they knew; for, as we have said, the cast of his thought was very much the same in everything that he approached; the humour of *Alice* and the other books was one manifestation of an original and perhaps somewhat eccentric genius. And those who know him only through his books have a real knowledge of him; they are not looking at a mere fanciful product of his leisure, though they learn from others how natural it seemed that a clever, simple-hearted, and religious man should express himself in books for children of all ages.

NOTES

1. Thomas Banks Strong (1861–1944), Student and Dean at Christ Church, later was bishop successively of Ripon and Oxford.
2. H. L. Thompson: see pp. 52–4 below.

Stories True and False*

T. B. STRONG

It is with considerable hesitation that I have undertaken to write a short article on Mr Charles Lutwidge Dodgson. I think that he would have disliked greatly to be made the subject of any such treatment, and it will be impossible in a note of this kind to give an impression of the various aspects of his character and work. But the approach of the centenary has led a number of people to send reminiscences to various papers, consisting usually of isolated events or expressions, and it may be possible in a longer note to give a more concrete idea of his mode of life in college, where he spent a large part of his life. . . .

My knowledge of him was acquired within the 'House'. . . .

At the time of his appointment the Dean and Canons were the governing body of the whole House; the Students had no votes in any of the business of the House, and, unless they held College offices, such as Censor or Tutor, there was no reason why a Student should come across any undergraduates. It is true that Dodgson was shy, and was not naturally attracted to undergraduates, as there was a certain unexpectedness in their proceedings – sometimes there is even now – and this kept him at bay. . . . he never was a Tutor and was therefore never responsible for more than mathematical teaching. Few men read for honours in mathematics and the main part of Dodgson's teaching must have been concerned with the arithmetic and Euclid

* From the Bishop of Oxford (Strong), 'Mr Dodgson: Lewis Carroll at Oxford', *The Times*, 27 Jan 1932, pp. 11–12.

necessary for Responsions. Those who went to his lectures probably went in a class and not singly.

Efforts which he occasionally made to enliven the proceedings did not always succeed. There was a rule-of-three question which he told me he occasionally set – in hopes of ascertaining whether his pupils had thought at all of the relevance of arithmetic to things. If it takes 10 men so many days to build a wall, how long would it take 300,000 men? The answer would come, giving a very short space of time. Then Dodgson would comment: 'You don't seem to have observed that that wall would go up like a flash of lightning, and that most of those men could not have got within a mile of it.' A baffling comment such as this upon a successful calculation cannot have encouraged confidence. There was another feature of the old Oxford which would have tended to keep Dodgson and his pupils apart. Mere seniority counted a great deal more than it does now, and it erected a barrier which was never quite overcome. After Dodgson's death one of the old Students who was about eight years senior to him came to see me. We talked of the loss the House had suffered, and my old friend wound up the conversation by saying. 'I was very fond of Dodgson: although he was a junior man, I was very fond of Dodgson.' I do not suppose that Dodgson's aloofness was much greater than that of other Students who were not Tutors: a large part of it was simply the custom of the place.

The rule-of-three sum mentioned above was not, I think, a mere whimsical test of intelligence: it raised a real question which, I think, always interested and perplexed him. Why should a sum worked out accurately with figures fail when it comes in contact with mere details of fact? It would be natural to assume that figures, if trustworthy at all, would lead to infallible results. His system of logic was really an attempt to deal with ordinary sentences and ideas as if they were mathematically defined, so that, by processes of a quasi-mathematical character, infallible conclusions could be reached. The syllogism in the old formal logic dealt only with the relations between three terms, but if you had terms the exact force of which you knew, you could get extended processes of reasoning leading to conclusions from a whole series of propositions. At one time, while the *Symbolic Logic* was in process of being written Dodgson used to correspond with me at great length on these matters. At first I tried to raise the general question of the relation of words and things, but he always declined to write upon this problem: if the words were clear and certain in their meaning, the results of combining them must be clear and certain too. The book is full of whimsical propositions, which were, no doubt, intended to amuse, but the author shows by his preface that he regarded his book seriously as 'giving clearness of thought – the ability to *see your way* through a puzzle . . . more valuable than all, the power to detect fallacies, and to tear to pieces the flimsy, illogical arguments which you will so continually encounter in books, in newspapers, in speeches, and even in sermons, and which so easily delude those who have never taken the trouble to master this fascinating art.' I think, then, that Dodgson's aloofness was due partly to the circumstances of university life and partly to his preoccupation with a highly abstract aspect of words and things.

It will be clear from what has already been said that Dodgson had abundance of leisure: he had few duties involving peremptory claims upon his time. I do not suppose he was ever idle; but I doubt whether he read many books. Even in mathematics, I have heard it said, he might have attained a much more distinguished position, for this was his main subject, if he had read more.[1] I do not think he had much interest in history. So far as dates went, he had an elaborate *memoria technica* by which he remembered them.[2] But he used to tell a story of his experience in the *viva-voce* examinations in the Final Classical Schools. Herodotus was one of the subjects and the examiner questioned him on it without much success. At last he said, 'Well, Mr Dodgson, is there any fact mentioned by Herodotus which you remember?' Then Dodgson brightened up. He remembered the name of a Libyan tribe of which Herodotus records nothing but that they painted themselves red and ate apes. (*History*, IV.,194.)

He gave elaborate thought and took elaborate pains about everything he had to do. . . .

He was attracted by whimsical subjects and correspondents. People who thought they had 'squared the circle' had an interest for him: he entered into discussion with them occasionally, but never succeeded in persuading any one of them of his errors. All of them, he said, made some injustifiable assumption, but could never be got to see that they had made an assumption or that it was unjustifiable. Sometimes his elaborateness of method cost him dear.[3] He agreed at the request of a Delegacy to examine in mathematics in the Local Examinations. He then considered carefully how best to ensure absolute fairness of judgment in regard to all the papers, and decided that the only safe way was to read them all at one sitting. The bundles arrived in increasing numbers till at last a bundle appeared with a note to the effect that his results were expected next morning. He accordingly went to his room after Hall and piled up the papers in a heap which reached to his shoulders – he worked always at a standing desk – he then read them all through the night and finished his task just in time for morning Chapel, next day. 'Of course,' he used to say, 'I never examined again.' I do not think it occurred to him that other methods were possible.

There were thus two very different strains in Dodgson's mind which were never very far apart. On the one side, he delighted in everything that was whimsical or paradoxical, and readily caught this aspect of things. On the other, he had a deep conviction of the importance of rigid processes of thought and inference; and this appeared, not without the other, in his *Symbolic Logic* and other works of the kind. Even in *Alice* the devastating repartees of the Caterpillar and the other characters in the books combine, in a way, the two elements in his way of looking at things. They appeared also in his conduct of the business of the Common Room as Curator, but in this connexion their effect was less enchanting than in the books. When one came to know him and work with him it was clear that he was one man and not two, and that in his mind the two elements of whimsical imagination and the love of rigid definition and inference were always present.

This leads me to attempt a refutation of two of the legends which are often repeated about him. One is often told that this or that particular person was the original from which the Hatter or some other character in the books was drawn. People say this, I think, because they cannot imagine that so simply convincing a character as the Hatter can have failed to exist in the world of fact, and because they cannot believe that anyone could have invented it. I do not think Dodgson observed people enough to construct his characters in that way. It will be remembered that he himself said that the last line of *The Hunting of the Snark* occurred to him by itself, and that the poem was written to explain it.[4] I am sure that this was much more like the way he went to work than the other.

The other legend, frequently repeated, as to which I am wholly sceptical, is that some one presented a copy of *Alice in Wonderland* to the Queen, who asked to have any future works by the author sent to her, and that he sent her a work on the Theory of Numbers or some such subject. I disbelieve this for two reasons. It would have been contrary to Dodgson's whole attitude towards the Throne and to his good manners to put a gibe of this sort upon the Queen. And it was entirely contrary to his attitude towards his books. He always refused to admit to any but specially privileged persons that he was Lewis Carroll.[5] The class of persons who knew, legitimately so to say, became a very large one, especially as his child friends became so numerous, but nothing offended him more inevitably than an allusion to his other self in general conversation – in Common Room, for instance, when strangers were present. No doubt he deceived himself as to the number of people who knew his secret; but it would have been clean contrary to all his practice to identify himself as author of *Alice* with the author of his mathematical works.

There is one more aspect of his life and work which it would not be right to pass by. He was ordained on the title of his Studentship, but he never proceeded to priest's orders. Why he stopped at the diaconate I do not know, but I think his stammer in speech may have had something to do with it. He was rather sensitive about this, and it made him shy of taking clerical duty in church. And again, he may have thought that if he took priest's orders he ought to have gone out into parochial life, as his father, also a Student of Christ Church, had done before him. No one who knew him could doubt that he took his position as an ordained man seriously, or that his religion was a great reality to him, controlling his thoughts and actions in a variety of ways. His power with children, which he could not fail to know was great, was a matter of serious responsibility in his mind, and he regarded it, rightly, as in a true sense part of his 'work'. . . . His whimsical humour is [present in letters he wrote to children,] as it is in *Alice*, but I do not think that any one could criticize the tone and character of his letters and teaching.

Owing to the stammer, as I have said, he did not often take duty. When he did, he preferred preaching to the reading of prayers and lessons. He prepared his sermons with elaborate care and could, to a large extent, arrange to avoid the words which tripped him up in speech. He preached fairly often at a service for College servants which used to be held in the Cathedral on Sunday evenings, and he once addressed a congregation mainly of undergraduates in St Mary's. His sermons were picturesque in style, and strongly emotional; there could be no doubt that they came from real and sincere devotion: he delivered them slowly and carefully, and he held his audience.

As one saw more of him it became natural to think of him in connexion with the two sides of his mind, and to understand their real unity, and to know behind them the kind and thoughtful Devout Christian man.

NOTES

1. The myth that Dodgson did not read much has been exploded by the publication of his *Diaries* and *Letters*. For evidence that he was abreast of all important work in mathematics and logic, see *Lewis Carroll's Symbolic Logic, Part I and Part II*, ed. W. W. Bartley III (1977) esp. pp. 30–1.

2. Dodgson's *Memoria Technica* is an adaptation of Dr Richard Grey's system of 1730 for remembering dates. Dodgson assigns two consonants to each number, fills in vowels to make words, and sets the words in rhymed couplets to make them easier to remember. The metrics and the rhymes alone are enormous improvements upon Grey's cumbersome system.

3. For more on Dodgson and circle-squaring, see *Handbook*, pp. 117, 158.

4. See p. 221n, below.

5. Dodgson added the following postscript to the Preface of the second edition of his *Symbolic Logic, Part I* (1896):

I take this opportunity of giving what publicity I can to my contradiction of a silly story, which has been going the round of the papers, about my having presented certain books to Her Majesty the Queen. It is so constantly repeated, and is such absolute fiction, that I think it worth while to state, once for all, that it is utterly false in every particular: nothing even resembling it has ever occurred.

His Own Invention*

FREDERICK YORK POWELL[1]

This letter on 'Lewis Carroll' was found in MS. with the first pages missing. The form and the conclusion show that it was meant for the press, but it seems never to have gone there: inquiry has failed to trace it. It must have been written in support of the memorial to Dodgson, which took the form of a cot in the Children's Hospital, Great Ormond Street. It would therefore be dated 1897. [Elton]

He was a born inventor; he invented a *memoria technica* for the calendar, so as to be able to calculate week-days in past years when the month-day was given without needing writing materials,[2] and many other 'dodges' of the kind: he invented logical signs, mathematical expressions, games with and without pieces, methods of calculating, of account-keeping, of sorting out weekly bills, and a thousand other devices for lightening the labour of keeping one's things and papers in order. Some of these were over-ingenious, of course, but he did not mind that, and he would smile over the recollection of having once induced a body to which he belonged to try a method of election which would have ended, if it had not been promptly renounced, in a result entirely against every one's wishes or expectations: though to the end of his life, I believe, he clung to the idea that every vote must be regarded as an individual expression of opinion and not as a means to the desired end. He had an almost pious devotion to the vulgate 'Euclid', maintained that it was the best introduction to geometry, and carried on more than one controversy in its defence.

He was a great worker but not a very great reader. His library was full of the unexpected. At one time he had the first editions of most of G. Meredith's books (to my intense envy), but I believe he parted with them in one of those clearances by which he sternly kept the number of his books within bounds. He had many of the rarer first editions of Tennyson, but he was never a bibliophile, and ignored all questions of original shape, keeping of covers, uncut paper, &c. He admired Tennyson's poetry greatly and once made a useful index to *In Memoriam*,[3] copies of which he gave to many friends. He loved *Notes*

---

* From Oliver Elton, *Frederick York Powell* (1906) ii, 361–7.

and Queries and had a good complete set. He was fond of dictionaries of quotations and the like. He bought no books except to read, and most of these, once read, he would get rid of at clearing-times. He was a reader of medical books, knew his 'bones', and had a good layman's knowledge of the main medical facts. He had a love of pictures rather than a taste for art: his favourites were Sir Noël Paton, Sir J. Tenniel, Miss Thompson, and Holiday. His criterion was the drawing of a pretty young English girl-child, and provided the face was sweet and the figure in proportion he did not ask for more. He liked Frost's humorous drawings, preferred Leech to Keene and Sambourne to both, and admired (very rightly) Miss Greenaway's wee toddlers in their old-fashioned garb. He was an exceptionally good after-dinner speaker, but it was rarely one could get him to undertake the unthankful task, and then he would only do it when *inter amicos*. The whimsical thought, the gentle satire, the delicate allusions to the various characteristic ways of his hearers, the pleasant kindness that somehow showed through the veil of fun, made his few post-prandial orations memorable. He seldom preached, but those who heard him spoke of his preaching as remarkable for its simple earnestness and apt cleverness of phrase. His last books were the outcome of his idea that perhaps he had not made full use of his opportunities to enforce what he held to be important truths. To the stage he was greatly attracted, and loved what he thought a good play, but the slightest infraction of the strictest decorum or a word that sounded 'irreverent' to his ears would ensure such a rebuke, public or private, as he thought best fitted for the occasion. His faith was of the old-fashioned evangelical school, and he was shocked at the playing of cricket on Sunday, which was encouraged by some worthy and sensible country parsons of his acquaintance.

He was a man who thought it right to see that his charity was well bestowed, and he took care to see that what he gave was given in quarters where it would reach those he wished to benefit. He was especially alive, as might be expected, to the duties we owe to children, both the helpless and the poor and those who, though better off, are unduly neglected; and he was so anxious to care for the little ones that one feels in penning these lines that the cause for which they are written would excuse those biographic details that he would have thought best withheld.

He remembers the amusement caused by the Oxford skits, that, both before and after *Alice*, delighted the whole University. It is probable that the awful controversy as to Jowett's salary will be chiefly remembered by the famous tract in which the elimination of 'π' was discussed. And the demands, incessant though no doubt legitimate, of the scientific men upon the University funds were never so funnily criticized as in his pamphlet where the necessity of a small plot for the cultivation of 'roots' was set forth. The fun of his 'Hiawatha the photographer', 'that would be like the sea', his burlesque of 'The Two Voices', would have placed him beside Calverley:[4] but the originality of his *Alice* parodies, the inimitable quality of his Jabberwock, and the intervention of the 'Waterford', as his 'found again' scheme of verse epigram (first published in *Sylive and Bruno*) has been called, give him an entirely unique place among the fun-makers of this century.

He reminded one at times in his topsy-turvy, unexpected, whimsy fancies of Lamb, but he was never so widely appreciative, so catholic as 'Charles the Great'. He never forgot his cloth, he had neither the weaknesses nor the pathetic gleams of the man whose criticism was the soundest and most sympathetic, and whose autobiographic sketches were the finest, of any written in his generation. Dodgson never forgot the realities, he never played at being other than was – a cleric, a don, a Christian clergyman with sworn duties, a Student of the House. Consequently, while his range was necessarily limited and his self-correction and self-examination necessarily severe, he wisely chose a sphere of literature, small but his own, in which he could move freely, and he preferred to write for children, innocent and happy and intelligent, [rather] than for the world of grown-up men and women, with the weight of sorrow and sin on them, and the consciousness of the cares of this world and (as he thought) of the world to come weighing on them. For them he could preach and pray, for the children he could write and all his wonderful gifts of fun and fancy he used for their pleasure and profit.

He took marvellous trouble to get his books printed, illustrated, and bound exactly as he thought best. He was a most careful and expensive proof-corrector. He had an ideal for every illustration, which he would press on the artist till he was satisfied with the result. He studied such details as ink and type and paper, for any book he issued, regardless of cost or expense of time. Hence the wonderful correctness of his text, and the unity of letterpress and illustration that prevails in his books.

His life at Oxford was simple in the extreme. He rose early, worked nearly all day standing at his desk, with the barest apology for lunch; a brief smart walk now and then in the afternoon, or call at some friend's house, were his only diversion. Hall-dinner and a chat with a friend in his own room afterward, with more work after, till he went to bed. He rarely dined out, and only occasionally invited particular friends to dine with him. He wanted all his time for his work, he said, and he often told us he found the days too short. He had very good health and was seldom out of sorts for a day. His vacations he spent partly at the seaside, where he took some part of the work he had in hand, and often made much progress. But he would give himself some leisure away from his Oxford room, which was his home and his workshop.

The quiet humour of his voice, a very pleasant voice, the occasional laugh, – he was not a man that often laughed, though there was often a smile playing about his sensitive mouth, – and the slight hesitation that whetted some of his wittiest sayings, – all those that knew him must remember; but his kindly sympathies, his rigid rule of his own life, his unselfish love of the little ones, whose liegeman he was, his dutiful discharge of every obligation that was in the slightest degree incumbent on him, his patience with his younger colleagues, who were sometimes a little ignorant and impatient of the conditions under which alone Common-room life must be in the long run ruled, his rare modesty, and the natural kindness which preserved him from the faintest shadow of conceit, and made him singularly courteous to every one, high or low, he came across in his quiet academic life, – these his less-known characteristics will only remain in the memories of his colleagues and contemporaries. Dodgson and Liddon long made the House Common-room a resort where the weary brain-worker found harmless mirth and keen but kindly wit. Liddon, on his days, was a fine talker, full of humour and observation, an excellent mimic, a maker of beautiful and fine-coloured phrase, a delightful debater. Dodgson was a good teller of anecdote, a splendid player at the game of *quodlibet*, which St Louis commended as an after-dinner sport, a fantastic weaver of paradox and propounder of puzzle, a person who never let the talk flag, but never monopolized it, who had rather set others talking than talk himself, and was as pleased to hear a twice-told tale as to retail his own store of reminiscence; a quality egregious, but, as all know, rare.

That this kind, conscientious lover of children should be commemorated not in glass or brass or marble, but in a way that should be actively useful in the relief of children's suffering and sorrow, would have surely pleased his soul. And though he shrank from all publicity, and led his modest dutiful life in quiet academic shade, the books that enshrined so much of his best thought and most sympathetic work have made him the intimate and playmate of many little ones in many homes, and they will not be sorry to know that their unknown friend was a man that they could respect as well as love. It may be true that his art is especially that of a day, exclusively nineteenth century, peculiarly Victorian and insular, and even Church of England: *tant mieux*: here is a production that can never be really imitated or in any way cheapened by the future, a curious little piece of fantasy such as will never be wrought out again, a thing *per se*: and it is none the less valuable because it is as frankly modern as the 'turn out' of our newest novelist or last-arrived draughtsman. Dodgson and the talented and humane author of *Struwwelpeter* were contemporaries and died within a few months of each other.[5] If to their names we add the greater names of Marryat and Grimm and Stevenson and the lower name of Andersen, we shall have gone over the roll of those who have made English nurseries happy by their genius, and struck those chords that find harmonious echoes in the delicate, sensitive, sympathetic minds of childhood. It is no little privilege to have earned the love of these little ones, and it is a pleasure, surely, to help to honour in so becoming a way as you, Sir, have suggested, the memory of one that had worthily won this distinction.

NOTES

1. Frederick York Powell (1850–1904) was Lecturer in Law, Student of Christ Church, Regius Professor of Modern History at Oxford, and the author of numerous historical works. Powell's biographer writes that he was 'in the habit of bringing strange foreigners to High Table – "Powell's assassins", Dodgson called them. They were . . . learned men as a rule, but not infrequently they were political refugees, not wholly unworthy (probably) of Dodgson description' – Oliver Elton, *Frederick York Powell* (1906) II, 427. Powell wrote a verse on the posthumous sale of Dodgson's effects (ibid., II, 393).

2. On 8 March 1887, Dodgson wrote in his *Diaries* (p. 449), 'Discovered a Rule for finding the day of the week for any given day of the month. There is less to remember than in any other Rule I have met with.' He published 'To Find the Day of the Week for Any Given Date' in *Nature*, 35 (31 Mar 1887) 517.

3. In 1862, Tennyson's publisher, Edward Moxon, printed *An Index to 'In Memoriam'*, suggested and edited by Dodgson but largely compiled by one or more of his sisters.

4. Dodgson took a genuine interest in college and university affairs, and he often expressed himself boldly and frankly on controversial issues, not only in letters to *The Times* and other papers but in pamphlets he had printed and circulated privately. *Notes by an Oxford Chiel* (1874) assembled six of Dodgson's essays on Oxford affairs, one of which, *The New Method of Evaluation as Applied to* π (1865), pokes fun in algebraic terms at the discussion that raged in Oxford over the question of whether or not to raise the salary of the Regius Professor of Greek, Benjamin Jowett, whom some members of the university considered a heretic. *The Offer of the Clarendon Trustees* (1868), another *Oxford Chiel* essay, is a parody listing a number of suggestions to advance mathematical activities at the New Museum. One of the suggestions is for a 'piece of open ground for keeping Roots and practising their extraction . . .'. 'Hiawatha's Photographing', a poetic fantasy of a photographer's efforts to take sittings of an ordinary family, is an outright lampoon of the mid-Victorian rage to photograph everything in sight. The verse is in the meter of Longfellow's Indian poem; it first appeared in the *Train*, Dec 1857. Earlier (Nov 1856), Dodgson had published, also in the *Train*, 'The Three Voices' (his parody of Tennyson's 'Two Voices'), which tells of a mild-mannered man's encounter with a shrew at the seashore.

5. In fact Heinrich Hoffmann died in 1874, twenty-four years before Dodgson.

'An excellent after-dinner speaker'*

FREDERICK YORK POWELL

Mr Dodgson was an excellent after-dinner speaker, though he did not like to have to speak. He made a wonderfully humorous speech at the Censor's dinner, but I can only recall the very delightful impression. It was a *soufflé* of a speech, light, pleasant, digestible, and nourishing also.

I can't remember anything of his stories. He did not often make stories. He told old stories very well with a (Charles) Lamb-like stutter.

He made me laugh once till I nearly cried in Hall over a story that was true, of a child, too small to talk much, being put to bed and calling to its nurse, 'Nursey, my feet, my feet!' So nurse took it out of its cot, and brought it into the nursery, and got some hot water and vinegar and bathed its legs and feet, and got it some warm milk and gave it to drink, and put it to bed again. But again the child cried out, 'Nursey, my feet, my feet! I feel so untumfy.' So she had it out again, and couldn't find anything amiss with its feet and legs. However, she thought it wouldn't do it any harm to bathe them again, so she put a little more vinegar in the water and bathed them, and then rubbed and dried them very carefully, and put the child, who was now very sleepy, back again. But again came the cry, 'Nursey, my feet, my feet! I'm so untumfy.' So she took a light and bethought her of examining the cot, when she found that the elder brothers had made it an 'apple-pie' bed, so that its feet could not get down to the comfortable length.

The comic idea of the child wondering how hot water and vinegar were to make its feet comfortable under the circumstances roused me in the sense of incongruity that lies at the root of much laughter. But I have met many people who wouldn't admit that this was a funny story. It certainly amused Dodgson, and I still laugh when I think of it.

* From *Picture Book*, pp. 356–7.

A Mind of 'twofold activity'*

LIONEL A. TOLLEMACHE[1]

The obituary notices of the man of genius who is best known as the literary father of the *Alice*s have agreed in calling attention to one great peculiarity which marked him. His mind had a twofold activity. He might be described – roughly – as made up of Euclid and La Fontaine fused together. To speak more precisely: as a mathematician, he did his work well; as a fabulist, admirably. The intellectual athlete who kept his balance on the rugged and bewildering heights of Conic Sections and Determinants could freely disport himself in a *waking-dreamland*, a land whose phantasmagoria

Of shoes and ships and sealing-wax
And cabbages and kings

was interspersed with such 'fearful wild-fowl' as pedestrian oysters and plaintive mock-turtles. But the point to note is that his intellect, vigorous and versatile on these oddly remote and dissimilar levels, was unwieldy on intermediate levels. He could soar and dive far better than he could walk. This may partly account for his unreadiness in conversation. Not, indeed, that he was unable at times to talk brilliantly. With his ready command of homely and witty illustrations, he could hardly fail to achieve this. Indeed, I have obtained distinct testimony on the point from one of his intimate friends, who writes

Of his brilliancy there can be no manner of doubt; but it was at the same time very difficult to define or focus. You ask me for some of his brilliant flashes; I am quite unable to give you any. All he said, all his oddities and clever things, arose out of the conversation –

* From *Old and Odd Memories* (1908) pp. 307–15 (repr. from 'Reminiscences of "Lewis Carroll" ', *Literature*, 5 Feb 1898, pp. 144–5).

conversation quite of an ordinary everyday sort; to explain it at all you would want shorthand notes of everything that was said, and even then you would not follow it, unless you knew the people who were talking, the peculiarities of this man, and the deafness of that, and so on. It was *Alice*, all kinds of queer turns given to things. You never knew where he would take you next; and all the while there seemed to be an odd logical sequence, almost impelling your assent to most unexpected conclusions. He had a great fund of stories; these again were never told independently, they were fished up from his stores by some line dropped down in ordinary talk. He always said he never invented them (and my own impressions is that he did not), but that they had been read somewhere or told him by some one. He never told stories against people, was never bitter or cruel, never attempted to 'score off' others.

It may be instructive to contrast my correspondent's view of Dodgson's conversational powers with the view taken by another of his friends, a man of science. The latter tells me that, to his thinking, Dodgson was not a brilliant talker; he was too peculiar and paradoxical; and the topics on which he loved to dwell were such as would bore many persons; while, on the other hand, when he himself was not interested, he occasionally stopped the flow of a serious discussion by the intrusion of a disconcerting epigram. This glaring discrepancy of opinion may in part be explained as follows: The correspondent from whom I have quoted is orthodox, whereas my scientific friend inclines towards modern views. Now, I suspect that Dodgson's pleasantry, however seemingly extravagant, had a method in it; and that, even if none of his paradoxes had, like those of Mansel,[2] a more or less clearly defined theological purpose, at any rate his wit would play with the greatest ease and effect among orthodox and sympathetic listeners. Nor is it likely that among such listeners his sallies would be rated at less than their full value. As a general rule, orthodoxy, combined with brilliancy, is like glycerine combined with vaccine – it enables a little of it to go a very long way!

From a comparison of these discordant accounts it may be inferred that Dodgson was not a steady, or what may be termed a *safe* talker. He could not be relied on to bear his part in the give-and-take of serious conversation – to keep the shuttlecock flying at neither more nor less than the convenient height. Indeed, the greatest praise which his most partial friends could claim for him as a talker would be that which Wellington bestowed on Talleyrand, namely, that he was generally dull, but now and then said things which his hearers would never forget. Thus, then, we may conclude that he had no eye for the middle distance of the intellectual landscape. The lower generalizations of philosophy and the higher generalizations of daily experience, which together form the common ground where men of parts and men without parts can freely meet and converse – these *axiomata media* of discourse were almost a sealed, were (let us say) an *uncut*, book to our mathematical romancist.

He was, indeed, addicted to mathematical and sometimes to ethical paradoxes. The following specimen was propounded by him in my presence: 'Suppose that I toss up a coin on the condition that, if I throw heads once, I am to receive a 1*d.*; if twice in succession, an additional dole of 2*d.*; if thrice, a further addition of 4*d.*, and so on, doubling for each successful toss: what is the value of my prospects? The amazing reply is that it amounts to infinity; for, as the profit attached to each successful toss increases in exact proportion as the chance of success diminishes, the value of each toss will be identical, being in fact a halfpenny; so that the value of an infinite number of tosses is an infinite number of half-pence. Yet, in fact, would any one give me sixpence for my prospect? This', concluded Dodgson, 'shows how far our conduct is from being determined by logic.' The solution of this astounding paradox is of course that, in order to bring out his result, we must suppose a somewhat monotonous eternity to be consumed in the tossing process.

He told me of a simple, too simple, rule by which, he thought, one could be almost sure of making something at a horse-race. He had on various occasions noted down the fractions which represented the supposed chances of the competing horses, and had observed that the sum of these chances amounted to more than unity. Hence he inferred that, even in the case of such hard-headed men as the backers, the wish is often father to the thought; so that they are apt to overrate the chances of their favourites. His plan, therefore, was to bet against all the horses, keeping his own stake the same in each case. He did not pretend to know much about horse-racing, and I probably know even less; but I understand that it would be impossible to adjust the hedging with sufficient exactitude – in fact, to get bets of the right amount taken by the backers.[3]

Two other 'dodges' of his may be mentioned here. He said that, if a dull writer sent you a copy of his books, you should at once write and thank him, and should add, with Delphic ambiguity, that you will *lose* no time in perusing them! Being a strict moralist, he must assuredly have meant so palpable an equivocation to be regarded as a mere *jeu d'esprit*. He was doubtless more serious in asserting that whenever a mother held up an uncomely infant for his inspection, he met her wistful gaze with the exclamation. 'That *is* a baby!' Might not Falconbridge have condoned such an evasion in an extreme case as being, at worst, 'a virtuous sin'? To be frank would be a mortal offence; and to avert a mother's wrath, one might be tempted to invoke a principle of limited application, '*Salus amicitiae suprema lex.*'[4] Better this than to set up the more widely applicable and therefore more abusable plea, '*De minimis non curat moralitas*.'[5]

Dodgson had an ingenious *memoria technica* to impress and illustrate harmonic progression. According to him, it is (or was) the rule at Christ Church that, if an undergraduate is absent for a night during term time without leave he is for the first offence sent down for a term; if he commits the offence a second time, he is sent down for two terms; if a third time, Christ Church knows him no more. This last calamity Dodgson designated as 'infinite'. Here, then, the three degrees of punishment may be reckoned as 1, 2, infinity. These three figures represent three terms in an ascending series of harmonic progression, being the reciprocals of 1, $\frac{1}{2}$, 0, which are three terms in a descending arithmetical progression.

After the foregoing manifestations of the riddling spirit which possessed this ποικιλῳδός[6] Oxonian Sphinx, we are not surprised to learn that, though he generally delighted children, he has been known to bore them with arithmetical puzzles. Also, his favourites sometimes complained that his interest in them passed away with their childhood. He related to me a quaint incident, which is said to be highly characteristic of him. He mentioned that he took no great interest in little boys, and that once on receiving a letter from a child with an hermaphrodite name, Sydney or Evelyn, he supposed the writer to be a boy, and answered somewhat curtly. Learning afterwards that his small correspondent was a girl, he made his peace by writing to her with great cordiality and with a mock-serious playfulness. His letter concluded with the postscript: 'If you see Nobody come into the room, please give him a kiss from me.' Was he prompted thus to personify Nobody by the recollection of a famous scene in the *Odyssey*?[7] At all events, being sorely perplexed as to the manner of bestowing a ghostly embrace on visible and incarnate nothingness, the poor child acknowledged her embarrassment in a charmingly naïve letter which he read aloud to me.

He spoke of the difficulties which he had to encounter before his *Alice* could make her appearance on the stage.[8] Especially he dwelt on the corrections which were needed in 'The Walrus and the Carpenter'. His intention had been that this farcical interlude should be represented in its original form. But he discovered that the tranquil massacre of the oysters was a catastrophe too tame for dramatic effect. Thereupon he conceived the happy thought of making the ghosts of the victims jump on the sleeping forms of their assassins and give them bad dreams. With pardonable – or rather with amiable – vanity he informed me that the spirit shown by the defunct oysters in inflicting this (somewhat mild) retaliation drew loud applause from the spectators.

Owing to the immense popularity of this fable without a moral, or with a queer moral (for, in very truth, the loquacious and companionable oysters are more like children bewitched into the shape of oysters), I am tempted to repeat a minute criticism upon it. Referring to the form in which it was originally written, I asked its author about its concluding stanza, and especially about the line, 'Shall we be trotting home again?' The humorous fatuity of this line, addressed, as it is, to the eaten oysters, would assuredly tally far better with the unctuous and gratuitous wheedling of the Walrus than with the commonplace bluntness of the Carpenter; why, then, is it put into the Carpenter's mouth? Dodgson frankly owned that the objection had never occurred to him. He said something about the number of syllables in the first line of the stanza, but he presently remarked that this line might be written, 'O Oysters dear, the Walrus said'. On the whole, he left on my mind the impression that, if he had woven anew the quaintly and brilliantly variegated threads of the threefold wonder-tale of Alice (*Tergeminam Aliciam, tria virginis ora creavit*), 'a triune Alice, one fair maid in three', this trifling blemish in its best-remembered, oftenest-quoted episode would have been removed.

My sketch of Lewis Carroll would be incomplete if I made no mention of his solicitude to avoid every form of pleasantry which could possibly give offence. Everybody remembers the triumphant conclusion of *Alice in the Looking-Glass*. After not a few singular adventures, the heroine crosses a fateful stream; whereupon a crown is set on her head; and, entering a stately mansion, she is welcomed with the rejoicings of her friends, rejoicings which are in no wise lessened by the infliction of a sudden and severe, if not capricious, punishment on a member of the opposite party. All this, ever since my first perusal of the book, has reminded me of the closing scene of that favourite of my boyhood, *The Pilgrim's Progress*. I mentioned this association of ideas to Dodgson; and I let him discern my curiosity to know whether the coincidence was undesigned. He took the matter more seriously than I had expected. With evident annoyance, he assured me that the thought of imitating Bunyan had never occurred to him; such trespassing on sacred ground would have seemed to him highly irreverent; and, sooner than be guilty of that irreverence, he would have re-written this portion of the book. At the same time, he acknowledged that he had nearly been betrayed into an oversight which he would have regretted exceedingly. Mill was once provoked into saying that a certain wise man was remarkable, not only for seeing what ordinary men could not see, but also for not seeing what they could see. It was with a somewhat similar sense of anomaly and incongruity that I learnt that, without the least suspicion of profanity, such an accomplished man as Dodgson had, in the first draft of *Alice in Wonderland*, made the passion-flower do duty for a flower in a passion. Fortunately he showed the manuscript to a lady friend, who informed or reminded him of the sacred source from which that flower derives its name. The correction was at once made; and the passion-flower yielded its place to the tiger-lily.

NOTES

1. Dodgson and Tollemache were only briefly acquainted. Lionel Arthur Tollemache (1838–1919), second son of the 1st Baron Tollemache, Scholar, Balliol College, Oxford, author, enters Dodgson's *Diaries* on 28 June 1872 (p. 311): 'To town with [his Christ Church colleague Augustus George Vernon] Harcourt [1834–1919, Student, Tutor and Dr Lee's Reader in Chemistry at Christ Church]. Taught Dr Lewin's [speech therapy] system to his cousin Tollemache.'

2. Henry Longueville Mansel (1820–71), the metaphysician. Dodgson was certainly aware of his works for Mansel enters his *Examination Statute* (1864) and *The Elections to the Hebdomadal Council* (1866); see *Handbook*, pp. 24, 39.

3. Dodgson's essay 'The Science of Betting' appeared in the *Pall Mall Gazette*, 19–20 Nov 1866, and was reprinted in *The Times*, 20 Nov. 'Write all the possible events in a column,' Dodgson instructs the bettor,

placing opposite to each the odds offered against it: this will give two columns of figures. For the third column add together the odds in each case, and find the least common multiple of all the numbers in this column. For the fifth and sixth columns multiply the original odds by the several numbers in the fourth column. These odds are to be given, or taken, according as the sum total of the sixth column is greater or less than the least common multiple. The last two columns give the *relative amounts* to be invested in each bet. . . .

4. A paraphrase of Cicero's 'Salus populi suprema est lex' (*De Legibus*, III.iii.8), becoming here 'the preservation of friendship is the supreme law'.

5. 'Morality does not concern itself with trifles.'

6. 'Perplexing'.

7. In book IX of the *Odyssey*, Odysseus, after telling the Cyclops Polyphemus that his name is Noman, blinds the one-eyed giant. When the Cyclops' kinsmen gather round and ask the reason for his distress, he explains that ' "Norman is slaying me. . . ." And they answered . . .: "If then no man is violently handling thee in thy solitude, it can in no wise be that thou shouldest escape the sickness sent by mighty Zeus" ' (trs. S. H. Butcher and A. Lang).

8. For Dodgson's adventures in getting *Alice* onto the stage, see *Letters*, Index pp. 1199–200.

His 'Intense solemnity and earnestness'*

H. L. THOMPSON[1]

It is not easy to estimate the loss which Oxford has sustained in the unexpected death of Mr Dodgson. It might almost be said of him, as of another famous Christ Church Student of somewhat kindred genius, that he was *paucis notus, paucioribus ignotus.*[2] As 'Lewis Carroll' he had a world-wide reputation; but at Oxford he took no part in University business, and was seldom seen in general society. His habits were in some respects those of a recluse, and he had not many intimate friends. Yet those who were privileged to share his friendship know that their lives are now far poorer than before, and that there has passed away one of the most delightful of companions, whose keen intellect and playful fancy, united to a guilelessness and purity almost childlike in their simplicity, gave a rare and unique charm to a friendship now to be cherished only in memory. . . .

Of his work as a mathematician a layman must not venture to hazard an opinion. He was a strenuous student, and an independent thinker: and in *Euclid and his Modern Rivals* he is believed to have achieved his object, in ousting from public school teaching one at least of unsound modern manuals. Of late, he was profoundly interested in logical studies; and if his *Symbolic Logic* had been completed, it would certainly have merited the praise of ingenious and original treatment of a well-worn subject, encumbered perhaps with trivialities which sometimes, as they were propounded to bewildered friends during a country walk, recalled the useless puzzles of ancient sophistry.

His special gifts of fancy and humour, delicate, quaint, and quite inimitable, gave a character of its own to all that he touched. He used from time to time to contribute to the passing controversies of the University or Christ Church some infinitely humorous leaflet, which softened all bitterness and dissolved animosities in endless laughter. *The New Method of Evaluation as applied to* π, is now perhaps almost forgotten. It was a paper calculated in 1865, at the conclusion of the long controversy about the endowment of the Regius Professorship of Greek,

* From 'The Late Rev. C. L. Dodgson', *Oxford Magazine*, 26 Jan 1898, pp. 158–9.

and it described, under mathematical formulae, the various methods attempted for attaining the desired result. In 1865, when the Professor of Physics met an offer of the Clarendon Trustees by a detailed enumeration of the requirements in his own department of Natural Science, Mr Dodgson, in a 'Letter to Sandford',[3] using almost the exact phraseology of the Professor, described in a very amusing way the imaginary needs of the Mathematical School. He asked among other things for 'a room for reducing Fractions to their Lowest Terms. This should be provided with a cellar for keeping the Lowest Terms when found, which might also be available to the general body of Undergraduates for the purpose of "Keeping terms"', and 'a narrow strip of ground, railed off and carefully levelled, for investigating the properties of Asymptotes, and testing practically whether Parallel Lines meet or not: for this purpose it should reach, to use the expressive language of Euclid, "ever so far"'.

It is impossible to explain fully the secret of his charm as a writer for children. *Alice in Wonderland*, and *Through the Looking-Glass* almost defy analysis or criticism. But they were the outcome of a very beautiful life; and the insight into the mind of childhood no doubt came in a great measure from the singular innocence and refinement of his own mind, with its strong background of reverence and awe. He was in truth a deeply religious man, almost a puritan in strictness; always on the guard against the intrusion into conversation of any expression which savoured in the least degree of light estimation of Divine truth. Some will remember his sermon at St Mary's last Lent Term; the erect, gray-haired figure, with the rapt look of earnest thought; the slow, almost hesitating speech; the clear and faultless language; the intense solemnity and earnestness which compelled his audience to listen for nearly an hour, as he spoke to them on the duty of reverence, and warned them of the sin of talking carelessly of holy things.[4]

He was then revealing the secret of his life; and those who were his friends are thankful for his friendship, and desire, now that he has passed away,

σπένδειν νᾶμα πόθων, μνᾶμα φιλοφροσύνας.[5]

NOTES

1. Henry Lewis Thompson (1840–1905) was an old friend of Dodgson. He was Student and Censor at Christ Church, Vicar of St Mary the Virgin, Oxford, and author of numerous works, including a biography of Dean Liddell (1899) and a history of Christ Church (1900).
2. 'Known to few, unknown to fewer'.
3. The full title is *The Elections to the Hebdomadal Council. A Letter to the Rev. C. W. Sandford, M. A.*; it was published in 1866 (see *Handbook*, pp. 38–9).
4. Dodgson preached three times at St Mary's, on 6 December 1896, 7 March and

24 October 1897. Of the last occasion, he wrote in his *Diaries* (p. 541), '. . . I enjoyed the great privilege of preaching at St Mary's, one of the sermons for members of the University. I took as text Psalms 103.11, 12.'
   5. 'To shed streams of tears in memory of his kindness.'

Curator of Common Room*

ARTHUR HASSAL[1]

In 1883, when the present writer became a member of Christ Church, and during the succeeding ten years or so, the meetings in Common Room after dinner were much enlivened by the presence and conversation of such men as Dr Liddon and Mr Dodgson.

   The latter's curatorship was an opportunity, which he did not forgo, of issuing from time to time leaflets, which were often characterized by the delicate and delightful humour which made meetings with the author of *Alice in Wonderland* worthy of remembrance.

   At the same time Mr Dodgson regarded his office of Curator as one of great responsibility, and spent a vast amount of time in the management of the room and of the cellars. He was aided throughout his curatorship by the admirable and devoted serving of Mr Telling, the head Common Room servant, who died in harness, though an old man.[2]

   In February 1884 Mr Dodgson published a supplement to *Twelve Months in a Curatorship*, headed 'To the Members of Common Room', in which he characteristically explained what his relations to the Wine Committee would be, and in 1886 he issued a paper entitled *Three Years in a Curatorship*. In the preface he declared that 'long and painful experience has taught me one great principle in managing business for other people, viz. if you want to inspire confidence *give plenty of statistics*. It does not matter that they should be accurate or even intelligible, so long as there is enough of them. A curator who contents himself with simply *doing* the business of a Common Room, and who puts out no statistics, is sure to be distrusted. "He keeps us in the dark!" men will say. "He publishes no figures. What does it mean? Is he assisting himself?" But once circulate some abstruse tables of figures, particularly if printed in lines and columns, so that the

---

* From *Christ Church, Oxford* (1911) pp. 136–7.

ordinary reader can make nothing of them, and all is changed at once. "Oh, go on, go on!" they cry, satisfied with facts. "Manage things as you like! We trust you entirely!"'

The pamphlet was divided into four sections – No. I. dealing with *Airs, Glares and Chairs*, describing how he and committee . . . carried out the ventilation and the lighting of the Common Room, and moreover introduced two arm-chairs; No. II. was headed *De Re Nummaria*, and was a financial statement in which the question of the annual consumption of wine figures largely; and No.III. *De Combibonibus*, deals with the condition of the cellar.

In 1892, on resigning his curatorship, he issued a useful pamphlet entitled *Curiosissima Curatoria*, which contained among other matters a *résumé* of the resolutions passed by the members of Common Room during his period of office. In this pamphlet the history of the struggle for a smoking-room is narrated. In 1886 a committee was appointed . . . to deal with this question, and before long a smoking-room was established.

NOTES

1. Arthur Hassall (1853–1930), Student of Christ Church, became Examiner in History (1890). He became Curator of Common Room at Christ Church in 1893.

2. James Telling was the butler of Christ Church Common Room for almost half a century. On 19 February 1885, Dodgson, noting the periodic audit of Common Room records, wrote in his Diaries, 'Perhaps the most satisfactory thing done was the raising of Telling's wages by £10. He has served us 23 years.' Dodgson could also pun on the butler's name. Writing to an unidentified professor in a letter dated merely 30 January (MS, Berol Collection), he informs the recipient, 'I'll be telling the Common Room Man, *he*'ll be telling till further notice.'

'The walks were well worth the cricks!'*

MRS E. L. SHUTE[1]

In the early 'eighties I married and went to live in Oxford. I had been brought up in France, and knew even less Latin and Greek than Shakespeare; – facts that rather told against me with a certain section of Oxford Society, but my husband's friends (he was a Student of the

* From 'Lewis Carroll as Artist', *Cornhill Magazine*, Nov 1932, pp. 559–62.

House) were kind enough to extend their friendship to me, and C. L. Dodgson was one of the kindest.

He was thin, and very pale. His face presented the peculiarity of having two very different profiles; the shape of the eyes, and the corners of the mouth did not tally. He sometimes hesitated in his speech (your true raconteur's trick this, is it not?) and I fancied he would often deliberately use it to heighten expectancy by delaying the point of his stories. How many he told, and how well he told them! And how did he manage never to tell you the same one twice? He had a defect in hearing which he shared with some other great men (the great Duke of Wellington and Cannon Liddon amongst others), also my humble self. I mention myself as being of the one-eared company because it was such an annoyance to me when L. C. used to take me out for walks. Those were pre-bicycle, pre-car days, and people walked more then than they do now. I walked as diligently as any of Jane Austen's heroines, and many were the delightful rambles L. C. took me. By Mesopotamia, up Headington Hill to Joe Pullen's tree; down to Iffley; round the '4-mile grind', over Folly Bridge, along the towing path and back by Kennington; he talking all the way, and that is where the ear trouble comes in!

By all the laws of right and justice, *I* should have walked with my 'good' ear to him; but no! His 'bad' ear was also the right one, and if I managed for a little to dodge round and get on the side I wanted, he always circumvented me, and it would end in my giving up the struggle, and returning home with a crick in my neck from twisting by head round to bring my hearing ear into play.

The walks were well worth the cricks!

In those days, a woman had skirts and feet – no legs; and L. C. was the pink of propriety.

When a stile crossed our path, he went first, and with averted eyes, and his back turned as much as possible to me, would hold up his hand to help me over. Hikers of to-day! Can you believe this? When, after a few years, my husband died, I returned to live in London, and L. C. would sometimes come and draw from the model with me, at my studio in Chelsea. Everyone who knows his books, knows also his drawings; the extraordinary, whimsical imagination and point of them, which the absence of proportion and balance makes only the more funny.

I never heard of his drawing from the model except in my studio, taking his chance, as he said, of drawing whatever I happened to be at work on. Perhaps he never got the chance elsewhere. Anyway, he caught at the notion with great interest. His letters were full of it. He would send me lists of children willing to sit, many of them child-actresses. In one of his letters he sets forth his ideas on the subject of models. He confessed to having no interest in boy or grown-up female models, having the 'bad taste' to find more beauty in the undeveloped than the mature form. 'I think', he adds, '12 would be my ideal age: children are so thin from 7 to 10.'

I cannot say his drawings were very good, in spite of his concentration and enthusiasm, but I was always delighted when I got hold of a child to suit him, and he turned up.

Letters as late as 1896 allude to sittings in my studio. In the rests, he would lay himself out to amuse our model, and it was interesting to see how puzzled a new child might be at first; how, gradually, she would catch on, and finally give herself wholly up to the enchantment of his stories.

I made the tea; he supplied the cakes, and the lunch rest would get unduly prolonged, to everyone's satisfaction.

It sometimes strikes me as unfortunate that the immortal *Alice*'s have thrown his minor masterpieces into the shade. . . .

Who knows the fascinating poem of 'The Lang Coortin' ', as funny a thing as ever L. C. wrote, and 'I have a horse, a ryghtte good horse',[2] etc.; and 'Hiawatha's Photographing'? This can be most effectively rendered as a stage piece. Someone as 'chorus' recites the poem, while others come on, in the different characters, 'the governor, the father' and so on, and carrry out the verses in dumb show. We did it, one Christmas, in my very young days, and L. C. was much taken with the idea, when, years after, I met him and told him of it.

NOTES

1. Mrs Shute was born Edith Letitia Hutchinson (1854?–1952), younger daughter of General Frederick Hutchinson. She was married to Richard Shute (1849–86), Student and Tutor of Christ Church. Dodgson naturally knew Shute and photographed him. When he first met Mrs Shute, on 2 Nov 1882, he thought her 'lively and "taking"'. He admired her drawings and especially her children's book *Jappie-Chappie and How he Loved a Dollie* (1887), which he gave as a present to child friends.

2. The first line of 'Ye Carpette Knyghte'. All these verses appear in both *Phantasmagoria and Other Poems* (1869) and *Rhyme? and Reason?* (1883).

'Not an alluring personage'*

W. TUCKWELL[1]

Lewis Carroll . . . has been recently biographized, facsimile'd, Isa-Bowmanised, to the nth as he would say. Of course, he was one of the sights of Oxford: strangers, lady strangers especially, begged their lionising friends to point out Mr Dodgson, and were disappointed when they saw the homely figure and the grave repellent face. Except to little girls, he was not an alluring personage. Austere, shy, precise, absorbed in mathematical reverie, watchfully tenacious of his dignity, stiffly conservative in political, theological, social theory, his life mapped out in squares like Alice's landscape, he struck discords in the frank harmonious *camaraderie* of College life. The irrreconcilable dualism of his exceptional nature, incongruous blend of extravagant frolic with self-conscious puritan repression, is interesting as a psychological study now that he is gone, but cut him off while living from all except the 'little misses' who were his chosen associates. His passion for them was universal and undiscriminating; like Miss Snevellicci's papa, he loved them every one. Yet even here he was symmetrical and rigid; reaching the point where brook and river meet, the petted loving child friend was dropped, abruptly, remorselessly, finally. Perhaps it was just as well: probably the severance was mutual; the little maids put away childish things, he did not: to their maturer interests and grown-up day-dreams he could have made no response: better to cherish the recollection unimpaired than to blur it by later consciousness of unsuitability; to think of him as they think of nursery books, a pleasant memory, laid by upon their shelves affectionately, although no longer read. And to the few who loved him this faithlessness, as some have called it, seems to reveal the secret of his character. He was what German Novalis has called a 'grown-up child'. A man in intellectual range, severe self-knowledge, venturesome imagination, he remained a child in frankness, innocence, simplicity; his pedantry cloaking a responsiveness, which shrank from coarser, more conventional, adult contact, vibrated to the spiritual kinship of

---

* From *Remembrances of Oxford* (1900) pp. 161–3.

little ones, still radiant with the visionary light which most of us lose all too soon, but which shone on him through life.

NOTE

1. William Tuckwell (1829–1919), Fellow, New College, Oxford, Headmaster, Rector, biographer of Chaucer, Horace and Spenser. Tuckwell was probably unacquainted with Dodgson (he does not appear in the *Diaries*) and very likely wrote from hearsay, which would account for his likening Dodgson's undiscriminating [passion]' for 'little misses' to the one displayed by the Snevellicci in *Nicholas Nickleby*.

'The most prolific malcontent'*

MICHAEL SADLEIR[1]

[Michael Sadler was] . . . Steward of Christ Church for nine years, and [one of his duties was] . . . dealing with complaints from members of Common Room. The most prolific malcontent was 'Lewis Carroll' . . . who was Curator of Common Room and ever on the *qui vive* for negligence on the part of College servants or minor inconveniences affecting his own comfortable life. There survive originals or transcripts of no fewer than forty-eight letters from Dodgson to the Steward, calling attention to, or asking for the redress of miscellaneous grievances. The messengers sometimes clear the letter-boxes two minutes before the stated hour, so that important missives lose the post. Occasional letters go out from the Lodge *unstamped*, much to the annoyance of their recipients. How much milk is Mr Dodgson supposed to receive each morning and at what price? There is a 'dangerous effluvium caused by some defect of drainage' which makes the New Common Room 'quite uninhabitable'. The gas supply is inadequate to a new asbestos grate which Mr Dodgson wishes to instal. He requires an electric bell-push in each of his two bedrooms. Please tell the kitchen to send him *no more smoked ham*. If ginger-beer can be supplied in bottles with glass-ball stoppers instead of corked, Mr Dodgson, who is accustomed to stack them head-downwards to prevent effervescence, would not, out of a dozen, find five completely empty and two half empty. And so on; and so on. . . .

* From *Michael Ernest Sadler . . . A Memoir by his Son* (1949) pp. 90–1, 95.

REMINISCENCES OF LEWIS CARROLL

(Extracts from MES Diary)

Christmas Day, 1931

Went a walk with John Barclay (formerly J. Barclay Thompson) of Christ Church.

He told me that he knew Dodgson intimately for 40 years. When *Alice* was being printed, Dodgson used to say to him 'Come up to my room, Tenniel has just sent me another drawing.' Barclay used to take Dodgson to Mrs. Thomas Arnold's in North Oxford, as Dodgson liked to go a walk with the little girls, one of whom was afterwards Mrs Humphry Ward.

T. Vere Bayne was Curator of Common Room at Christ Church. He had no Wine Committee. He *would* lay in sherry. Dodgson worked out by Calculus that it would last – if he went on at that rate – for 300 years. Using this Dodgsonian calculation, Barclay moved at a Common Room meeting that there should be a wine committee. This was carried. Bayne resigned. Dodgson came over to Barclay in a corner of Common Room and said that he (Dodgson) would never become stiff and autocratic like Bayne. Dodgson was elected Curator. In a fortnight he had become 'clothed with brief authority' and was angrily irritable at any suggestion of change. He drew up a long list of rules. Quickly he himself broke them. Barclay called attention to this, in moving for amendment. Dodgson was very angry and a testy correspondence followed. Dodgson put into the College Library a record of the controversy from his (not including Barclay's) point of view.

In his last years, Dodgson came out as a preacher. Undergraduates flocked to hear him when he was in the pulpit. He wept when he came to the more serious parts of his sermons.[2]

NOTES

1. Michael Sadleir (1888–1957), author and publisher, was the son of Sir Michael Sadler (1861–1943), educational pioneer and art patron, Student and Steward of Christ Church, and Master of University College, Oxford.

2. The disagreement between Dodgson and Barclay Thompson as given here is one-sided. On 8 December 1882, Dodgson wrote in his *Diaries* (p. 411),

A Common Room Meeting. Barclay Thompson had (at the meeting of November 30) brought (by implication) charges of obstinacy and extravagance against the Curator. These I now attempted to rebut. Fresh powers were given to the Wine Committee, and then a new Curator elected. I was proposed by Holland, and seconded by Harcourt, and accepted office with no light heart: there will be much trouble and thought needed to work it satisfactorily: but it will take me out of myself a little, and so may be a real good.

Dodgson wrote a number of conciliatory letters to Barclay Thompson (see *Letters*, pp. 508–13), who nevertheless persisted on a contentious course. He was John Barclay Thompson, later John Barclay (1845–1936), Student and Tutor at Christ Church and Dr Lee's Reader in Anatomy.

'A just horror of the interviewer'*

G. J. COWLEY-BROWN[1]

The late Lewis Carroll (if Lewis Carroll can ever be called *the late*) had a just horror of the interviewer. He was a great deal too modest to blow his own trumpet, or to let any one else blow it for him. A few personal reminiscences, however, by one of his contemporaries, who had special opportunities of observing him, will be no breach of confidence, and may prove interesting to the readers. . . . It was my fortune to be matriculated at the same time with him, and to have some conversation with him as we walked . . . together. . . .

On coming into residence I had the advantage of reviving an acquaintance thus begun, being associated with . . . Dodgson in the same 'mess'. . . .

We all, however, I may safely say, sat in the same hall and some of us even at the same table with Dodgson without discovering (perhaps from our own want of it) the wit, the peculiar humour, that was in him. We looked upon him as a rising mathematician, nothing more. He seldom spoke, and the slight impediment in his speech was not conducive to conversation. One day, however, long after we had taken our degrees, he asked me to go for a walk with him to his rooms, he would show me some drawing by Tenniel. They were in pencil, on small squares of paper, and were the originals of the illustrations in *Alice*. He then confided to me that he was writing a book. One morning, not long after, he, like Bryon, woke 'to find himself famous'. . . .

It was Dr Pusey . . . who gave Dodgson his studentship. In those days the studentships of Christ Church (a species of fellowship) were,

* From 'Personal Recollections of the Author of *Alice in Wonderland*', *Scottish Guardian* 28 Jan 1898, p. 54.

with the exception of the Westminster ones, pieces of patronage which the Dean and Canons divided between them. Dodgson, however, though the son of one of Dr Pusey's *collaborateurs* in the *Library of the Fathers*,[2] was, if I may use the word, no 'Puseyite'. I may note here his telling me of a rendering by his father which he thought aptly imitated the alliteration of the original, the phrase, *a cœno ad cœlum* (somewhere, I think, in Tertullian), which he had rendered 'from the sty to the sky'. Dodgson was an unaffectedly religious man, as witness his *Easter Greeting*, with its now pathetic reference to his 'hope to look back upon' what he had written 'without shame and sorrow . . . when *my* turn comes to walk through the valley of shadows'.[3] He was no party man, neither was he a 'Puritan', as one of the party church newspapers last week thought proper to describe him. His shyness and the consciousness of his stammer did not at the time I am speaking of prevent his occasionally helping one of the city clergy; and I remember his enlisting my help also, during a short residence in Oxford, on behalf of one of the hard-working chaplains who held one of these churches. My subsequent interviews with him, our lot being now cast in different countries, were 'few and far between', but in occasional visits to Oxford he was always glad to see me. I recall one of these occasions on which he asked me to come to his rooms after Hall, and on ascertaining that I had a daughter of the age of 'Alice', he sent her a beautiful copy of the book with her name inscribed in it 'from the author'. I ventured to ask him once what made him take this *nom de plume*. He said, 'You see my name is Charles, and as Carolus is the Latin for it, I thought Carroll would do very well. My name also is Lutwidge, and Lewis comes near enough to it.'

My last conversation with him was on the occasion of the *Gaudy* last June. I sat by him during the customary speech in the chapter-house, and I remember his telling me that it fell to him once to make a speech there on *Hakluyt's Voyages*, Hakluyt having been an old Westminster student of the House.[4] He dined with us in Hall, but I saw him no more, having to leave that night, little thinking how soon he was to be taken from the society he had helped to sweeten. There were no signs of senility about him. The wine of his fancy ran clear to the last. '*Quando ullum invenient parem?*'[5]

NOTES

1. George James (Cowley-)Brown (1832–1924) was Chancellor and Canon of Edinburgh Cathedral. For a second account of his years at Oxford, see 'Christ Church, Oxford, Sixty Years Ago', *Oxford Magazine*, 34 (1915) 41–2, 56–7, 71–2.

2. Edward Bouverie Pusey (1800–82), Canon of Christ Church and Regius Professor of Hebrew, one of the most eloquent defenders of the Oxford Movement, and Dodgson's father were students together and friends at Christ Church in the 1820s. Pusey did

indeed nominate the young Charles Dodgson for his Studentship. In the latter 1830s, Pusey undertook to publish a 'Library of the Fathers', a series of translations of the early Christian Fathers, and engaged his old friend Dodgson *père* to do the Tertullian volume. It appeared in 1842.

3. Dodgson composed *An Easter Greeting to Every Child Who Loves 'Alice'* and had it privately printed as a four-page leaflet expressly to be inserted in *The Hunting of the Snark* (1876). 'I do not like', he wrote (*Diaries*, p. 350), 'to lose the opportunity of saying a few serious words to (perhaps) 20,000 children.' The serious words are meant to cheer his readers: he urges them not to fear the end of life, for purer and greater pleasures await them in the brighter sunrise after death.

4. It was customary for a Christ Church BA to deliver an oration at the Gaudy about a past distinguished member of the college, and for the Dean to assign the subject. Dodgson gave the oration on Richard Hakluyt (1552?–1616), the famous geographer, at the Gaudy in 1856. His manuscript is in Christ Church Library.

5. Horace, *Odes*, I.xxiv.8: 'when will they find anyone to equal him?'

'Known only to the world'*

CLAUDE M. BLAGDEN[1]

[Dodgson might be said . . . to be] known only to the world, for he had long ceased to do any tutorial work, he had no dealings with undergraduates, even on his own staircase, and most of his colleagues never set foot in his rooms, until they visited them out of curiosity after he was dead. He did not quite eschew our company, and he would preside in Hall, if he were the senior present, or in Common Room, if the Curator (that is, the President) were not there. He had, in fact, been at one time Curator himself, and in that capacity had given free play to his whimsies. He held the view that amateur wine-tasters deceived themselves when they professed to distinguish one vintage from another, and that they really were guided by the label supplied by the wine-merchant. To prove this he once secretly interchanged the labels on the bottles which the wine committee had met to taste, and maintained that his colleagues had reacted exactly as he had foretold. He acted up to his convictions when a crisis occurred in the cellar. His predecessor, following the fashion of the day, had neglected port and laid in great stores of brown sherry. When in the nineties port was again in fashion, and the sequence of

* From *Well Remembered* (1953) pp. 113–16.

appropriate vintages was lacking to the Christ Church cellar, Dodgson solved the problem by sending out to the grocer for some – 'Running the Common Room', said a most abstemious colleague, 'on the lines of a lower middle-class family.' In 1896 Dodgson's port was still circulating after dinner, but the curatorship had passed to other, less eccentric, hands.

His desire for anonymity carried him to strange lengths. 'If I had written them,' he once told an earnest enquirer who asked him if he were really the author of the *Alice* books, 'I should answer NO, No.' I myself witnessed a very painful scene in Common Room one night when he was presiding. The Senior Classical Tutor had dining with him a very eminent Latin scholar from Berlin, and foolishly, as he placed his guest on the right hand of the President, whispered to him that he was next to the author of *Alice*. The courteous German, as soon as he was introduced, opened the conversation by saying: 'Oh, Mr Dodgson, I am so glad to meet you, for I have enjoyed your *Alice* books so much.' The only answer was: 'That is a subject which I never discuss with anybody'; Dodgson turned his back on him, and addressed no other word to him for the rest of the evening. In the hey-day of his fame he was much worried by autograph hunters, who wrote to him from every quarter of the world. He never refused them an autograph, but those which he sent, purporting to come from Lewis Carroll, were not his. He used to waylay colleagues ... after morning chapel, and carry them back to his rooms to write his *nom de plume* for him, and I expect that there are still collectors who cherish this signature, and are not aware that it was written by a Bishop of Chichester or a Bishop of Oxford.

His treatment of the German professor was only equalled by his treatment of one of his own guests. He hated smoking, and no tobacco was allowed in his rooms. Once in my time he had staying with him Captain T. Gibson Bowles, M.P.[2] I saw him in Common Room with him, and then the two walked across the quadrangle to Dodgson's rooms. An hour or two later, Strong who had been to see the Junior Censor, found Bowles sitting disconsolately on the stairs. When he asked what he was doing there he found that Bowles, returning to Dodgson's rooms, had said very humbly: 'I suppose that I couldn't have a pipe here, could I?' and was met with the answer: 'You know that I don't allow smoking here. If I had known that you wanted to smoke, I would have ordered the Common Room Smoking Room to be got ready for you.' So he went out on to the cold dark stairs, and fortunately fell in with Strong, who carried him off to his rooms in Peckwater and entertained him for the rest of the evening.

Towards his colleagues his attitude was quite unpredictable. He might use them as a whetstone for the sharpening of his own wits, or, in his more humane moods, he would be the witty companion that he had been on Reading Parties long ago. He made J. S. Phillimore[3] speechless with anger one night at dinner, when he suddenly presented him with a problem which began 'Take a dodecahedron', and he drove Strong wild with his logical conundrums. In later life he chose logic as the special object of his study, and then he would constantly send his servant across to Strong with hard questions carefully written down for him to answer. Strong at first took these questions seriously, and set himself to give reasoned answers to them; but he soon discovered, on the receipt of an answer from Dodgson with hardly a moment's delay, that he was being used, not by a tireless seeker after the truth, but by a very determined and skilful games player, who had worked out all possible solutions, and was prepared to play a game of logic-chopping till the skies fell. Yet from time to time, alas! all too rarely, we had a glimpse of a very different man. Sometimes, if the audience was small and appreciative, he would sit in Common Room, and tell us stories in his own inimitable way. Then we realized what children must have found in him, and what supreme gifts he had to charm and hold them.

He was very simple and sincere in his religion. We used to see him kneeling devoutly in Cathedral at the College prayers, and once, long after service was ended, he was found on his knees quite unaware of time or place. Though in Holy Orders, he undertook no clerical duties till, not long before his death, he was persuaded by the Vicar of St Mary's to preach one of the Sunday evening sermons to undergraduates. The word was passed round the University that he was coming, and the church was thronged, but those who expected fireworks were doomed to disappointment. What they did hear was a plain, evangelical sermon of the old-fashioned kind, preached by one who held to the faith of his childhood, undisturbed by the learning or the criticism of any later age. His death in January 1898 made no ripple on the surface of University or college life. Lewis Carroll is among the immortals of literature, C. L. Dodgson was soon forgotten, except by the very few.

NOTES

1. Claude Martin Blagden (1874–1952), Scholar, Corpus Christi College, Oxford, became Student and Censor of Christ Church after Dodgson's death and later Bishop of Peterborough. He does not appear in Dodgson's *Diaries*.

2. Thomas Gibson ('Captain Tommy') Bowles (1842–1922), playwright, politician, was the founder of the society paper *Vanity Fair* (1868) and the journal for women the *Lady* (1885). Dodgson had known Bowles and his family since the 1870s. It was on 3 March 1879 that Bowles came to Oxford and stayed with Dodgson. On the morning of 4 March, Dodgson photographed him (*Diaries*, p. 378). Bowles published Dodgson's word-game *Doublets* in *Vanity Fair* (1879) and another word-game, *Syzygies*, in the *Lady* in 1891–2.

3. John Swinnerton Phillimore (1872–1926) was an undergraduate at Christ Church

in the 1890s and later Professor of Greek at Glasgow University. He does not appear in Dodgson's *Diaries*. For Bishop Strong's reminiscences, see above, pp. 32–9.

'He liked to "quiz" his neighbours'*

VISCOUNT SIMON[1]

It was very odd that Lewis Carroll, or rather Mr Dodgson of Christ Church, should have taken any special interest in me, but as a Freshman I may have attended some of his mathematical lectures, and we must have conversed, because he invited me to dine and I several times had the good fortune to be his guest at the House.

He did not like strangers to treat him as the author of Lewis Carroll's books. Do I not remember that when the first number of a weekly illustrated paper called *Black and White* appeared they published an indignant letter which Mr Dodgson had written to the Editor from Oxford, refusing the invitation to write for them a contribution 'by Lewis Carroll'? I suppose they would have paid handsomely for such an article, but the effect of his letter protesting that they should *assume* he was the author of *Alice in Wonderland* must have resulted in giving the paper an interesting paragraph for nothing.[2]

At the dinner table he liked to 'quiz' his neighbours with occasional conundrums with a mathematical air, which I at any rate found very entertaining. Here are two of them which I recall to have been posed in my hearing on these occasions.

1. A man wanted to go to the theatre, which would cost him 1*s*. 6*d*., but he only had 1*s*. So he went into a Pawnbroker's shop and offered to pledge his shilling for a loan. The Pawnbroker satisfied himself that the shilling was genuine and lent him 9*d*. on it.

The man then came out of the shop with 9*d*., and the Pawnbroker's ticket for 1*s*. Outside he met a friend to whom he offered to sell the Pawnbroker's ticket and the friend bought it from him for 9*d*. He now had 9*d*. from the Pawnbroker and another 9*d*. from the friend and so was able to go to the theatre.

'The question is,' said Lewis Carroll, 'who lost what?'

* From Derek Hudson 'Lewis Carroll (1954) pp. 312–14.

I remember much discussion round the table and I modestly advanced the answer that the friend lost 6*d*. as he had to repay the loan to the Pawnbroker in order to recover the shilling. Lewis Carroll turned to me and said: 'My young friend, your answer is not indeed right, but it does you the greatest credit, for it shows that you are so ignorant in the ways of Pawnbrokers that you think they do their business for nothing!' I had not allowed for the fact that the Pawnbroker charged interest.

2. Take two tumblers, one of which contains 50 spoonfuls of pure brandy and the other 50 spoonfuls of pure water. Take from the first of these one spoonful of the brandy and transfer it without spilling into the second tumbler and stir it up. Then take a spoonful of the mixture and transfer it back without spilling to the first tumbler.

'My question is,' said Lewis Carroll, 'if you consider the whole transaction, has more brandy been transferred from the first tumbler to the second, or more water from the second to the first?'

The answer, of course, is easy enough to work out, for the spoonful of the mixture will consist of 1/51 parts of brandy and 50/51 parts of water, so on the whole transaction 50/51sts of brandy has been transferred from the first tumbler to the second, and 50/51sts of water from the second tumbler to the first. But Lewis Carroll then observed that it was quite unnecessary to work out these fractions. You started with a tumbler containing 50 spoonfuls of brandy and at the end this tumbler still contained 50 spoonfuls, neither more nor less. Whatever it had lost in brandy it had gained in water, and as there had been no spilling the quantities were equal.

Lewis Carroll took special pleasure in concocting rather absurd but very elementary questions of this kind, and there are many more elaborate posers in one of his mathematical books called *Pillow Problems*,[3] e.g. A girl's school, consisting of X pupils goes a walk *en crocodile* every day, the girls walking Y abreast. How many days can they take this dull exercise without any girl walking more than once next to the same girl? The complication, of course, is that if they walk more than two abreast, a girl on the outside would only have *one* other girl next to her, but a girl in the middle would have *two*.

The truth about Lewis Carroll is that he was always engaged in genially pulling somebody's leg and he did this very amusingly by propounding a comic mathematical problem to a non-mathematical mind. That at least was the side of him which he showed to me at occasional dinner parties, and I think he found the Canons of Christ Church easy meat!

His parody of Euclid's third 'Postulate' is a good example of his wit.

That Postulate runs: 'Let it be granted that a circle can be described about any centre at any distance from that centre.' He transformed this into: 'Let it be granted that a controversy can be raised about any subject at any distance from that subject.'[4] How true that is!

NOTES

1. John Allsebrook Simon (1873–1954), 1st Viscount Simon, statesman and Lord Chancellor, was an undergraduate at Wadham College, Oxford, in the early 1890s, and in 1897 was elected a Fellow of All Souls. He does not enter Dodgson's *Diaries*.

2. No letter from Dodgson in fact appeared in *Black and White*.

3. In *Curiosa Mathematica, Part II: Pillow-Problems Thought Out during Sleepless Nights* (1893), Dodgson published a group of seventy-two problems in algebra, plane geometry, and trigonometry. He tackled the problems one by one during sleepless nights and wrote them down the next morning.

4. See Dodgson's *Dynamics of a Parti-cle* (1865) ch. 1.

'The living embodiment of the old Oxford'*

J. B.[1]

My earliest sight of 'Lewis Carroll' was when, as a Freshman, raw and abashed, I had once the honour of sitting opposite him at dinner. With all a boy's nervousness at dining for the first time at a college 'high table', in utter ignorance of the allusions which filled the talk, and tortured by a desire to escape to more congenial society, I found huge consolation in the fact that now I was regarding with my own eyes a god of my childhood. To one fresh from a very different place, and not yet habituated to the real Oxford, he seemed the living embodiment of the old Oxford of a boy's fancy. I desired to attend his lectures till I found that he was a mathematician. Dreary people in his own college, when questioned concerning their great man, confessed to having lived in ignorance that a prophet was among them. To certain [ones] he was simply an old mathematical tutor; to others a great name in letters which they had never connected with a local habitation; but to none was his figure noticeable. Few of Oxford's famous men have been so inconspicuous in her midst. Froude was

* From '"Lewis Carroll" at Oxford', *Academy*, 22 Jan 1898, pp. 99–100.

constantly to be observed; even Walter Pater was known by sight to a large part of the undergraduate world; but I scarcely remember to have seen 'Lewis Carroll' half a dozen times in the street.

In a sense he was the most old-world of all the elements in the place. The Oxford of ecclesiastical bustle and honest doubt, of Newman and Mark Pattison, of Arnold and Clough, though actually earlier in time, was years later in sentiment. . . . Though full of the wide human nature which delights in all things contemporary, his mind, alike in its piety, its ingenuities and its humours, belonged to an earlier and quieter world. His flue never lost 'its happy country tone'. His Oxford was sleepy and early Victorian, a haunt of people who played croquet and little girls with short frocks and smoothly brushed hair and quaint formal politeness. It seems to me that the exact subtlety of the humour of the *Alice* books could never be caught again, for the sleepy afternoon air, the quaint grace and the mock dignity are all the property of an elder and vanishing world.

In Oxford his works enjoyed a surprising popularity, and formed the storehouse for undergraduate nicknames. In my own day it even became a fashion for a man to set them in foolish paradox by the side of Shakespeare when incautiously questioned on his preference in letters. *The Hunting of the Snark* was popularly supposed to contain all the metaphysics in the world. I once heard a distinguished college authority explain his course of lighter reading during one vacation. 'The first week', he said, 'I read *Sylvie and Bruno*.' 'And then?' some one asked, 'And then', he said, 'I read the Second Part.' 'And then?' 'And then,' he murmured in doubt – 'then,' brightening up, 'ah, then, I went back to *Through the Looking-Glass*.'

NOTE

1. I have been unable to identify the author.

'His simplicity of mind and heart'*

FRANCIS PAGET[1]

We may differ, according to our difference of taste or temperament, in appraising Charles Dodgson's genius; but that that great gift was his, that his best work ranks with the very best of its kind, this has been owned with a recognition too wide and spontaneous to leave room for doubt. The brilliant, venturesome imagination, defying forecast with ever-fresh surprise; the sense of humour in its finest and most naïve form; the power to touch with lightest hand the undercurrent of pathos in the midst of fun; the audacity of creative fancy, and the delicacy of insight in these are rare gifts; and surely they were his. Yes, but it was his simplicity of mind and heart that raised them all, not only in his work but in his life, in all his ways, in the man as we knew him, to something higher than any mere enumeration of them tells: that almost curious simplicity, at times, that real and touching child-likeness that marked him in all fields of thought, appearing in his love of children and in their love for him, in his dread of giving pain to any living creature, in a certain disproportion, now and then, of the view he took of things – yes, and also in that deepest life, where the pure in heart and those who become as little children see the very truth and walk in the fear and love of God.

* From *Virtue of Simplicity*, a sermon Dean Paget preached on the Sunday after Dodgson's death, pp. 7–8.

NOTE

1. Francis Paget (1851–1911), Senior Student at Christ Church from 1874, succeeded Liddell as Dean in 1892 and became Bishop of Oxford in 1901.

His Scheme for Redistribution*

HENRY SCOTT HOLLAND[1]

Oh, Dodgson! Have you seen his incredible paper on Redistribution![2] It is the wildest form of serious joking that ever was seen. It will make you scream with laughter, if you just picture *every* single Member of Parliament (for he has sent it to all), starting gaily at page 8 – reaching the comfortable formula at the top of page 14 – and merrily rattling on over the interesting and even fascinating details of pages 18 and 19.

I carried [it] in my pocket to Downing St that day: and then felt it too absurd to give it to you. Yet Dodgson is most solemnly anxious about it, and lives in constant prayer that the Prime Minister may throw his eye over it, and recognize at a glance the conclusion of all the passionate dreams of his momentous career – the realization of his wildest hopes – the crown of his lifelong work. Would he look at it as a joke? as one of the most surious specimens of human mental culture ever produced in a Common Room? Perhaps he could be interested in it, as in Queen Elizabeth's shoe-strings, or in any of the treasures of our museums? It really is a curiosity – to come out of the same mind as *Alice* – and yet to think that same mind does not the least see the splendour of the joke! He is frightfully in earnest. You will know whether this would be a conceivable method of introducing it. It really is worth looking at, for this purpose of psychical study.

---

* *A Forty Years' Friendship: Letters from the Late Henry Scott Holland to Mrs Drew*, ed. S. L. Ollard (1919) pp. 79–80.

NOTES

1. Henry Scott Holland (1847–1918), Senior Student, Lecturer, and Tutor at Christ Church, Canon of St Paul's, Regius Professor of Divinity at Oxford, editor and author, was the one who proposed Dodgson for Curator of Senior Common Room at Christ Church. Holland, according to Bishop T. B. Strong,

always thought Dodgson had to a certain extent missed his age: that he ought to have lived in the Middle Ages in the palmy days of Scholasticism. His peculiar gifts of mind would . . . have enabled him to rout all other Schoolmen, and to produce subtitles and dialectical terms which would have beaten and confounded the whole of Europe. He pictured Dodgson lecturing (as is said of one of the Schoolmen) to eleven thousand enthusiastic students. They would have flocked to him from all the Universities – Paris, Padua, Bologna, etc., to hear him turn the theories of all other great men inside out and upside down

(Sidney Herbert Williams and Falconer Madan,
A Handbook of the Literature of the Rev. C. L. Dodgson. . . . [1931] p. 212).

The recipient of Holland's letter was Mary Drew (d. 1927), third daughter of W. E. Gladstone.

2. Holland makes too light of Dodgson's work on reforming parliamentary elections. Indeed Dodgson was actively involved in the public controversy over proportional representation. Four of his letters on the subject appeared in the *St James's Gazette* in May and June 1884, and an article on the subject in the same paper on 5 July. He had separate copies of this article struck off, sent one to Lord Salisbury with a covering letter, and then exchanged a number of letters with Lord Salisbury on the subject. Dodgson's proposals have been dealt with at length by Duncan Black in *The Theories of Committees and Elections* (1958) and elsewhere (see *Letters,* esp. pp. 544–5).

'His tantalizing taciturnity'*

H. A. L. FISHER[1]

To none . . . old or young, did this wayward and original spirit open out its curious treasures. His intense shyness and morbid dislike of publicity made him a figure apart. Only in Common Room, when the port had gone round, and only then on a lucky night, would a tiny drop of fantasy fall from Mr Dodgson's lips, after which the venerable humorist would resume his tantalizing taciturnity. A dull and steady routine governed the days of this fantastic friend of all children. Every afternoon he could be seen in his tall silk hat and flowing clerical black striding out to take the air with his inseparable companion the genial and benevolent Vere Bayne,[2] yet another Christ Church cleric, upon whose shoulders, equally with Dodgson's, sacerdotal duty lay with a gossamer weight. The old Life Fellowships, often much abused, justified themselves in the case of this admirable pair.

* From *Unfinished Autobiography* (1940) p. 54.

NOTES

1. Herbert Albert Laurens Fisher (1865—1940), historian, statesman, Warden of New College, Oxford. His father had been a Student at Christ Church. H. A. L. Fisher and

Dodgson must have been acquainted: Dodgson called on him in Oxford on 17 March 1897 (*Diaries*, p. 533).

2. Thomas Vere Bayne (1829–1908) was Dodgson's oldest friend, a relationship that reached back to their childhood in Daresbury. They were contemporaries as undergraduates and dons at Christ Church, and Bayne was Dodgson's predecessor as Curator of Common Room. A 'stately, whiskered' man who, 'when he was not wearing academic dress, was always dressed in top-hat and frock-coat', he was 'the very personification of Christ Church' – Claude M. Blagden, *Well remembered* (1953) pp. 112–13. Bayne witnessed Dodgson's will. For Dodgson's photograph of Bayne, see *Letters*, facing p. 477.

A Production of *Alice**

ALAN MACKINNON[1]

I cannot forbear . . . from mentioning an admirable little performance of *Alice in Wonderland*, which took place in June 1895, and was personally superintended by the author. The scenes were admirably arranged. . . . There was, indeed, a quaint charm about the performance which exactly suited the dainty fantasy of the story.

During the rehearsals in Worcester College Gardens, Dodgson occasionally used to look in, but being a shy man he never allowed himself to come forward; all we ever saw of him was a sly face peeping out from behind a tree and smiling. . . .

* From *The Oxford Amateurs* (1910) pp. 200–1.

NOTE

1. Alan Murray Mackinnon (b. 1870) was an undergraduate at Trinity College, Oxford, and took his BA in 1883; he was also a student of the Inner Temple.

On Homer*

The Dons of Christ Church one evening in Common Room were discussing the authorship of the works of Homer, some supporting the

* 'Varia', *Church Times*, 18 Feb 1898, p. 6.

traditional view, and others denying even the existence of such a person. Dodgson, who was sitting quietly smiling at the eagerness with which each speaker defended his opinion, was at length appealed to for his views, and replied with gravity befitting the occasion that 'he had long made up his mind on this controversy; it appeared to him perfectly clear that the poems attributed to Homer were not written by him, but by another man of the same name!'

'He fined me 10s.'*

LORD KILBRACKEN[1]

In or about the year 1867, I being then an undergraduate of Balliol College, Oxford, was one evening playing billiards with a friend after Hall in a public billiard room. To us entered suddenly a pro-proctor. . . . Having ascertained my name and college, he desired me to call upon him next day in his rooms in Christ Church: I did so, and after giving me a short lecture he fined me 10s. This pro-proctor was Lewis Carroll, otherwise known as the Rev. C. L. Dodgson. *Alice* had then been published about two years, and in the intervals of his proctorial duties he was no doubt elaborating the story of *Through the Looking-Glass*, which appeared a few years later.

* From a letter to *The Times*, 23 Dec 1931, p. 6.

NOTE

1. John Arthur Godley (1847–1932), 1st Baron Kilbracken, Fellow of Hertford College, Oxford, barrister (Lincoln's Inn), Gladstone's private secretary, was a Balliol undergraduate in the late 1860s.

Oxford Women Adore his Memory*

LAURENCE HUTTON[1]

[H]e liked young women, who all liked him; and Oxford is now full of women, mature and immature, who adore the gentle memory of the creator of *Alice*. One of them, still a young woman, who was but a baby when *Wonderland* was originally visited, says of him that 'he was a man whom one had to read backwards'. He had to be looked at 'As Through a Looking-Glass'. She describes him as moody, and as a man of strong dislikes. But he liked her; and, hand in hand, on the roofs of the College, she, as a child, and he used to wander, he always amiable and full of queer conceits of speech and of imagination.

* From *Literary Landmarks of Oxford* (1903) pp. 77–8.

NOTE

1. I have been unable to identify the author.

His 'dry and perfunctory manner'*

HERBERT MAXWELL[1]

Dimly through the mist of 68 years does your leading article about Lewis Carroll bring before me the lean, dark-haired person of Charles Lutwidge Dodgson, before whom as mathematical lecturer we undergraduates of Christ Church used to assemble. Very few, if any,

* Letter to *The Times*, 19 Dec 1931, p. 6.

of my contemporaries survive to confirm my impression of the singularly dry and perfunctory manner in which he imparted instruction to us, never betraying the slightest personal interest in matters that were of deep concern to us. Yet this must have been the very time when he was framing the immortal fantasia of *Alice*.

NOTE

1. Sir Herbert Eustace Maxwell (1845–1937), 7th Bart of Monreith, country gentleman, MP, a lord of the Treasury, author of a life of Wellington, was an undergraduate at Christ Church in the mid 1860s.

A Joke*

EDWARD LEE HICKS[1]

[From Hicks's Diary 1870:] N.B. – Heard this evening the last new joke of the author of *Alice in Wonderland*: He (Dodgson) knows a man whose feet are so large that he has to put on his trousers over his head.

* From John H. Fowler, *Life and Letters of Edward Lee Hicks* (1922) p. 25.

NOTE

1. Edward Lee Hicks (1843–1919) was variously Fellow and Tutor of Corpus Christi College, Oxford; select preacher at Oxford; and Bishop of Lincoln. He does not enter Dodgson's Diaries.

He was 'extremely lucid'*

JOHN H. PEARSON[1]

I was up at Christ Church as an undergraduate early in the eighties, he being my mathematical tutor and certainly his methods of explaining the elements of Euclid gave me the impression of being

* From a letter to *The Times*, 22 Dec 1931, p. 6.

extremely lucid, so that the least intelligent of us could grasp at any rate 'the Pons Asinorum'. I remember he gave me a copy of a game he had invented, something after the manner of chess, which he termed 'Lanrich Mead'; my treasure is lost in the limbo of the past.[2] I wonder whether any other copies are in existence.

NOTES

1. John Henry Pearson (b. 1858), Vicar of Combe-Longa, Oxford, Patron of Lincoln College, Oxford, was an undergraduate at Christ Church in the early 1880s.

2. The limbo of the past claimed the precise name of the game. Dodgson invented *A Game for Two Players* in 1878; in its earliest form he called it 'Natural Selection'; ultimately it became *Lanrick*. It is a game for two players using sixteen men, a chess or draughts board, and nine markers the size of chess squares. Players need good memories to retain the complicated definitions and rules. The point of the game is to be first to get all one's men into a 'Rendezvous', defined by one of the players at the outset of the game. 'Lanrick: A Game for Two Players' appeared in the *Monthly Packet*, Dec 1880, pp. 613–14; and as a separate publication, printed by Oxford University Press, in 1881.

A First Tutorial*

WATKIN H. WILLIAMS[1]

Though 65 years have elapsed since I, in company with eight or 10 other Freshmen attended my first mathematical lecture with Mr Dodgson (*Alice in Wonderland* had not been written, and the name Lewis Carroll was unknown), my memory of the incident is still vivid. He took me last, and, glancing at a problem of Euclid which I had written out, he placed his finger on an omission. 'I deny your right to assert that.' I supplied what was wanting. 'Why did you not say so before? What is a corollary?' Silence. 'Do you ever play billiards?' 'Sometimes.' 'If you attempted a cannon, missed, and holed your own and the red ball, what would you call it?' 'A fluke.' 'Exactly. A corollary is a fluke in Euclid. Good morning.'

* Letter to *The Times*, 12 Jan 1932, p. 6.

NOTE

1. Watkin Herbert Williams (1845–1944), Dean of St Asaph, Bishop of Bangor, took his BA at Christ Church in 1870.

'Deaf on one side'*

G. S. D.[1]

Some of your correspondents seem to be wrong in suggesting that the humour of C. L. Dodgson was quite unsuspected till it flooded the pages of Lewis Carroll. A dear old Oxford don, who fully appreciated that his own fame rested in no wise on his taciturnity, told me this tale with joy. He found himself at a dinner party seated between a lady and Dodgson, whose suggestion that they should change places he naturally resented. 'You see,' explained Dodgson, 'I am deaf on one side and I want to have the good ear toward the lady and the bad one against you.'

* Letter to *The Times*, 28 Dec 1931, p. 6.

NOTE

1. I have been unable to identify the author.

'Homer nods'*

MINNIE TOLLINGTON[1]

My father, the late Bishop Boyd Carpenter, delivered the Bampton Lectures in Oxford in the year 1887. Referring to the conflict between religion and science and the occasions when each blamed the other for an unhappy difference or opinion, my father added. 'Why, this is the old domestic quarrel in which each parent says to the other, Clearly this fault in our child is the outcome of characteristics well known to belong to your family.' An audible if suppressed, titter ran through the learned congregation. A letter of protest was sent, of all people, by

* From a letter to *The Times*, 24 Dec 1931, p. 5.

'Lewis Carroll' to my father, depreciating the introduction of any element of amusement into a sermon. Homer nods. Did a sense of humour for once fail the delightful author of *Alice*?

NOTE

1. The daughter of William Boyd Carpenter (1841–1918), Bishop of Ripon. The letter that Dodgson wrote is reproduced in H. D. A. Major, *The Life and Letters of William Boyd Carpenter* (1925) p. 184; and in *Letters*, pp. 677–8. When Dodgson heard the Bishop preach at Oxford on another occasion, he noted in his Diaries that he thought the Bishop had delivered 'a very remarkable extempore sermon'.

His 'innate kindness'*

'THE LAST OF THE SERVITORS'

As one connected with the House first in the same year as Mr Dodgson took his degree, 1854, I should like to . . . bear witness to the innate kindness of his disposition. On entering the House as an undergraduate in 1864 I received from him a note, asking me to call upon him. I went to his rooms in Tom . . . and he said, 'Mr——, if you are intending to read mathematics, I shall be glad to give you any help you need.'

* From a letter to *The Times*, 30 Jan 1932, p. 6.

PART III

Child Friends

The Friendship that Sparked *Alice's Adventures**

ALICE (LIDDELL) HARGREAVES[1]

Here they come; the two men carrying luncheon-baskets, with the three little girls in shady hats clinging to their hands. The man with the rather handsome, and very interesting face is Mr Dodgson, while the other one is Mr Duckworth, afterward Canon of Westminster, who gave his name to the 'Duck' in 'The Pool of Tears'. Ina, the tallest of the three girls, has brown hair, and very clean-cut features; Alice, the second, has almost black hair cut in a fringe across her forehead; while Edith arrests our attention by her bright auburn hair. Lorina Charlotte, the eldest sister, becomes the Lory in 'The Pool of Tears', while her initials make the name Elsie (L. C.) in the story of the three sisters who lived at the bottom of a well; Lacie, the second 'well' sister, is merely what would nowadays be called an anagram for Alice; Edith becomes Tertia in the dedicatory poem, the Eaglet in 'The Pool of Tears', and Tillie in 'The Three Sisters'. This last was because the other two sisters often called her Matilda, a nickname they had invented for her. Being now introduced, we can follow them down to Salter's, where the rowing boats are kept, and watch them choose a nice roomy boat, and plenty of comfortable cushions. Now Alice can tell us her story free from the many interruptions which would have been sure to come from the other two seventy years ago.

'Soon after we went to live in the old grey stone-built Deanery, there were two additions to the family in the shape of two tiny tabby kittens. One called Villikens, was given to my eldest brother Harry, but died at an early age of some poison. The other, Dinah, which was given to Ina, became the special pet, and lived to be immortalized in the *Alice*. Every day these kittens were bathed by us in imitation of our own upbringing. Dinah I was devoted to, but there were some other animals of which we were terrified. When my father went to Christ

* From 'Alice's Recollections of Carrollian Days, as Told to her Son', *Cornhill Magazine*, 73 (July 1932), 1–12. A different version of this article appeared as 'The Lewis Carroll that Alice Recalls', *New York Times*, 81 (1 May 1932) section 5, pp. 7, 15.

Church, he had some carved lions (wooden representations of the Liddell crest) placed on top of each of the corner posts in the banisters going upstairs and along the gallery. When we went to bed we had to go along this gallery, and we always ran as hard as we could along it, because we *knew* that the lions got down from their pedestals and ran after us. And then the swans on the river when we went out with Mr Dodgson! But, even then, we were always much too happy little girls to be really frightened. We had some canaries, but there was never a white rabbit in the family. That was a pure invention of Mr Dodgson's. . . .

'One Boxing Day [the pony I was riding] crossed its legs, and came down with me on the Abingdon Road. . . . [As a consequence] I was on my back for six weeks with a broken thigh. During all these weeks Mr Dodgson never came to see me. If he had, perhaps the world might have known some more of Alice's Adventures. As it is, I think many of my earlier adventures must be irretrievably lost to posterity, because Mr Dodgson told us many, many stories before the famous trip up the river to Godstow. No doubt he added some of the earlier adventures to make up the difference between *Alice in Wonderland* and *Alice's Adventures Underground*,[2] which latter was nearly all told on that one afternoon. Much of *Through the Looking-Glass* is made up of them too, particularly the ones to do with chessmen, which are dated by the period when we were excitedly learning chess. But even then, I am afraid that many must have perished for ever in his waste-paper basket, for he used to illustrate the meaning of his stories on any piece of paper that he had handy.

'The stories that he illustrated in this way owed their existence to the fact that Mr Dodgson was one of the first amateur photographers, and took many photographs of us. He did not draw when telling stories on the river expedition. When the time of year made picnics impossible, we used to go to his room in the Old Library, leaving the Deanery by the back door, escorted by our nurse. When we got there, we used to sit on the big sofa on each side of him, while he told us stories, illustrating them by pencil or ink drawings as he went along. When we were thoroughly happy and amused at his stories, he used to pose us, and expose the plates before the right mood had passed. He seemed to have an endless store of these fantastical tales, which he made up as he told them, drawing busily on a large sheet of paper all the time. They were not always entirely new. Sometimes they were new versions of old stories: sometimes they started on the old basis, but grew into new tales owing to the frequent interruptions which opened up fresh and undreamed-of possibilities. In this way the stories, slowly enunciated in his quiet voice with its curious stutter, were perfected. Occasionally he pretended to fall asleep, to our great dismay. Sometimes he said 'That is all till next time', only to resume on being told that it was already next time. Being photographed was therefore a joy to us and not a penance as it is to most children. We looked forward to the happy hours in the mathematical tutor's rooms.

'But much more exciting than being photographed was being allowed to go into the dark room, and watch him develop the large glass plates. What could be more thrilling than to see the negative gradually take shape, as he gently rocked it to and fro in the acid bath? Besides, the dark room was so mysterious, and we felt that any adventures might happen then! There were all the joys of preparation, anticipation, and realization, besides the feeling that we were assisting at some secret rite usually reserved for grown-ups! Then there was the additional excitement, after the plates were developed, of seeing what we looked like in a photograph. Looking at the photographs now, it is evident that Mr Dodgson was far in advance of his time in the art of photography and of posing his subjects.

'We never went to tea with him, nor did he come to tea with us. In any case, five-o'clock tea had not become an established practice in those days. He used sometimes to come to the Deanery on the afternoons when we had a half-holiday. . . . On the other hand, when we went on the river for the afternoon with Mr Dodgson, which happened at most four or five times every summer term, he always brought out with him a large basket full of cakes, and a kettle, which we used to boil under a haycock, if we could find one. On rarer occasions we went out for the whole day with him, and then we took a larger basket with luncheon – cold chicken and salad and all sorts of good things. One of our favourite whole-day excursions was to row down to Nuneham and picnic in the woods there, in one of the huts specially provided by Mr Harcourt for picnickers. On landing at Nuneham, our first duty was to choose the hut, and then to borrow plates, glasses, knives and forks from the cottages by the riverside. To us the hut might have been a Fairy King's palace, and the picnic a banquet in our honour. Sometimes we were told stories after luncheon that transported us into Fairyland. Sometimes we spent the afternoon wandering in the more material fairyland of the Nuneham woods until it was time to row back to Oxford in the long summer evening. On these occasions we did not get home until about seven o'clock.

'The party usually consisted of five – one of Mr Dodgson's men friends as well as himself and us three. His brother occasionally took an oar in the merry party, but our most usual fifth was Mr Duckworth, who sang well. On our way back we generally sang songs popular at the time, such as,

> Star of the evening, beautiful star,

and

> Twinkle, twinkle, little star,

and

> Will you walk into my parlour, said the spider to the fly,

all of which are parodied in the *Alice*.

'On one occasion two of Mr Dodgson's sisters joined the party, making seven of us, all in one boat. They seemed to us rather stout, and one might have expected that, with such a load in it, the boat would have been swamped. However, it was not the river that swamped us but the rain. It came on to pour so hard that we had to land at Iffley, and after trying to dry the Misses Dodgson at a fire, we drove home. This was a serious party, no stories nor singing: we were awed by the "old ladies", for though they can only have been in their twenties, they appeared dreadfully old to us.

'In the usual way, after we had chosen our boat with great care, we three children were stowed away in the stern, and Mr Dodgson took the stroke oar. A pair of sculls was always laid in the boat for us little girls to handle when being taught to row by our indulgent host. He succeeded in teaching us in the course of these excursions, and it proved an unending joy to us. When we had learned enough to manage the oars, we were allowed to take our turn at them, while the two men watched and instructed us. [The "Feather, feather" of the Old Sheep must have been a familiar injunction.]³ I can remember what hard work it was rowing upstream from Nuneham, but this was nothing if we thought we were learning and getting on. It was a proud day when we could "feather our oars" properly. The verse at the beginning of the *Alice* describes our rowing. We thought it nearly as much fun as the stories. Sometimes (a treat of great importance in the eyes of the fortunate one) one of us was allowed to take the tiller ropes: and, if the course was a little devious, little blame was accorded to the small but inexperienced coxswain.

'Nearly all of *Alice's Adventures Underground* was told on that blazing summer afternoon with the heat haze shimmering over the meadows where the party landed to shelter for awhile in the shadow cast by the haycocks near Godstow. I think the stories he told us that afternoon must have been better than usual, because I have such a distinct recollection of the expedition, and also, on the next day I started to pester him to write down the story for me, which I had never done before. It was due to my "going on going on" and importunity that, after saying he would think about it, he eventually gave the hesitating promise which started him writing it down at all. This he referred to in a letter written in 1883 in which he writes of me as the "one without whose infant patronage I might possibly never have written at all". What a nuisance I must have made of myself! Still, I am glad I did it now; and so was Mr Dodgson afterwards. It does not do to think what pleasure would have been missed if his little bright-eyed favourite had not bothered him to put pen to paper. The result was that for several years, when he went away on vacation, he took the little black book about with him, writing the manuscript in his own peculiar script, and drawing the illustrations. Finally the book was finished and given to me. But in the meantime, friends who had seen and heard bits of it while he was at work on it, were so thrilled that they persuaded him to publish it. I have been told, though I doubt its being true, that at first he thought that it should be published at the publisher's expense, but that the London publishers were reluctant to do so, and he therefore decided to publish it at his own expense. In any case, after Macmillans had agreed to publish it, there arose the question of the illustrations. At first he tried to do them himself, on the lines of those in the manuscript book, but he came to the conclusion that he could not do them well enough, as they had to be drawn on wood, and he did not know how. He eventually approached Mr (later Sir John) Tenniel. Fortunately, as I think most people will agree, the latter accepted. As a rule Tenniel used Mr Dodgson's drawings as the basis for his own illustrations and they held frequent consultations about them. One point which was not settled for a long time and until after many trials and consultations, was whether Alice in Wonderland should have her hair cut straight across her forehead as Alice Liddell had always worn it, or not. Finally, it was decided that Alice in Wonderland should have no facial resemblance to her prototype.

'Unfortunately my mother tore up all the letters that Mr Dodgson wrote to me when I was a small girl. I cannot remember what any of them were like, but it is an awful thought to contemplate what may have perished in the Deanery waste-paper basket. Mr Dodgson always wore black clergyman's clothes in Oxford, but, when he took us out on the river, he used to wear white flannel trousers. He also replaced his black top-hat by a hard white straw hat on these occasions, but of course retained his black boots, because in those days white tennis shoes had never been heard of. He always carried himself upright, almost more than upright, as if he had swallowed a poker.

'On the occasion of the marriage of King Edward and Queen Alexandra, the whole of Oxford was illuminated, and Mr Dodgson and his brother took me out to see the illuminations. The crowd in the street was very great, and I clung tightly on to the hand of the strong man on either side of me. The colleges were all lit up, and the High Street was a mass of illuminations of all sorts and kinds. One in particular took my fancy, in which the words "May they be happy" appeared in large letters of fire. My enthusiasm prompted Mr Dodgson to draw a caricature of it next day for me, in which underneath those words appeared two hands holding very formidable birches with the words "Certainly not". Even if the joke was not very good, the drawing pleased me enormously, and I wish I had it still!

Little did we dream then that this shy but almost brilliant logic tutor with a bent for telling fairy stories to little girls, and for taking photographs of elderly dons, would before so many years be known all over the civilized world, and that his fairy stories would be translated into almost every European language, into Chinese and Japanese, and some of them even into Arabic! But perhaps only a brilliant logician could have written *Alice in Wonderland*!'

That is my mother's story as it was written down in 1931, before she or I knew anything about Lewis Carroll Centenary Celebrations. 'That blazing afternoon' of story-telling, we know from Lewis Carroll's diary, was 4 July 1862, when 'Alice' herself was 10 years old. On this day, he notes, he 'made an expedition *up* the river to Godstow with the Liddells: we had tea on the bank there, and did not reach Christ Church till half-past eight.' And against this he afterwards added the note – 'on which occasion I told them the fairy-tale of Alice's Adventures Underground, which I undertook to write out for Alice.'

That was the birthday of the story: three years later he celebrated the day with a certain whimsical appropriateness, arranging that when the story came out as a book under its new name it should have the same birthday, for *Alice in Wonderland* was published on 4 July 1865. . . .

As Mr Dodgson says in one of his later letters to my mother, which she still has, she 'was through so many years, my ideal child friend. I have had scores of child friends since your time: but they have been quite a different thing.' Perhaps that is why they none of them inspired him to write another *Alice*.

NOTES

1. Alice Pleasance Liddell (1852–1934) married (1880) Reginald Gervis Hargreaves (1852–1926), of Cuffnells, Hampshire, JP. Her older sister was Lorina Charlotte, known as 'Ina' (1849–1930); she married (1874) William Baillie Skene (1838–1911), Fellow of All Souls, barrister, Student and Treasurer of Christ Church. The third daughter was Edith Mary (1854–76), who was engaged to be married when she died. Sir William Blake Richmond painted the trio as 'The Three Sisters' (see Anne Clark, *Lewis Carroll* [1979] p. 101), and Dodgson photographed them in various combinations (see *Letters*, facing pp. 92, 124, 509, 672; *Life and Letters*, pp. 94, 366; Gernsheim, plate 45; *Diaries*, facing pp. 311, 326). Caryl Liddell Hargreaves (1887–1955), Wing-Commander, Alice's third and youngest son, recorded these recollections.

2. As published, *Alice's Adventures in Wonderland* is twice as long as the version that Dodgson originally wrote out for Alice, which was later published as *Alice's Adventures Under Ground*.

3. Bracketed material by Caryl Hargreaves.

'The inner life of a famous man'*

ISA BOWMAN[1]

It is not easy to make an effort and to remember all the little personalia of some one one has loved very much, and by whom one has been loved. And yet it is in a measure of one's duty to tell the world something of the inner life of a famous man; and Lewis Carroll was so wonderful a personality, and so good a man, that if my pen dragged ever so slowly, I feel that I can at least tell something of his life which is worthy the telling. . . .

I cannot set down a critical estimate, a cold, dispassionate summing-up of a man I loved, but I can write of a few things that happened when I was a little girl, and when he used to say to me that I was '*his* little girl'. . . .

He was so good and sweet, so tender and kind, so certain that there was another and more beautiful life waiting for us, that I know, even as if I heard him telling it to me, that some time I shall meet him once more.

In all the noise and excitement of London, amid all the distractions of a stage life, I know this, and his presence is often very near to me, and the kindly voice is often at my ear as it was in the old days.

To have even known such a man as he was is an inestimable boon. To have been with him for so long as a child, to have known so intimately the man who above all others has understood childhood, is indeed a memory on which to look back with thanksgiving and with tears.

Now that I am no longer 'his little girl', now that he is dead and my life is so different from the quiet life he led, I can yet feel the old charm, I can still be glad that he has kissed me and that we were friends. Little girl and grave professor! it is a strange combination. Grave professor and little girl! how curious it sounds! yet strange and curious as it may seem, it was so. . . .

. . . even in mathematics his whimsical fancy was sometimes suffered to peep out, and little girls who learnt the rudiments of

* Extracts from *The Story of Lewis Carroll* (1899).

calculation at his knee found the path they had imagined so thorny set about with roses by reason of the delightful fun with which he would turn a task into a joy. But when the fun was over the little girl would find that she had learnt the lesson (all unknowingly) just the same. Happy little girls who had such a master. . . .

As a lecturer to his grown-up pupils he was also surprisingly lucid, and under his deft treatment the knottiest of problems were quickly smoothed out and made easy for his hearers to comprehend. 'I always hated mathematics at school,' an ex-pupil of his told me a little while ago, 'but when I went up to Oxford I learnt from Mr Dodgson to look upon my mathematics as the most delightful of all my studies. His lectures were never dry.' . . .

Lewis Carroll was a man of medium height. When I knew him his hair was a silver-grey, rather longer than it was the fashion to wear, and his eyes were a deep blue. He was clean shaven, and, as he walked, always seemed a little unsteady in his gait. At Oxford he was a well-known figure. He was a little eccentric in his clothes. In the coldest weather he would never wear an overcoat, and he had a curious habit of always wearing, in all seasons of the year, a pair of grey and black cotton gloves.

But for the whiteness of his hair it was difficult to tell his age from his face, for there were no wrinkles on it. He had a curiously womanish face, and, in direct contradiction to his real character, there seemed to be little strength in it. . . . He was as firm and self-contained as a man may be, but there was little to show it in his face.

Yet you could easily discern it in the way in which he met and talked with his friends. When he shook hands with you – he had firm white hands, rather large – his grip was strong and steadfast. . . . Every one says when he shook your hand the pressure of his was full of strength, and you felt here indeed was a man to admire and to love. The expression in his eyes was also very kind and charming.

He used to look at me, when we met, in the very tenderest, gentlest way. Of course on an ordinary occasion I knew that his interested glance did not mean anything of any extra importance. Nothing could have happened since I had seen him last, yet, at the same time, his look was always so deeply sympathetic and benevolent, that one could hardly help feeling it meant a great deal more than the expression of the ordinary man.

He was afflicted with what I believe is known as 'Housemaid's knee', and this made his movements singularly jerky and abrupt. Then again he found it impossible to avoid stammering in his speech. He would, when engaged in an animated conversation with a friend, talk quickly and well for a few minutes, and then suddenly and without any very apparent cause would begin to stutter so much, that it was often difficult to understand him. He was very conscious of this impediment, and he tried hard to cure himself. For several years he read a scene from some play of Shakespeare's every day aloud, but despite this he was never quite able to cure himself of the habit. Many people would have found this a great hindrance to the affairs of ordinary life, and would have felt it deeply. Lewis Carroll was different. His mind and life was so simple and open that there was no room in them for self-consciousness, and I have often heard him jest at his own misfortune, with a comic wonder at it.

The personal characteristic that you would notice most on meeting Lewis Carroll was his extreme shyness. With children, of course, he was not nearly so reserved, but in the society of people of maturer age he was almost old-maidishly prim in his manner. When he knew a child well this reserve would vanish completely, but it needed only a slightly disconcerting incident to bring the cloak of shyness about him once more, and close the lips that just before had been talking so delightfully.

I shall never forget one afternoon when we had been walking in Christ Church meadows. On one side of the great open space the little river Cherwell runs through groves of trees towards the Isis, where the college boat-races are rowed. We were going quietly along by the side of the 'Cher', when he began to explain to me that the tiny stream was a tributary, 'a baby river' he put it, of the big Thames. He talked for some minutes, explaining how rivers came down from hills and flowed eventually to the sea, when he suddenly met a brother Don at a turning in the avenue.

He was holding my hand and giving me my lesson in geography with great earnestness when the other man came round the corner.

He greeted him in answer to his salutation, but the incident disturbed his train of thought, and for the rest of the walk he became very difficult to understand, and talked in a nervous and preoccupied manner. One strange way in which his nervousness affected him was peculiarly characteristic. When, owing to the stupendous success of *Alice in Wonderland* and *Through the Looking-Glass*, he became a celebrity, many people were anxious to see him, and in some way or other to find out what manner of man he was. This seemed to him horrible, and he invented a mild deception for use when some autograph-hunter or curious person sent him a request for his signature on a photograph, or asked him some silly question as to the writing of one of his books, how long it took to write, and how many copies had been sold. Through some third person he always represented that Lewis Carroll the author and Mr Dodgson the professor were two distinct persons, and that the author could not be heard of at Oxford at all. On one occasion an American actually wrote to say that he had heard that Lewis Carroll had laid out a garden to represent some of the scenes in *Alice in Wonderland*, and that he (the American) was coming right away to take photographs of it. Poor Lewis Carroll, he was in terror of Americans for a week!

Of being photographed he had a horror, and despite the fact that he was continually and importunately requested to sit before the camera, only very few photographs of him are in existence. [. . . despite his love for the photographer's art, he hated the idea of having his own picture taken for the benefit of a curious world. The shyness that made him nervous in the presence of strangers made the idea that any one who cared to stare into a shop window could examine and criticize his portrait extremely repulsive to him.][2] Yet he had been himself a great amateur photographer, and had taken many pictures that were remarkable in their exact portraiture of the subject.

It was this exactness that he used to pride himself on in his camera work. He always said that modern professional photographers spoilt all their pictures by touching them up absurdly to flatter the sitter. When it was necessary for me to have some pictures taken he sent me to Mr H. H. Cameron,[3] whom he declared to be the only artist who dared to produce a photograph that was exactly like its subject. I thought that Mr Cameron's picture made me look a dreadful fright, but Lewis Carroll always declared that it was a perfect specimen of portrait work.

I had an idle trick of drawing caricatures when I was a child, and one day when he was writing some letters I began to make a picture of him on the back of an envelope. I quite forget what the drawing was like – probably it was an abominable libel – but suddenly he turned round and saw what I was doing. He got up from his seat and turned very red, frightening me very much. Then he took my poor little drawing, and tearing it into small pieces threw it into the fire without a word. Afterwards he came suddenly to me, and saying nothing, caught me up in his arms and kissed me passionately. I was only some ten or eleven years of age at the time, but now the incident comes back to me very clearly, and I can see it as if it happened but yesterday – the sudden snatching of my picture, the hurried striding across the room, and then the tender light in his face as he caught me up to him and kissed me.

I used to see a good deal of him at Oxford, and I was constantly in Christ Church. He would invite me to stay with him and find me rooms just outside the college gates, where I was put into charge of an elderly dame, whose name, if I do not forget, was Mrs Buxall. I would spend long happy days with my uncle, and at nine o'clock I was taken over to the little house in St Aldate's and delivered into the hands of the landlady, who put me to bed.

In the morning I was awakened by the deep reverberations of 'Great Tom' calling Oxford to wake and begin the new day. Those times were very pleasant, and the remembrance of them lingers with me still. Lewis Carroll at the time of which I am speaking had two tiny turret rooms, one on each side of his staircase in Christ Church. He always used to tell me that when I grew up and became married he would give me the two little rooms, so that if I ever disagreed with my husband we could each of us retire to a turret till we had made up our quarrel!

And those rooms of his! I do not think there was ever such a fairy-land for children. I am sure they must have contained one of the finest collections of musical-boxes to be found anywhere in the world. There were big black ebony boxes with glass tops, through which you could see all the works. There was a big box with a handle, which it was quite hard exercise for a little girl to turn, and there must have been twenty or thirty little ones which could only play one tune. Sometimes one of the musical-boxes would not play properly, and then I always got tremendously excited. 'Uncle' used to go to a drawer in the table and produce a box of little screw-drivers and punches, and while I sat on his knee he would unscrew the lid and take out the wheels to see what was the matter. He must have been a clever mechanist, for the result was always the same – after a longer or shorter period the music began again. Sometimes when the musical-boxes had played all their tunes he used to put them into the box backwards, and was as pleased as I at the comic effect of the music 'standing on its head', as he phrased it.

There was another and very wonderful toy which he sometimes produced for me, and this was known as 'The Bat'. The ceilings of the rooms in which he lived at the time were very high indeed, and admirably suited for the purpose of 'The Bat'. It was an ingeniously constructed toy of gauze and wire, which actually flew about the room like a bat. It was worked by a piece of twisted elastic, and it could fly for about half a minute.

I was always a little afraid of this toy because it was too lifelike, but there was a fearful joy in it. When the music-boxes began to pall he would get up from his chair and look at me with a knowing smile. I always knew what was coming even before he began to speak, and I used to dance up and down in tremendous anticipation.

'Isa, my darling,' he would say, 'once upon a time there was some one called Bob the Bat! and lived in the top left-hand drawer of the writing-table. What could he do when uncle wound him up?'

And then I would squeak out breathlessly, 'He could really FLY!'

Bob the Bat had many adventures. There was no way of controlling the direction of its flight, and one morning, a hot summer's morning, when the window was wide open, Bob flew out into the garden and alighted in a bowl of salad which a scout was taking to some one's rooms. The poor fellow was so startled by the sudden flapping apparition that he dropped the bowl, and it was broken into a thousand pieces.

There! I have written 'a thousand pieces', and a thoughtless exaggeration of that sort was a thing that Lewis Carroll hated. 'A thousand pieces?' he would have said; 'you know, Isa, that if the bowl had been broken into a thousand pieces they would each have been so tiny that you could have hardly seen them.' And if the broken pieces had been get-at-able, he would have made me count them as a means of impressing on my mind the folly of needless exaggeration.

I remember how annoyed he was once when, after a morning's sea bathing at Eastbourne, I exclaimed, 'Oh this salt water, it always makes my hair as stiff as a poker.'

He impressed it on me quite irritably that no little girl's hair could ever possibly get as stiff as a poker. 'If you had said, "as stiff as wires", it would have been more like it, but even that would have been an exaggeration.' And then, seeing that I was a little frightened, he drew me a picture of 'The little girl called Isa whose hair turned into pokers because she was always exaggerating things.'

That and all the other pictures that he drew for me are, I'm sorry to say, the sole property of the little fishes in the Irish Channel, where a clumsy porter dropped them as we hurried into the boat at Holyhead.

'I nearly died of laughing' was another expression that he particularly disliked; in fact any form of exaggeration generally called from him a reproof, though he was sometimes content to make fun. . . .

Lewis Carroll's ordinary handwriting . . . [was] not a particularly legible one. When, however, he was writing for the press no characters could have been more clearly and distinctly formed than his. Throughout his life he always made it his care to give as little trouble as possible to other people. 'Why should the printers have to work overtime because my letters are ill-formed and my words run into each other?' he once said, when a friend remonstrated with him because he took such pains with the writing of his 'copy'. . . .

They were happy days, those days in Oxford, spent with the most fascinating companion that a child could have. In our walks about the old town, in our visits to cathedral or chapel or hall, in our visits to his friends he was an ideal companion, but I think I was almost happiest when we came back to his rooms and had tea alone; when the fire-glow (it was always winter when I stayed in Oxford) threw fantastic shadows about the quaint room, and the thoughts of the prosiest of people must have wandered a little into fancy-land. The shifting firelight seemed to almost ætherealize that kindly face, and as the wonderful stories fell from his lips, and his eyes lighted on me with the sweetest smile that ever a man wore, I was conscious of a love and reverence for Charles Dodgson that became nearly an adoration.

It was almost pain when the lights were turned up and we came back to everyday life and tea.

He was very particular about his tea, which he always made himself, and in order that it should draw properly he would walk about the room swinging the teapot from side to side for exactly ten minutes. The idea of the grave professor promenading his book-lined study and carefully waving a teapot to and fro may seem ridiculous, but all the minutiæ of life received an extreme attention of his hands, and after the first surprise one came quickly to realize the convenience that his carefulness ensured.

Before starting on a railway journey, for instance (and how delightful were railway journeys in the company of Lewis Carroll), he used to map out exactly every minute of the time that we were to take on the way. The details of the journey completed, he would exactly calculate the amount of money that must be spent, and, in different partitions of the two purses that he carried, arrange the various sums that would be necessary for cabs, porters, newspapers, refreshments, and the other expenses of a journey. It was wonderful how much trouble he saved himself *en route* by thus making ready beforehand. Lewis Carroll was never driven half frantic on a station platform because he had to change a sovereign to buy a penny paper while the train was on the verge of starting. With him journeys were always comfortable. . . .

For his little girl friends, of course, he reserved the most intimate side of his nature, but on occasion he would throw off his reserve and talk earnestly and well to some young man in whose life he took an interest.

Mr Arthur Girdlestone[4] is able to bear witness to this, and he has given me an account of an evening that he once spent with Lewis Carroll, which I reproduce here from notes made during our conversation.

Mr Girdlestone, then an undergraduate at New College, had on one occasion to call on Lewis Carroll at his rooms in Tom Quad. At the time of which I am speaking Lewis Carroll had retired very much from the society which he had affected a few years before. Indeed for the last years of his life he was almost a recluse, and beyond dining in Hall saw hardly any one. . . .

All through the University, except in an extremely limited circle, Lewis Carroll was regarded as a person who lived very much by himself. 'When', Mr Girdlestone said to me, 'I went to see him on quite a slight acquaintance, I confess it was with some slight feeling of trepidation. However I had to go on some business, and accordingly I knocked at his door about 8.30 one winter's evening, and was invited to come in.

'He was sitting working at a writing-table, and all round him were piles of MSS. arranged with mathematical neatness, and many of them tied up with tape. The lamp threw his face into sharp relief as he greeted me. My business was soon over, and I was about to go away, when he asked me if I would have a glass of wine and sit with him for a little.

'The night outside was very cold, and the fire was bright and inviting, and I sat down. He began to talk to me of ordinary subjects, of the things a man might do at Oxford, of the place itself, and the affection in which he held it. He talked quietly, and in a rather tired voice. During our conversation my eye fell upon a photograph of a little girl – evidently from the freshness of its appearance but newly taken – which was resting upon the ledge of a reading-stand at my elbow. It was the picture of a tiny child, very pretty, and I picked it up to look at it.

'"That is the baby of a girl friend of mine", he said, and then, with an absolute change of voice, "there is something very strange about very young children, something I cannot understand". I asked him in what way, and he explained at some length. He was far less at his ease than when talking trivialities, and he occasionally stammered and sometimes hesitated for a word. I cannot remember all he said, but some of his remarks still remain with me. He said that in the company of very little children his brain enjoyed a rest which was startlingly recuperative. If he had been working too hard or had tired his brain in any way, to play with children was like an actual material tonic to his whole system. I understood him to say that the effect was almost physical!

'He said that he found it much easier to understand children, to get his mind into correspondence with their minds when he was fatigued with other work. Personally, I did not understand little children, and they seemed quite outside my experience, and rather incautiously I asked him if children never bored him. He had been standing up for most of the time, and when I asked him that, he sat down suddenly. "They are three-fourths of my life", he said. "I cannot understand how any one could be bored by little children. I think when you are older you will come to see this – I hope you'll come to see it."

'After that he changed the subject once more, and became again the mathematician – a little formal, and rather weary.'

Mr Gridlestone probably had a unique experience, for it was but rarely that Mr Dodgson so far unburdened himself to a comparative stranger, and what was even worse, to a 'grown-up stranger'. . . .

I am going on to talk about my life with him at Eastbourne, where I used, year by year, to stay with him at his house in Lushington Road. . . . At Eastbourne I was happier even with Lewis Carroll than I was at Oxford. We seemed more free, and there was the air of holiday over it all. Every day of my stay at the house in Lushington Road was a perfect dream of delight.

There was one regular and fixed routine which hardly ever varied, and which I came to know by heart; and I will write an account of it here, and ask any little girl who reads it, if she ever had such a splendid time in her life.

To begin with, we used to get up very early indeed. Our bedroom doors faced each other at the top of the staircase. When I came out of mine I always knew if I might go into his room or not by his signal. If, when I came into the passage, I found that a newspaper had been put under the door, then I knew I might go in at once; but if there was no newspaper, then I had to wait till it appeared. I used to sit down on the top stair as quiet as a mouse, watching for the paper to come under the door, when I would rush in almost before uncle had time to get out of the way. This was always the first pleasure and excitement of the day. Then we used to go downstairs to breakfast, after which we always read a chapter out of the Bible. So that I should remember it, I always had to tell it to him afterwards as a story of my own.

'Now then, Isa dearest,' he would say, 'tell me a story, and mind you begin with "once upon a time". A story which does not begin with "once upon a time" can't possibly be a good story. It's *most* important.'

When I had told my story it was time to go out.

I was learning swimming at the Devonshire Park baths, and we always had a bargain together. He would never allow me to go to the swimming-bath – which I revelled in – until I had promised him faithfully that I would go afterwards to the dentist's.

He had great ideas upon the importance of a regular and almost daily visit to the dentist. He himself went to a dentist as he would have gone to a hairdresser's, and he insisted that all the little girls he knew should go too. The precaution sounds strange, and one might be inclined to think that Lewis Carroll carried it to an unnecessary length; but I can only bear personal witness to the fact that I have firm strong teeth, and have never had a toothache in my life. I believe I owe this entirely to those daily visits to the Eastbourne dentist.

Soon after this it was time for lunch, and we both went back hand-in-hand to the rooms in Lushington Road. Lewis Carroll never had a proper lunch, a fact which always used to puzzle me tremendously.

I could not understand how a big grown-up man could live on a glass of sherry and a biscuit at dinner time. It seemed such a pity when there was lots of mutton and rice-pudding that he should not have any. I always used to ask him, 'Aren't you hungry, uncle, even *to-day*.'

After lunch I used to have a lesson in backgammon, a game of which he was passionately fond, and of which he could never have enough. Then came what to me was the great trial of the day. I am afraid I was a very lazy little girl in those days, and I know I hated walking far. The trial was, that we should walk to the top of Beachy Head every afternoon. I used to like it very much when I got there, but the walk was irksome. Lewis Carroll believed very much in a great amount of exercise, and said one should always go to bed physically wearied with the exercise of the day. Accordingly there was no way out of it, and every afternoon I had to walk to the top of Beachy Head. He was very good and kind. He would invent all sorts of new games to beguile the tedium of the way. One very curious and strange trait in his character was shown on these walks. I used to be very fond of flowers and of animals also. A pretty dog or a hedge of honeysuckle were always pleasant events upon a walk to me. And yet he himself cared for neither flowers nor animals. Tender and kind as he was, simple and unassuming in all his tastes, yet he did not like flowers! I confess that even now I find it hard to understand. He knew children so thoroughly and well – perhaps better than any one else – that it is all the stranger that he did not care for things that generally attract them so much. However, be that as it may, the fact remained. When I was in rapture over a poppy or a dogrose, he would try hard to be as interested as I was, but even to my childish eyes it was an obvious effort, and he would always rather invent some new game for us to play at. Once, and once only, I remember him to have taken an interest in a flower, and that was because of the folk-lore that was attached to it, and not because of the beauty of the flower itself.

We used to walk into the country that stretched, in beautiful natural avenues of trees, inland from Eastbourne. One day while we sat under a great tree, and the hum of the myriad insect life revealed the murmur of the far-away waves, he took a foxglove from the heap that lay in my lap and told me the story of how they came by their name; how, in the old days, when, all over England, there were great forests, like the forest of Arden that Shakespeare loved, the pixies, the 'little folk', used to wander at night in the glades, like Titania, and Oberon, and Puck, and because they took great pride in their dainty hands they made themselves gloves out of the flowers. So the particular flower that the 'little folks' used came to be called 'folks' gloves'. Then, because the country people were rough and clumsy in their talk, the name was shortened into 'Fox-gloves', the name that every one uses now.

When I got very tired we used to sit down upon the grass, and he used to show me the most wonderful things made out of his handkerchief. Every one when a child has, I suppose, seen the trick in which a handkerchief is rolled up to look like a mouse, and then made to jump about by a movement of the hand. He did this better than any one I ever saw, and the trick was a never-failing joy. By a sort of consent between us the handkerchief trick was kept especially for the walk to Beachy Head, when, about half-way, I was a little tired and wanted to rest. When we actually got to the Head there was tea waiting in the coastguard's cottage. He always said I ate far too much, and he would never allow me more than one rock cake and a cup of tea. This was an invariable rule, and much as I wished for it, I was never allowed to have more than one rock cake.

It was in the coastguard's house or on the grass outside that I heard most of his stories. Sometimes he would make excursions into the realms of pure romance, where there were scaly dragons and strange beasts that sat up and talked. In all these stories there was always an adventure in a forest, and the great scene of each tale always took place in a wood. The consummation of a story was always heralded by the phrase, 'The children now came to a deep dark wood.' When I heard that sentence, which was always spoken very slowly and with a solemn dropping of the voice, I always knew that the really exciting part was coming. I used to nestle a little nearer to him, and he used to hold me a little closer as he told of the final adventure.

He did not always tell me fairy tales, though I think I liked the fairy tales much the best. Sometimes he gave me accounts of adventures which had happened to him. There was one particularly thrilling story of how he was lost on Beachy Head in a sea fog, and had to find his way home by means of boulders. This was the more interesting because we were on the actual scene of the disaster, and to be there stimulated the imagination.

The summer afternoons on the great headland were very sweet and peaceful. I have never met a man so sensible to the influences of Nature as Lewis Carroll. When the sunset was very beautiful he was often affected by the sight. The widespread wrinkled sea below, in the mellow melancholy light of the afternoon, seemed to fit in with his temperament. I have still a mental picture that I can recall of him on the cliff. Just as the sun was setting, and a cool breeze whispered round us, he would take off his hat and let the wind play with his hair, and he would look out to sea. Once I saw tears in his eyes, and when we turned to go he gripped my hand much tighter than usual.

We generally got back to dinner about seven or earlier. He would never let me change my frock for the meal, even if we were going to a concert or theatre afterwards. He had a curious theory that a child should not change her clothes twice in one day. He himself made no alteration in his dress at dinner time, not would he permit me to do so. Yet he was not by any means an untidy or slovenly man. He had many little fads in dress, but his great horror and abomination was high-heeled shoes with pointed toes. No words were strong enough, he thought, to describe such monstrous things.

Lewis Carroll was a deeply religious man, and on Sundays at

Eastbourne we always went twice to church. Yet he held that no child should be forced into church-going against its will. Such a state of mind in a child, he said, needed most careful treatment, and the very worst thing to do was to make attendance at the services compulsory. Another habit of his, which must, I feel sure, sound rather dreadful to many, was that, should the sermon prove beyond my comprehension, he would give me a little book to read, it was better far, he maintained, to read, than to stare idly about the church. When the rest of the congregation rose at the entrance of the choir he kept his seat. He argued that rising to one's feet at such a time tended to make the choirboys conceited. I think he was quite right.

He kept no special books for Sunday reading, for he was emphatically of opinion that anything tending to make Sunday a day dreaded by a child should be studiously avoided. He did not like me to sew on Sunday unless it was absolutely necessary.

One would hardly have expected that a man of so reserved a nature as Lewis Carroll would have taken much interest in the stage. Yet he was devoted to the theatre, and one of the commonest of the treats that he gave his little girl friends was to organize a party for the play. As a critic of acting he was naïve and outspoken, and never hesitated to find fault if he thought it justifiable. . . .

He was a fairly constant patron of all the London theatres, save the Gaiety and the Adelphi, which he did not like, and numbered a good many theatrical folk among his acquaintances. Miss Ellen Terry was one of his greatest friends. Once I remember we made an expedition from Eastbourne to Margate to visit Miss Sarah Thorne's theatre, and especially for the purpose of seeing Miss Violet Vanbrugh's Ophelia. He was a great admirer of both Miss Violet and Miss Irene Vanbrugh as actresses. Of Miss Thorne's school of acting too he had the highest opinion, and it was his often expressed wish that all intending players could have so excellent a course of tuition. Among the male members of the theatrical profession he had no especial favourites, excepting Mr Toole and Mr Richard Mansfield.[5]

He never went to a music-hall, but considered that, properly managed, they might be beneficial to the public. It was only when the refrain of some particularly vulgar music-hall song broke upon his ears in the streets, that he permitted himself to speak harshly about variety theatres.

Comic opera, when it was wholesome, he liked, and was a frequent visitor to the Savoy theatre. The good old style of Pantomime too was a great delight to him, and he would often speak affectionately of the pantomimes at Brighton during the régime of Mr and Mrs Nye Chart.[6] But of the up-to-date pantomime he had a horror, and nothing would induce him to visit one. 'When pantomimes are written for children once more,' he said, 'I will go. Not till then.'

Once when a friend told him that she was about to take her little girls to the pantomime, he did not rest till he had dissuaded her. . . .

[Lewis Carroll was] the greatest friend to children who ever lived. Not only did he study children's ways for his own pleasure, but he studied them in order that he might please them. . . . Year after year he retained the same sweet, kindly temperament, and, if anything, his love for children seemed to increase as he grew older. . . .

Over all matters connected with letter writing, Lewis Carroll was accustomed to take great pains. All letters that he received that were of any interest or importance whatever he kept, putting them away in old biscuit tins, numbers of which he kept for the purpose. . . .

He was so modest about . . . [his books], that it was extremely difficult to get him to say, or write, anything at all about them. I believe it was a far greater pleasure for him to know that he had pleased some child with *Alice* or *The Hunting of the Snark*, than it was to be hailed by the press and public as the first living writer for children. . . .

Socially, Lewis Carroll was of strong conservative tendencies. He viewed with wonder and a little pain the absolute levelling tendencies of the last few years of his life. . . .

And now I think I have done all that has been in my power to present Lewis Carroll to you in his most delightful aspect – as a friend to children. . . . I hope I have done something to bring still nearer to your hearts the memory of the greatest friend that children ever had.

NOTES

1. 'Among the celebrated theatrical families who from their childhood upwards have been cherished by the playgoing public none have filled a more prominent position for the last decade than the Bowman sisters', wrote a critic in *Era* on 14 June 1902 (p. 11). Dodgson had a good deal to do with putting that family on the stage and with its great success. He first encountered Isa, who had a small part in the original stage production of *Alice*, at a rehearsal, and before long met the other Bowman children, three younger sisters and a brother. With Dodgson's help, all went on to act professionally – the girls to full-time stage careers. The parents of these gifted children were Charles Andrews Bowman (b. 1851), pianist and organist, and his wife Helen Herd, born Holmes. Isabella ('Isa', 1874–1958) was the eldest. She later married (1899) George Reginald Bacchus (1873–1945), an Oxford graduate and journalist. It appears that she grew estranged from her husband and became the common-law wife of one Frank Barclay, whose name she adopted. Isa acted the leading role in the 1888 revival of *Alice* at the Globe Theatre.

2. Passage in brackets appears later in Isa Bowman's book.

3. Henry Herschel Hay Cameron, youngest son of Charles Hay Cameron (1795–1880) and his famous photographer wife, Julia Margaret Cameron (1815–1880), became a professional photographer with a studio near Cavendish Square, 'advertising himself as "a photographic artist". . . . [He] seemed to have added acting to his other interests in life, for one of his great-nieces remembers seeing him as the Carpenter in a production of *Alice in Wonderland* . . .' – Brian Hill, *Julia Margaret Cameron* (1973) p. 174. Dodgson visited Cameron's studio on 16 September 1887, and bought some 'lovely photos' (p. 455). He took Isa to the studio on 27 September, presumably to be

photographed. Dodgson visited the studio at least once more, on 16 January 1888, and bought more photographs (p. 457).

4. Arthur Henry Girdlestone (1869–?) matriculated at New College in 1888.

5. Sarah Thorne (1836–99), actress–manager, taught many aspiring young people at her theatres in Margate and Chatham and took some of them on tour. Violet and Irene Vanbrugh were students of Miss Thorne (for more about the Vanbrughs, see p. 188n, below). For more about Dodgson and Ellen Terry, see p. 241n, below; for more on J. L. Toole, see p. 188n, below. The Bowman sisters toured with the distinguished actor Richard Mansfield (1857–1907) in the United States in 1889.

6. Another established theatrical family. They were Henry Nye Chart (1822–76) actor—manager, and his wife Ellen Elizabeth Rollason, manager. Their son, Henry Nye Chart (1868–1934), began a distinguished acting career as a ten-months-old baby when he was carried onto the stage of the Theatre Royal, Brighton.

Some of his Child Friends were 'married women with children of their own'*

BEATRICE HATCH[1]

Though no longer children in years there were many to whom 'Lewis Carroll' still gave . . . [the title Child-Friends]:

'I make very few new child-acquaintances now, but I have still so many old child-friends, some of them married women with children of their own', was a remark he made to me recently, with one of those delightful smiles which usually accompanied such sayings. It is, therefore, in the capacity of one of his oldest 'child-friends', and one who as such saw perhaps more of him in the last few years than most others, that I venture to give some recollections of our 'Mr Dodgson', for the sake of those who know him less intimately.

'Lewis Carroll' is known almost throughout the world by his incomparable *Alice*, and yet in many respects that author and the Don of Christ Church, Oxford, were two distinct persons, and he preferred that the public should act as if this were the case. 'I claim no authorship with any such book', was his invariable answer to letters that came addressed to 'the Rev. C. L. Dodgson' on the subject of his fictitious works; while, on the other hand, the unfortunate people who

* From 'In Memoriam. Charles Lutwidge Dodgson (Lewis Carroll)', *Guardian*, 19 Jan 1898, pp. 11–12.

sent any communications to 'Lewis Carroll, Christ Church, Oxford', had their notes returned unopened on the plea that no such person lived at that address. It was his horror of being lionized which made him thus repel would-be acquaintances, interviewers, and the persistent petitioners for his autograph, and he would afterwards relate the stories of his success in silencing all such people with much satisfaction and amusement. Not long ago Mr Dodgson happened to get into correspondence with a man whom he had never seen, on some questions of religious difficulty, and he invited him to come to his rooms and have a talk on the subject. When, therefore, a Mr X. was announced to him one morning he advanced to meet him with outstretched hand and smiles of welcome. 'Come in, Mr X., I have been expecting you.' The delighted visitor thought this a promising beginning and immediately pulled out a note-book and pencil, and proceeded to ask 'the usual questions'. Great was Mr Dodgson's disgust! Instead of his expected friend here was another man of the same name, and one of the much-dreaded interviewers, actually sitting in his chair! The mistake was soon explained, and the representative of the press was bowed out as quickly as he had come in. On another occasion the editor of a collection of biographies wrote to ask for the honour of including his in the forthcoming volume. Mr Dodgson would not even allow him the satisfaction of an autograph letter in reply, but sent over to the present writer of this paper to request that a copy of his refusal should be made and forwarded by her.

But to his 'child-friends' he was the most gentle, affectionate, and sympathetic of companions. It is hardly necessary, perhaps to say they were always of the weaker sex. He did not like boys any more than he liked *very* young children, though it is difficult to believe that, after the delightful creation of 'Bruno'.[2] But girls of all sorts interested him – old and young, plain and pretty; from princesses, whose photographs and letters to himself he would show with some pride, down to lowly born children in a poor parish, where a sweet face would attract him from the band of hope or school audience assembled to hear him tell stories and draw pictures on a blackboard for their special amusement. . . .

It is difficult to realize, even while the bell is tolling in our ears this sad morning, that Oxford will no longer see that thin, upright figure walking rapidly through the streets, seeing no one, greeting no one, intent on his own thoughts, alone, or with a child-friend as companion, as he fetches her to have tea in his rooms, or takes her home again. He very rarely associated with any men of his own standing, beyond dining in Hall, and of later years he refused all invitations into society. A rule once made must never be broken was evidently a motto of his. I have known him reply to an invitation for a particular day, 'Because you have *asked* me, therefore I cannot come, but I will come the next day'; and those who know of this rule were careful not to *invite*, but merely to give information that they would be at home on a certain day at a certain hour, and to leave it to him whether he would come or not. Unless it were understood that no other guests would be there he would even then not come. But what of his own 'parties'? – for he was fond of entertaining, and a truly excellent host. The number of guests invited seldom exceeded *one*, though I have known two and even three. He preferred to have his friends singly, and in the case of two sisters whose mother wished them to come together he has been known to decline the pleasure of their company altogether. At one time it was always 'a walk and tea', to which one was invited, and this grew into 'dinner parties'. Never lunch, for he did not take it, and he liked to work uninterruptedly all the morning until nearly two o'clock. But now the last is over – the climb up the winding, wooden staircase in the corner of Tom Quad; the unlocking of the great oak door with 'the Rev. C. L. Dodgson' painted in white letters over it; yet another small door to be opened, and there we are in the large familiar room, with its huge windows overlooking St Aldate's. Under the bookcase are the cupboards which I loved as a child, for besides the mystery of their being unlocked by a special key on Mr Dodgson's own bunch, they contained such delights in the way of musical boxes, a brown bear that walked when it was wound up, and packets innumerable of photographs, held together by india-rubber bands, and catalogued with exquisite neatness. . . .

But let us go on to more recent years, since 'dinner parties' began. You are seated in a corner of the red sofa in front of the large fireplace, over which hang some painted portraits of his child-friends. . . . Logic is still, as it always has been, his great subject, and *Symbolic Logic*, of which Part I. was published in February, 1896, the particular branch. Indeed, he would almost make you believe that this study was an essential of life, and was glad of any opportunity to impart instruction to his girl-acquaintances. When dinner is announced you are led into another room much smaller than the first, and you may be quite sure you will never get the same *menu* that you had last time; for, besides other registers, lists and catalogues of letters, books, &c., Mr Dodgson keeps a list of the dishes supplied every time he has guests at his table, and is careful always to look this up when he invites you, that you may not have the same thing twice. Two courses, and only two, is another of his rules – meat and pudding – and no one could wish for more. After dinner . . . there are games of his own invention, 'Mish-mash', 'Lanrick', and so on; also his own Memoria Technica to be explained and possibly learnt. And so the evening slips away, and it is time to be escorted home again.

I have never heard Mr Dodgson preach, and shall always regret it.

It was but rarely that he did so; not that I believe his stammer was any hindrance to him in this. He has often told me that he never wrote out his sermons. He knew exactly what he wished to say, and completely forgot his audience in his anxiety to explain his point clearly. He thought of the subject only, and the words came of themselves. Looking straight in front of him he saw, as it were, his argument mapped out in the form of a diagram, and he set to work to prove it point by point, under its separate heads, and then summed up the whole. He took a serious view of life, and had a very grave vein running through his mind. The simplicity of his faith was very beautiful, though he had his prejudices, and some rather curious ideas on religious subjects. But he was liberal to all men, and always ready to help where he could. I have known him take a great deal of trouble over a very small matter, in order to aid or give pleasure to a friend, or even a friend's friend. We shall miss him for a long time to come – not for his books, for his story-telling days were past, but for himself. The well-known bright smile whenever we met; the long calls, when one felt oneself a child again for old sake's sake and life one vast holiday; the familiar and characteristic handwriting in the frequent and amusing notes; above all, the true affection that grows scarcer in these latter days – these are now things of the past, and we mourn.

But the lover of children himself 'as a little child' is reaping his reward of rest and peace beyond the veil.

NOTES

1. Dodgson was a friend of the Hatch family for more than twenty-five years. He photographed the children, gave them inscribed copies of his books, visited them often, took them on outings, and helped to advance their careers. The father of the family was Edwin Hatch (1835–89), controversial theologian, Vice-Principal of St Mary Hall, Oxford, and University Reader; the mother was born Bessie Cartwright Thomas (1839–91). The three girls, whom Dodgson christened collectively 'BEE' (the first initials of their three given names), were his favourites. The were Beatrice Sheward (1866–1947), who later grew interested in social work and was appointed the first probation officer in Oxford; Ethel Charlotte (1869–1975), who studied at the Slade School and became an artist; and Evelyn Maud (1871–1951), Benjamin Jowett's godchild, who was a student at St Hugh's, Oxford, and during the First World War worked for the War Office in London. Evelyn collected and edited *A Selection from the Letters of Lewis Carroll to His Child-Friends* (1933).
2. Dodgson's 'Bruno's Revenge' and *Sylvie and Bruno* (see p. 195n, below).

'Never . . . did any man make more friends among children'*

BEATRICE HATCH

[I]t is from a 'child-friend's' point of view that I wish to make a sketch of him, and to show something of what the real man was – not as lecturer, mathematician, or college don, but as a friend.

There are very many who could draw a similar picture of him, for never, surely, did any man make more friends among children than he did during the earlier and middle parts of his life. Latterly, however, he had not increased his acquaintance much, but the 'child-friends' of past years were still honoured by the old title, even though childhood had long been left in the far distance. Boys did not share this honour, nor babies. They were only tolerated for their sisters' sakes; but girls, little and big, were admitted into friendship at once. Sometimes on the sea-shore, sometimes in a railway carriage, the magnetic power began, and, in many cases, continued for life. It was impossible for Mr Dodgson to pass by the smallest opportunity of speaking to a child, and his winning manner gained the hearts, and generally the tongues, of all whom he met.

It was this love for children, combined with his inventive faculty, that led him to tell that most original story which afterwards developed into *Alice in Wonderland*. . . .

Puzzles and problems of all sorts were a delight to Mr Dodgson. Many a sleepless night was occupied by what he called a 'Pillow problem'. In fact, his mathematical mind seemed to be always at work on something of the kind, and he loved to discuss and argue a point connected with his logic if he could but find a willing listener. Sometimes while paying an afternoon call he would borrow scraps of paper, and leave neat little diagrams or word puzzles to be worked out by his friends. . . .

In his estimation, logic was a most important study for everyone. No pains were spared to make it clear and interesting to those who

* From '"Lewis Carroll"', *Strand Magazine*, Apr 1898, pp. 413–23.

would but consent to learn of him, either in a class, that he begged to be allowed to hold in a school or college, or to a single individual girl, who showed the smallest inclination to profit by his instructions. He never spared himself in any detail: everything was done in the neatest and most methodical manner. The arrangement of his papers, the classification of his photographs, the order of his books, the lists and registers that he kept about everything imaginable – all this betokened his well-ordered mind.

There was a wonderful letter-register of his own invention, which not only recorded the names of his correspondents, and the dates of their letters, but which also summarized the contents of each communication, so that in a few seconds Mr Dodgson could tell you what you had written to him about on a certain day in years gone by.

The plan of this letter register is explained by the inventor in his booklet called *Eight or Nine Wise Words about Letter-Writing*, which he published together with an 'Alice' Stamp-case in [1890]. . . .

Another register contained a list of every menu supplied to every guest who dined at Mr Dodgson's table! This sounds like the doing of an epicure, but Mr Dodgson was not that – far from it. . . . But everything that he did must be done in the most perfect manner possible; and the same care and attention would be given to other people's affairs, if in any way he could assist or give them pleasure. If he took you up to London to see a play at the theatre, you were no sooner seated in your railway carriage than a game was produced from his bag, and all occupants of the compartment were invited to join in playing a kind of 'halma' or 'draughts' of his own invention, on the little wooden board that had been specially made at his design for railway use, with 'men' warranted not to tumble down, because they fitted into little holes in the board! And the rest of those happy days spent with him were remarkable for the consideration that was shown for your comfort and happiness. If you went to see Mr Dodgson in the morning you would find him, pen in hand, hard at work on neat packets of MS. Carefully arranged around him on the table, but the pen would instantly be laid aside, and the most cheerful of smiles would welcome you in for a chat as long as you liked to stay. He was always full of interest, and generally had something fresh to show: an ingenious invention of his own for filing papers, or lighting gas, or boiling a kettle!

My earliest recollections of Mr Dodgson are connected with photography. He was very fond of this art at one time, though he had entirely given it up for many years latterly. He kept various costumes and 'properties' with which to dress us up, and, of course, that added to the fun. What child would not thoroughly enjoy personating a Japanese, or a beggar-child, or a gipsy, or an Indian? . . . Sometimes there were excursions on to the roof of the College, which was easily accessible from the windows of the studio. Or you might stand by your tall friend's side in the tiny dark room, and watch him while he poured the contents of several little, strong-smelling bottles on to the glass picture of yourself that looked so funny with its black face. And when you grew tired of this, there were many delights to be found in the cupboards in the big room downstairs. . . .

Opposite to the big window, with its cushioned seat, is the fireplace; and this is worthy of some notice on account of the lovely red tiles, which represent the story of *The Hunting of the Snark*. Over the mantelpiece hang three painted portraits of child-friends, the one in the middle being a picture of a little girl in a blue coat and cap, who is carrying a pair of skates. But the room is a study, and not a drawing-room, and the big tables and the tall reading-desks bear evidence to the genuine work that is done there. . . .

Mr Dodgson seats his guest in a corner of the red sofa in front of the fireplace, and the few minutes before dinner are occupied with anecdotes about other 'child-friends', small or grown up, or anything particular that has happened to himself, such as more applications from interviewers, collectors of autographs, and other persecutors. . . .

Dinner is served in a smaller room, which is also filled with bookcases and books. But we will imagine the repast concluded, for those who have had the privilege of enjoying a College dinner need not to be told how excellent it is, and we must not rouse envy in those who have not! The rest of the evening slips away very quickly, there is so much to be done, and to be shown. You may play a game . . . or you may see pictures, lovely drawings of fairies, whom your host tells you 'you can't be sure don't really exist'. Or you may have music, if you wish it, and Mr Dodgson will himself perform. You look round (supposing you are a stranger) for the piano. There is none. But a large square box is brought forward, and this contains an organette. Another box holds the tunes, circular perforated cards, all carefully catalogued by their owner. One of the greatest favourites is 'Santa Lucia', and this will open the concert. The handle is affixed through a hole in the side of the box, and the green baize lining of the latter helps to modulate the sound. The picture of the author of *Alice*, keenly enjoying every note, as he solemnly turns the handle, and raises or closes the lid of the box to vary the sound, is more worthy of your delight than the music itself. Never was there a more delightful host for a 'dinner-party', or one who took such pains for your entertainment, fresh and interesting to the last.

Sometimes I have spent an evening with Mr Dodgson in conversation only. With all his humour he took a serious view of life, and had a very grave vein running through his mind. The simplicity of his faith, his deep reverence, and his child-like trust in the goodness of God were very striking. His look of surprise, and gentle reassurance to a girl who told him she was nervous when she travelled by rail, fearing an accident, come into mind as I write. 'But surely you *trust* God! Do you think He would let you come to harm? To be *afraid* is to distrust.' These and other similar words of his give us an insight into the pure and open mind, in whose clear waters Heaven's sunshine could find an unsullied reflection. . . .

One form in which Mr Dodgson took his recreation was by going to the theatre, and with his strict views of morality, and refined taste, he was able many a time to induce stage managers to correct, or omit, anything that might jar on sensitive ears. Of course, the plays that he cared to go to were very limited in number. He particularly enjoyed seeing children act, and many a little actress would receive a note or a card, accompanied by a copy of one of his books, handed in at the stage-door the morning after the performance; and this was often the beginning of much kindness shown to her and a true friendship. . . .

All of these things belong now to the past, and we must open a new chapter in our lives, in which that well-known figure will not appear. But the benefaction which he bestowed upon the world is still with us – the benefaction of a wit that was never sarcastic, a humour that was always sympathetic; and the embodiment in himself of the three essentials of Life: Faith, the light by which to live; Hope, the goal for which to labour; Charity, the wide horizon, on which his soul looked out in love.

'They have such wrong ideas about him'*

ETHEL HATCH

During the last few years there have been portrayals of Lewis Carroll which seemed to me to give a very false impression of his character. . . .

They have such wrong ideas about him – that he was a recluse, and that he made friends with little girls but was too shy to talk to grown-ups. On the contrary, apart from his college work, he was many-sided in his interests. For over thirty years photography was his great hobby, and as well as writing children's books and books on logic and mathematics, and inventing games and puzzles, his chief delight was

* From 'Lewis Carroll Remembered', *Listener*, 4 Aug 1966, p. 167.

in the theatre. He knew all the chief professional actors and actresses of the day, especially Ellen Terry, who became a great friend. He also had many artist friends, among them Sir John Millais and Rossetti.

When he sometimes took me to visit friends in London, he was always perfectly at his ease, and had extremely good manners. In Oxford he had many friends among the married and unmarried dons. . . .

He disliked parties, especially dinner-parties – 'bandying small talk with dull people' was his description of them – and if he did not talk it was not from shyness but from boredom. But he seems to have enjoyed Lady Salisbury's house-parties at Hatfield, and would sit up till one in the morning talking to his fellow guests in the smoking-room. And the dons in the Senior Common Room at Christ Church delighted in his witty talk. In ordinary conversation his stammer was so slight as to be hardly noticeable, but it was probably more pronounced when he was lecturing.

He once said that the greatest happiness in life was in making others happy, and he certainly succeeded in doing this. Though I had a happy childhood on the whole, the days I spent with him were days – to use his own expression – 'to be marked with a white stone', and apart from his kind of thoughtful deeds for others, his books after all these years still give great happiness to many who never knew him.

'He was always staid and dignified'*

ETHEL HATCH

Beatrice remembered when she was five or six years old that when we were getting ready to depart he callled up the stairs to her: 'Hansom or growler?' and, thinking of hansom as an adjective, she promptly called back 'Handsome!' He had given her a large wax doll with fair hair brushed back, very like the pictures of Alice, who could say 'Papa' and 'Mama' quite plainly when she was pinched. Once when Beatrice had gone away for a little visit he wrote her a most amusing letter pretending that he had met the doll just outside Tom Gate trying to find the way to his rooms and crying because she had been

---

* From 'Recollections of Lewis Carroll', *Listener*, 30 Jan 1958, pp. 198–9, 202.

left all alone. So, he said, he took the doll into his rooms and sat her on his knees, 'but she exclaimed at being too near the fire and said: "You don't know how careful we have to be, we dolls. There was a sister of mine, would you believe it, she went up to the fire to warm her hands and one of them dropped right off." Of course it dropped right off, I said, because it was the right hand. "And how do you know it was the right hand", the doll said. So I said I think it must have been the right hand because the other hand was left. The doll said, "I shan't laugh, it's a very bad joke."'

After the photographic days Mr Dodgson often came to see us in our new house in Canterbury Road, but never by invitation as he always refused invitations. Once my mother sent him one for a tea party with '4–6' written on it. His answer came: 'Dear Mrs Hatch, What an awful proposition. To drink tea from 4–6 would try the constitution of the most hardened tea-drinker; to me, who hardly ever touch it, it would probably be fatal.' My mother loved entertaining and was a very good amateur actress. When we lived in Park Town theatricals were easy to arrange as there were folding doors between the dining-room and drawing-room. Though Mr Dodgson was very keen on the theatre he would never go to see amateurs acting, but he wrote an amusing prologue for my brother Wilfred and Beatrice to repeat before the performance; they were then about eight and seven years old. The whole prologue was reproduced in facsimile in *The Strand Magazine* in 1898. It is too long for me to repeat, but it began:

Wilfie! I'm sure that something is the matter!
All day there's been – oh, such a fuss and clatter!
Mamma's been trying on a funny dress –
I never *saw* the house in such a mess.

Then, when she hears there is to be a play, she says: 'How nice.' Wilfred says, 'But will it please the rest?' 'Oh, yes,' she says, 'because you know they'll do their best.' The play evidently did please some of the audience. I think it was a farce because my mother said the Miss Liddells, Alice and her sisters, the three who had first heard the story of Alice at the memorable picnic to Godstow, sat in the front row and had laughed so much, especially Edith, the one who died a few years later.

An afternoon walk was a regular habit of Mr Dodgson's, and we often met him out. I can recall him now, walking with his friend Mr Bayne, in St Giles'. He was tall and thin, with thick, dark hair turning iron-grey, clear-cut features, and light-blue eyes which seemed to take in everything as he looked about him; and his thin lips were generally twisted into a humorous smile. He was dressed in the usual clerical dress of that day, a black frock-coat and white cravat, and a top-hat rather at the back of his head. . . .

One of us was sometimes his companion on a walk. In a letter he wrote to me, inviting me to a walk and to tea in his rooms afterwards, he said he preferred children one by one, to two by two or even forty by forty. I particularly remember a lovely walk I had with him through the two Hinkseys, starting over Folly Bridge, and being at once on a country road with hedges each side. No houses had then been built on Boars Hill above. The Hinkseys were isolated country villages,[1] quite unspoilt, and walking through the fields between them we had a lovely view of Oxford as Matthew Arnold might have seen it. I had been taught that little girls should be seen and not heard and was shy of talking much, but Mr Dodgson had plenty to tell me, and talked too of the amusing things some little girls said to him. . . .

One afternoon he came to see us to ask what books he had given to each of us. He had given Beatrice several – *Through the Looking-glass, The Hunting of the Snark, Doublets*, and others. Evelyn had also received some from him. He was quite distressed when he found he had never given me a book and said I must have a copy of the next one that came out. The very next morning my nurse called me with a package addressed to me by Mr Dodgson. This was a book of the songs from *Alice* with the music – all well-known tunes which were evidently the tunes he would wish them sung to. I still have the book in its paper cover, with my name on it, and his usual monogram: CLD. A little later on he wrote about a book that he was going to send me but was not sure when it would be ready and added: 'If anticipation brings happiness, what should forty years of anticipation bring? – Why, forty years of happiness.' That was characteristic of his logical mind. The book happened to be *Rhyme? and Reason?* with which I was delighted when it arrived, as I loved *The Hunting of the Snark* as well as 'Hiawatha's Photographing', which it contained. We all received other books from him as they came out – *The Game of Logic, Sylvie and Bruno*, etc. – and of course the usual presents invented by him – the Wonderland Stamp Case and the biscuit-tin covered with pictures from *Alice* – but his many kindnesses to us are far too many to enumerate.

In spite of much fun and laughter in the games he played with us I can never remember his romping with us; he was always staid and dignified. One of our greatest treats was to be taken up to London for the day, fetched by him in a hansom for the 9 a.m. train, travelling second class (third class was unheard of in those days). On the journey games and books were brought out of a large black bag to pass the time. At Paddington we got into a hansom and drove to the Academy or some other exhibition, and after lunch, sometimes at the house of some of his old friends, we went to a *matinée*.

My fifteenth birthday was a red-letter day in my life when I went to the theatre for the first time; the Oxford Theatre had not been built then. The play was *Claudian*,[2] at the Princess's Theatre in Oxford

Street, Wilson Barrett taking the chief part. . . . The same day I was introduced to two of his artist friends. We visited Miss Heaphy at Heatherley's Studio, and Miss Gertrude Thomson, who had illustrated William Allingham's poem of the fairies,[3] joined up for the theatre. Mr Dodgson had suggested my bringing a book of my childish drawings to show them – on Ruskin's advice I had had no lessons – and afterwards both the artists wrote me kind letters giving me some advice. They were forwarded through Mr Dodgson, who wrote saying they made him green with jealousy as the only thing he ever had time to draw were the corks from all the bottles of beer that he drank.

Later on there were many more theatre expeditions, often to the Lyceum to see Ellen Terry and Irving. I especially remember seeing them in *Olivia*,[4] with Irving as the Vicar of Wakefield. Isa Bowman, Mr Dodgson's new child-friend, came with us. Beatrice was taken to *Much Ado*, and afterwards she received a photograph from Ellen Terry with 'To Beatrice from Beatrice' written underneath, and the words: 'There was a star danced, and under that was I born.' After one *matinée* Mr Dodgson took me to Guildford to spend the week-end with him and his sisters, three elderly maiden ladies, in their Victorian house, The Chestnuts, up above the town near the castle.

After my father died and my mother was in bad health he came to visit her frequently and she always enjoyed long serious talks with him. He still took an interest in my drawing, and was most anxious to send me to Herkomer's School at Bushey, offering to pay all expenses; he was so wonderfully generous. But some bad oil paintings that I had just attempted to do at a local class were not accepted when I sent them up for admission to the school, I am afraid Mr Dodgson was very disappointed, as I was at the time. But I have never regretted it since, as later on I went to the Slade School in London. Though he had the reputation of dropping his child-friends when they grew up he certainly kept up his friendship with us. After my mother's death our home in Oxford was given up, and my sister Evelyn and I went to London, and Mr Dodgson would often come up at the weekends and take one of us out to a *matinée* on a Saturday afternoon.

My sister Beatrice lived on in Oxford with our friends Canon and Mrs Sanday in their beautiful old house in Christ Church, so she was then in close touch with Mr Dodgson. She used to enjoy the *tête-à-tête* dinners she had with him in his rooms. From her earliest years she had been a great favourite of his, and in an entry in his diary he mentions that she is expected, adding: 'always a most welcome visitor'. I regret that I never had a *tête-à-tête* dinner with him at Christ Church although I did once have an invitation. I had gone down to stay with our friends in Christ Church for a weekend and my sister Evelyn, who was then at St Hugh's, was coming to spend the evening. So I refused his invitation, saying that I wanted to stay with my sisters. He then wrote me a most amusing letter. He said I was the new Cinderella who was so devoted to her sisters that she could not bear to be parted from them, and that they all went together to the ball and danced all the evening together, with their arms round each other's waist, and the prince was quite out of it. I had had *tête-à-tête* meals with him of course when I stayed with him in his lodgings in Eastbourne – but my visit there was overshadowed by my mother's serious illness and has left very little impression on me, though I know he arranged some entertainment for me every day. His next visitor was Irene Vanbrugh whose father was an old friend of Mr Dodgson's. He was most anxious that I should stay longer and meet her but I was not able to.

In 1897 he came to lunch with me in London before asking me to a *matinée*. I saw him again at the end of the year when he took me to the Court Theatre and two other young friends joined us. So it was quite unexpected and a great shock when a few weeks later, one morning in January, the maid brought in the newspaper, saying: 'Your sister says, you will be sorry to see the death of an old friend.' One never thought of him as old, and though he did sometimes suffer from ill-health he never showed it outwardly and was always the same cheery self to his friends. We had lost someone who had been in the background of our lives ever since I could remember anything.

Now I am speaking from a room in Kensington where he sometimes sat, though when I came to live here some years ago I did not know that George MacDonald had lived in this house in the eighteen-sixties and that Mr Dodgson often visited him here. It was also from this house that the suggestion was made that the book *Alice* should be published. He had sent the manuscript to Mrs MacDonald to read to the children and they had been so delighted with the story that she wrote urging him to publish it. He acted on her advice in 1865.

I am sitting in the same armchair in which he sometimes sat when he came to call on us in Oxford. At the end of his letter in 1884 wishing me forty years of happiness, he added: 'Think of me in the year 1924' – and now I am thinking of him in 1958.

NOTES

1. North and South Hinksey, no more than two miles south-west of Oxford.
2. Dodgson recorded in his Diaries that on 17 May 1884 he went 'to town, with Ethel Hatch, by the 9 a.m. train. We called . . . on Theo [Heaphy] at her studio. Then to Miss Thomson's, and after seeing her cartoon, etc., we 3 dined at Verrey's, and then went to [Henry Herman and W. G. Wills'] *Claudian*, which both my companions enjoyed much. We went back to Miss T., and had tea there. . . . I got Ethel home by about 8½.'
3. Dodgson was acquainted with the conventional portrait and narrative painter Thomas (Frank) Heaphy (1813–73) as early as 1867 and after Heaphy's death befriended the Heaphy family, especially his favourite of the eleven children, Theodosia

Laura (b. 1859). She followed in her father's footsteps with a modest success as a painter. For more on the Heaphys, see *Letters*, esp. p. 105. Dodgson and E. G. Thomson became acquainted in January 1879, and he gave copies of William Allingham's *The Fairies: A Child's Song* (1883), which she illustrated, as gifts to child friends. For more on Miss Thomson, see p. 236n, below.

4. On 27 June 1891, Dodgson went 'to London with Ethel Hatch. We went to the Royal Academy, lunched at Charing Cross. Then to see *Olivia* [W. G. Wills' adaptation of Goldsmith's *The Vicar of Wakefield*] at the Lyceum' (*Diaries*, p. 484).

The 'fresh beauty' of his Child Friends Appealed to 'his very keen artistic sense'*

EVELYN M. HATCH

As time went on, his fondness for children became more and more of a hobby. He made friends with little girls wherever he went, and occasionally with their small brothers also – his professed dislike of little boys allowing for some exceptions – and the circle got wider and wider, until his child-friends could be numbered by the hundred. The secret of their fascination for him lay chiefly in the appeal which their fresh beauty made to his very keen artistic sense, and in the stimulus which their ready acceptance of anything new or strange gave to his powers of invention. Their naïve sayings, also, were a continual delight to him. His child-friends belonged to his leisure moments – for he was a most industrious worker – and the very fact of their being associated with holiday and hours of recreation gave an additional gaiety to his enjoyment of their society. Here, too, were ample opportunities for carrying out his philosophy of life, that 'the truest kind of happiness, the only kind that is really worth the having, is the happiness of making others happy too'. . . .

Mr Dodgson was very much a part of Oxford, and those who lived there in their childhood all share the same recollections of him.

. . . if alone, he always seemed to have pleasant thoughts, if with a

* From Introduction to *A Selection from the Letters of Lewis Carroll . . . to His Child-Friends* (1933) pp. 1–13.

companion, young or old, he was usually telling some amusing story. And a child on the opposite side of the road would be greeted by a wave of the hand, or thrown a kiss, and would go home delighted, with the news 'I met Mr Dodgson!'

... The letters written by Mr Dodgson to the Oxford children consisted usually of short notes, in purple ink, on a half-sheet of paper, enclosed in a small square envelope and containing an invitation to 'a walk and tea and bread-and-butter' or 'to dine with me – only two courses' (generally including the famous Christ Church meringues), or perhaps an even more delightful proposal for a day in London, with a visit to the Pantomime or to a theatre.

The walks with Mr Dodgson bring back many pleasant associations. His favourite haunts were through the Parks and over the ferry to Marston fields, starred in early spring with celandines and daisies; round Christ Church Meadows or Magdalen Walks in May-time, when the trees were white and red with hawthorn, and buttercups were glowing in the sunshine; or further afield, into real country, through the quiet villages of the Hinkseys, before the gorse-covered slopes of Boar's Hill had been converted into suburbs of red brick. Walks were the special privilege of little-girl friends and he preferred to take only one at a time, considering 'three the worst possible number for a party'. During the walk he entertained his small guest with stories, riddles and jokes, and on their return to have 'tea and bread-and-butter' in the familiar big study with its oriel window overlooking St Aldate's. . . .

With the same thoroughness and energy which he applied to everything which he undertook, Mr Dodgson spared no pains as a host, and always made special efforts to overcome the shyness of a timid child – a feeling with which he had a secret sympathy. Yet a silent child-guest was a perplexity to him, and he was undoubtedly more at ease with one who would chatter unrestrainedly. Spoilt or greedy children were anathema: he would have nothing to do with them.

Some of the Oxford children still retained his friendship after they were grown up, but many of them passed out of his sight. He complained in one of his letters that 'usually a child becomes so entirely a different being as she grows into a woman, that our friendship has to change too, and that it usually does by sliding down from a loving intimacy into an acquaintance that merely consists of a smile and a bow when we meet'. In certain cases even the smile and the bow became a thing of the past, but this may be accounted for by the refusal of some parents to allow their daughters to go to his rooms unchaperoned – a point on which he was very sensitive.

During the last period of his life, when he was busy with his books on Logic and was giving classes at the High School and at Lady

Margaret and St Hugh's Hall, he was inclined to choose his new acquaintance from among older girls, although, as he pointed out in a letter . . . , he regarded them – and indeed treated them – as 'child-friends still'.

The present writer remembers how, on the first occasion of his coming to hold a Logic class at St Hugh's, about a dozen students assembled solemnly in the library, armed with note-books and pencils, prepared to listen to a serious lecture on a difficult subject. To their surprise, and also somewhat to their dismay, Mr Dodgson produced from his black bag twelve large white envelopes, each containing a card marked with a diagram, and a set of counters in two colours. These he dealt out to his audience. 'Now,' he said cheerfully, 'I will teach you to play the game of Logic!' And then, when he proceeded to illustrate his explanations with examples, his pupils found that they were actually expected to *laugh*! But though such propositions as:

> Some new Cakes are nice
> No new Cakes are nice
> All new Cakes are nice

and

> All teetotalers like sugar
> No nightingale drinks wine

sounded rather like extracts from a child's reading-book, it was soon discovered that considerable intelligence, as well as much skill and attention were required to learn the game and work out a conclusion on the diagram. How patiently he bore with our stupidity! To him we were all still very young! In these days dinner-parties with 'one young lady as guest' became his favourite form of entertainment, and he would spend the evening discussing Logic problems, playing games, or drawing on his fund of stories about the amusing sayings of children he had known. . . .

Children everywhere, when they were very small, took an intense delight in sitting on his knee or nestling in a group around him, while he told them some of his wonderful stories, illustrated by rapid sketches on the back of an envelope. Mr Dodgson was no draughtsman, but at least he could make his figures full of expression in a few dramatic strokes – hair on end with fright, hands raised in horror, or faces broad with smiles. Every story had some unexpected and marvellous ending. There was the one which finished with the words: 'My dear, you are a *Perfect Goose*!' and lo and behold, the drawing which had gone alongside the tale of a little man and woman who lived in a house with one window, by the side of a lake, and had been frightened by imaginary burglars, was turned upside down and there was a *Perfect Goose*! It was the way Mr Dodgson told it, rather than the story itself, which always gave the never-to-be-forgotten thrill. . . .

Part of Mr Dodgson's enjoyment of children came from the pleasure of watching them. For this reason he used to spend his summer vacations at the seaside, at one time at Whitby, later at Sandown in the Isle of Wight, and finally, for many years, at Eastbourne. There he loved to sit and look at the children playing on the sands. Sometimes he tried to sketch them, and he usually ended by enticing one of them to come and talk to him, but, with a true artist's sense of discrimination, he had his likes and dislikes and made his choice deliberately. As in the train, where he would while away the tedium of a long railway journey with every kind of distraction, he would bring a wire-puzzle out of his pocket, ask a riddle, tell a story, or teach some new game to his delighted listener. Of course he remained incognito, but would reveal himself at last as 'Lewis Carroll' by sending one of his books with an inscription 'from the author' to greet his new acquaintance on her return home. The thought of the shock of surprise that the opening of the parcel would bring gave him much amused satisfaction. . . .

He had many friends among the residents at Eastbourne, and during the latter part of his life he used to give Logic classes at some of the girls' schools there. Perhaps because it was vacation-time, he seems to have been more sociable at Eastbourne than in Oxford, where he refused all invitations, and at Mrs Barber's school he would go to supper with the girls and mistresses and hold informal classes after. It was Eastbourne, too, that, from about 1887 onwards, he would have children and girl-friends to stay with him.

Ellen Terry called Mr Dodgson 'a splendid theatre-goer', and her correspondence with him . . . shows the interest which he always took in dramatic art. He knew all the Terrys – Kate, who became Mrs Arthur Lewis and was always ready to welcome him and to let him bring a child-friend to her house on Campden Hill; Florence, who retired from the stage in 1882; and especially Ellen and Marion, for whose brilliant talents he had a great admiration. How many a gracious act of kindness can be attributed to the part of these two charming sisters, who were always ready to send a photograph or a bouquet of flowers or some other little attention to a child-friend brought to the theatre by Mr Dodgson! . . .

The dramatization of his books brought him into close touch with the stage-world. *Alice in Wonderland* was first produced at the Prince of Wales's Theatre in December 1886, as an operetta, with Phoebe Carlo as heroine. Mr Dodgson got to know all the performers and gave them each one of his books. . . . I am able to quote the letter which he wrote on this subject to the author and producer, Mr Savile Clarke:

'I want to give to every child (*i.e.* every boy and girl under 14) who has acted in this play, a book as a memento of the thing. . . . In the case of any child so young that he, or she, cannot yet read, perhaps the mother, or other guardian, will choose the book?' . . .

To his letter-writing he applied the meticulous care and precision which were characteristic of all his undertakings; the handwriting is clear and legible and the punctuation is always in the right place. The monogram 'C. L. D.' – so contrived that it could be written and intertwined without taking pen from the paper – was an invention of his youth, and seems to have indicated a certain degree of friendliness when used as a signature.

He wrote to children as he would talk to them – to the very young ones in simple language, to those over ten with the assumption that they would understand his jokes and not take his teasing too seriously. If 'Lewis Carroll' often appears, especially in the earlier letters, it must be remembered that he and 'Mr Dodgson' were one and the same person, and that it was in his relations with child-friends that the creator of the immortal 'Alice' gave the most complete revelation of himself.

'Out of temper'*

EVELYN M. HATCH

[His] taste for contrivance was shown in his *Memoria Technica* for remembering dates. I possess some notes in his own handwriting giving rhymes for the dates of Oxford colleges, as follows: –

Ch. Ch.
  Ring Tom when you please
  We ask small fees.

B. N. C.
  With a nose that is brazen
  Our gate we emblazon.

Each of the last three consonants denotes a number, l for 5, f for 4, and s for 6, so that the date for Christ Church is 1546, while in the

From 'Memories of Lewis Carroll', *Guardian*, 29 Jan 1932, p. 5.

case of Brazenose l, z, n, give 1509, it being always taken for granted that 1 is the first figure.

In spite of the jokes in the examples, Mr Dodgson regarded his *Game of Logic* as a serious system, into which he had put much hard work, and he used to speak of his disappointment that he could not persuade other teachers of logic to adopt his methods.

What I remember most about Mr Dodgson is his kindness and his love of giving pleasure. He was generous with presentation-copies of his books and his letters were always delightful, signed with the familiar monogram C. L. D. . . .

Only once did I ever see him out of temper. It was in the early days and we were being photographed in the attic which he had arranged as a studio. He was summoned to go downstairs to receive Mrs X, who had brought a lady to call upon him. He returned very shortly, considerably ruffled. 'There is one thing that I cannot stand,' he said, 'and that is to be pointed out as: "That's the man who wrote *Alice in Wonderland*!"'

'It is the stupidest book I ever read!'*

EVELYN M. HATCH

Every summer he used to spend some weekends at Eastbourne, where he liked to sit on the sands and watch the children digging castles.

There he made many young friends, and the intercourse usually led up to the question: 'Have you ever read a book called *Alice in Wonderland*?' Sometimes the reply was disconcerting, and he often related with a grim chuckle how a small girl had answered: 'Yes, and I think it is the stupidest book I have ever read!'

But he carefully concealed his identity, and if the answer happened to be, 'No, I have never heard of it' – a copy would be despatched as a surprise to arrive the day after the child had arrived home, with the inscription: 'From the Author'!

Lewis Carroll declared that *Alice* and *Looking-Glass* were made up of

* From 'Author who Hated Sport', *Daily Record and Mail (Glasgow)*, 1 Mar 1932, p. 12.

bits and scraps, single ideas which came of themselves – hence their originality. His mind was always busy with inventions – riddles, games, stories, jokes, but he said that they came to him so suddenly and unexpectedly that at night he would have to strike a light to jot down an idea, or he had to stop in the midst of a walk to make a note of some brilliant thought. Like all true artists, he could not write to order. . . .

Among many families in Oxford he was an ever-welcome guest. He would appear unexpectedly one afternoon, join in a game of 'bears' under the dining-room table or sit by the fire and tell stories, which he had a way of turning into pictures. . . .

When we were older we used to get invitations for a day in London to visit the Royal Academy and see a matinée – a rare treat in those days. Going to the theatre was one of Mr Dodgson's favourite recreations, and with his usual precision he kept a 'play-record' which showed how often young friends were taken to share his pleasure. . . .

Mr Dodgson held strong opinions on many subjects and had a rigid code of morals. He hated hypocrisy in any form and had a horror of sport as a cruel pastime. Behind all his jokes there was a seriousness and an undercurrent of idealism. His aim was to give happiness and to make life richer both for his known and his unknown friends.

A Lecturer with a Black Handbag*

EVELYN M. HATCH

When I was a student at St Hugh's Hall, Oxford, in the nineties, I remember how my old friend Mr Dodgson offered to come and give us a lecture on logic. With great eagerness my fellow-students prepared to meet the famous mathematical tutor who was the authour of *Alice in Wonderland*, and assembled in the library armed with notebooks and pencils. To their surprise the lecturer appeared with a large black handbag, from which he proceeded to draw a number of white envelopes to be distributed among his audience. Each envelope proved to contain a card marked with two square diagrams and nine counters, some pink and some grey. Notebooks and pencils were not required: we were to play a game!

* From a letter to *The Times*, 7 January 1932, p. 6.

The envelope with its contents, as well as a book of explanation which went with it – a gift from the author and containing his signed initials elaborately intertwined with the date – are still in my possession. The book is called *The Game of Logic* and was first published by Macmillan and Co. in 1887.[1] It is almost as good reading as *Alice*, and the examples of premises given as exercises are in the true Lewis Carroll style. I quote the following:

> No bald person needs a hairbrush.
> No lizards have hair.

> A prudent man shuns hyaenas.
> No banker is imprudent.

> Bores are terrible.
> You are a bore.

The *Game* is as amusing as a good cross-word puzzle, and the author concludes a characteristic preface by saying: 'A second advantage possessed by this Game is that besides being an endless source of amusement . . . it will give the Players a little instruction as well. But is there any great harm in *that*, so long as you get plenty of amusement?'

Mr Dodgson often talked of his strange dreams and sudden inspirations, and his mind was evidently constantly busy with inventions. I remember a word-game called 'Mischmasch' which we used to play when he took me for his favourite walk round the Hinkseys, and can well recollect playing 'Lanrick' . . . , but I have never seen any written instructions for it. On the same occasion as the logic lecture at St Hugh's he taught us a 'Memoria Technica' for remembering dates, of which I have the notes in his handwriting.

NOTE

1. The first edition actually appeared in 1886.

The Fount of Stories that Never Ran Dry*

ENID SHAWYER[1]

Alice in Wonderland, as everybody knows, was told for the entertainment of three little girls on a river picnic. What few people realize is that that wonderful fount of stories never ran dry. I was his very last child-friend, and during all our many long afternoons together they continued to bubble up – fresh, original, and inimitable as ever. Two or three times a week he would come and 'borrow' me, and we would go off together, wholly content with each other's company, for afternoons which I shall never forget. I have, alas, forgotten the stories, because he never told the same one twice, but the Mad Gardener and the Spherical Proctor (in *Sylvie and Bruno*) originated on those walks, and there were a great many more of the Mad Gardener's songs ('He thought he saw . . .') than those which appeared in the book. If one seemed to him worth perpetuating, he would write it down when we got back to Christ Church, and I – great joy – would be allowed to type it.

The joys of our afternoons together were by no means ended when we returned to Christ Church. For hours on end we used to sit curled up together – the old man and the little girl – in a big arm-chair, playing games with words, working out ciphers together, or making up strange mathematical problems. We played games with ordinary apparatus too – backgammon, draughts, and sometimes chess – but they were odd variants of the usual games, and he took a great deal of trouble working out their rules. Often, the next morning, I would get a little note from him saying 'I think it would work better if . . .', and then a long exposition of a new rule. Chess was the most fun. He was, of course, a master of the game, but when he played with a child the knights and bishops became alive and held heated discussions over the rights of queens or the ownership of castles.

The word-games were always his favourites, and several of his own invention have been published in other books about him – *Mischmasch*, for instance, and the *Game of Logic* which he wrote and published

* From *Diaries*, pp. xxiv–xxvi.

himself. But his logical mind, with its odd turns and twists, tended to see absurdity in the common misuse of words that happens every day, and he loved to lead one through the most complicated mazes of reasoning to the conclusion that one had meant exactly the opposite of what one had just said.

When I was twelve I had scarlet fever, and for six long weeks I was shut away from all society. In all that time not a day passed without a letter from 'my old gentleman' (as the family always called him), bringing me an original puzzle, or a cipher to solve, or a new and absorbing game to play. Alas! all that treasure was assigned to the flames when I recovered, because it might harbour germs. I was furious about that at the time and have never since seen reason to revise my twelve-year-old opinion.

One of the most remarkable things about him was that in spite of the fact that he talked to his child friends exactly as if they were on an equal footing for himself, he never hesitated to correct a fault – never with a scolding, but in such a way that one saw its evil side and hated it, and one never forgot his talks. Never for one moment did one think of them as one did of the fault-finding of other grown-ups at school or at home. The truth of the matter is that he had the heart of a child himself, so when he spoke to a child she understood – even about the deeper things of life – because he spoke her own language.

Over and over again he begged my mother to let him take me away with him – sometimes to the seaside, sometimes to London. The Victorian mind saw possible evil even in the association of a child of twelve with an old man of sixty-three. He must have had wonderful patience, for he tried again and again, but I was never allowed to go and shall never to the end of my days cease to regret it. Days of close intercourse with one who, however whimsical his mind, was one of the few genuine scholar-saints were denied me because the saint was male and I was a little girl.

He did, however, manage to get permission to take me to my first play in Oxford. It was *Sweet Lavender*, with Edward Terry as Richard. Another great occasion was our visit to the Oxford University Press, where the Controller took us right through the production of a New Testament, from start to finish, and presented it to me at the end, with inscriptions both by himself and Mr Dodgson. I still treasure it.[2]

Mr Dodgson would have nothing to do with undergraduate activities. He regarded undergraduates as nothing but a necessary evil in University life, and such social occasions at Eights' Week were abhorrent to him. In Eights' Week 1893 he wrote inviting me to tea in his rooms as usual, adding, 'But are you sure you wouldn't rather go to the Eights. (Or if *that* isn't enough perhaps you would like to go to the Nines). Now *I* don't care for either Eights or Nines. All I want is to get a young lady of about $11\frac{1}{4}$ to come to tea – one that won't want to go down to the boats, but will just come up with me on the roof, where we can smoke our cigars in peace, and talk about Oliver Cromwell (my favourite subject you know).' When I went to tea with him in response to this note we played hide-and-seek among the chimney-pots above his rooms (the roof was one of our favourite playgrounds) and regarded the smart crowds returning from the races with pitying scorn.[3]

Another occasion of climbing with him was when he took me up Tom Tower to see the great bell which nightly rings the curfew. I was allowed to strike it once with a big hammer, causing glorious reverberations which must have greatly puzzled the inhabitants of Oxford.

I have gathered from the memoirs of other child-friends of his that their recollections of him consist mostly of 'occasions'. Our happy companionship was more like that of a grandchild with a much-loved grandfather. I never realized – as I do now – what jewels were being poured out for my entertainment. I know now that my friendship with him was probably the most valuable experience in a long life, and that it influenced my outlook more than anything that has happened since – and wholly for good. It was only when he was walking hand in hand with a child that expression came freely to him, and one such child here acknowledges to his memory a debt she can never repay.

NOTES

1. Dodgson first met Enid Gertrude Stevens on 27 February 1891, when he brought her oldest sister home after a walk. Enid (1882–1960) married (1904) James Anderson Shawyer (1879–1930), schoolmaster and inspector of schools. Her friendship with Dodgson during his last years was most gratifying to him. He commissioned his artist friend E. Gertrude Thomson (see p. 236n, below) to do a portrait of Enid, which then hung over his mantel at Christ Church. He dedicated *Sylvie and Bruno Concluded* with an acrostic verse to Enid. Enid's parents were Nicholas Henry Stevens (1826–82), London surgeon, and his second wife, Edith, born Headland (1841–1919).

2. On his birthdays, Dodgson preferred to give rather than receive presents. On his sixty-second (27 Jan 1894), his birthday 'treat' was to take Enid to a matinée of the Pinero play at the New Theatre. 'It was Enid's very *first* experience of a theatre, and I think she thoroughly enjoyed it', Dodgson wrote in his *Diaries* (p. 508). 'I am sure *I* did', he added. On April 7 1893, Dodgson borrowed Enid 'as usual' and took her to the University Press: 'The Controller took us through the Bible Department, which was as new a sight to me as to Enid. About 100 girls are employed, in glueing, covering, etc., and in superintending machinery which does folding, sewing, etc.' (*Diaries*, p. 498).

3. On 23 May 1896, Dodgson noted in his Diaries, '[My] 3 nieces went to the 8's – Violet with Mrs Lucy, and Beatrice and Gladys with Mrs Stevens and Enid. The latter 4 went, with my card, on to the Christ Church Barge, and came to me for tea between the races.'

'He was . . . terrified of my mamma'*

ENID SHAWYER

Although I wrote a foreword for the *Diaries of Lewis Carroll*, reviewed in last Sunday's *Observer* by Sir Harold Nicolson, I have not yet seen the book. But, as one of his 'child-friends' (he died when I was fourteen), I have such vivid memories of happy times spent in his company that I am unable to stand aside without protest while he is dismissed as 'dull'.

The highlights of my childhood, between the ages of nine and fourteen, were the afternoons when he used to take me for long walks, culminating in tea and games in his rooms in Christ Church. I know nothing about schizophrenia, but those afternoons were spent with Lewis Carroll – not any 'dull' Mr Dodgson. They were lit by fantasy worthy of the creator of the Jabberwock, the March Hare, and the Snark, and there was no 'mawkish pathos' about our friendship. Stories flowed from him, every bit as wonderful as those published in his books. Games with words, invented on the spur of the moment and later elaborated, delighted equally the old man and the little girl.

Arithmetical puzzles, and games founded on Logic (with the most gloriously funny examples) were kept for after tea, when pencils and paper were available, and wits had to be kept on tiptoe.

With grown-ups he was shy (he was obviously terrified of my mamma) – but then, so was I! It only made him more like oneself. His stammer (or, rather, stutter – it happened only on d's and t's) was unnoticeable except to himself, but I believe it did worry him.

I have, of course, no opportunity of knowing whether he was unpopular in Common Room – but he was certainly very welcome in the Dean's Lodgings in the days of Alice Liddell. Of the College servants I know a little more; for he used to take me down to the kitchen to be given the cook's famous eclairs, and they obviously loved him there.

As for being 'a lonely freak who wore black cotton gloves' – those who caused him to be lonely were unaware of what they were missing.

* Letter to the *Observer*, 14 Feb 1954, p. 22.

And why should he not wear black cotton gloves if he liked? (though, having walked miles and miles and in hand with him, I very much doubt whether he did).

Finally, these Diaries were never meant for publication. They are the methodical memoranda, stripped of all feeling, of the Rev. C. L. Dodgson, with no hint in them of the Lewis Carroll who was his *alter ego*. *Dull*? My goodness no! There was never a dull moment for a child in the company of Lewis Carroll – even though we had to call him Mr Dodgson.

'A tiny little note . . . asking me to tea'*

ENID SHAWYER

I first met him, I think, when I was nine: it was 1891, and I had a very bad cold and they had made me go to bed upstairs. He called on my mama and I was singing 'The Walrus and the Carpenter' at the top of my voice and he heard me. He didn't know there *was* me before that. I was not allowed down that day, but what happened the next morning was a perfectly delightful little note – oh, a tiny little note, the tiniest hand-writing – asking me to tea. That was the beginning of it. After that he used to fetch me – he used to call it borrowing me – two or three times a week, take me for long walks and take me back to tea in his rooms. He used to call for me in Canterbury Road and we generally took a tram to the Parks entrance; they were horse trams in those days, of course. Sometimes we went right round the Parks, but generally we went diagonally across the Parks and then along the river, past Parsons' Pleasure, to the ordinary Mesopotamia walk. Sometimes we went up Headington Hill from there, quite long walks.

He had a certain amount of don's work to do, but he did regard the undergraduate as a necessary evil, wholly an evil; he took no interest in undergraduate pursuits. I always remember once, he wrote asking me if I would like to come and have tea with him as usual – he always sent solemn little notes, that was because of my mamma. . . . Of course I said I would love to go, and we played hide and seek on the

* From Mrs E. G. Shawyer, 'More Recollections of Lewis Carroll – III', *Listener*, 6 Feb 1958, pp. 239, 243.

roof all among the chimney pots. We often did that; and watched all
the smart people coming back from the Eights with great scorn. We
often used the roof, as he had a special staircase up to it.

Stories poured out of him, one after another, and I can't remember
any of them because they never were repeated. During our walks he
was making up all the mad gardener and the spherical proctor verses
in *Sylvie and Bruno*, and there were far more of them than ever came
into print. But when he found one that he really thought he must
print, he would scribble it down and when we got back to the rooms I
was allowed to type it – tremendous joy.

Hours and hours we used to sit there; he had two enormous college
chairs, and he and I would be curled up in one of those and he would
continue the stories or else play games. We had lovely games. He had
backgammon and chess and all the possible things you can think of;
but he didn't play them as one had been taught to play them, he had
his own rules. Chess was the greatest fun. We were made to play
properly in chess, he was a master of this game – he couldn't bear to
do anything else; but for all the other games he had entirely new rules.
And he loved ciphers: he very often wrote letters to me in cipher, and
I had to solve them. What really pleased me was when I wrote him
back a letter in cipher and he couldn't solve it.

I don't remember which year it was that *Sylvie and Bruno* came out,
but anyway Harry Furniss used to come to his rooms and draw me by
the dozen; but I am told that the drawings of Sylvie in the book are
really Harry Furniss' own daughter. But Lewis Carroll always said I
was Sylvie. When the book came out, he dedicated the second volume
to me in an acrostic in which my name is the third letter in every line.

All that time we were the very greatest friends; I don't think
anybody else ever had so much of him as I had. I used to introduce
little friends of my own; he was always very sweet to them, but it
never got any further. He died when I was fifteen and a half. I was the
last child-friend; he had no others then at all. So I had no cause to be
jealous – ever.

To me he was Mr Dodgson*

E. M. ROWELL[1]

When I first saw Lewis Carroll I was a sixth-form girl at the Oxford High School. One morning at school the word went around that 'Mr Dodgson' was coming to give some lectures to the sixth on symbolic logic. To me the name 'Mr Dodgson' meant nothing, and when someone said casually, 'Lewis Carroll, you know', I acquiesced in the synonym, but my mind was blank as before.

I had of course always known *Alice in Wonderland*, but to me Alice and the White Rabbit and the Red Queen – and the Dormouse and the Mad Hatter and the Cheshire Cat – were endowed with all the vitality and reality and being of an age-old myth; and how they had managed to get into a book was really neither here nor there. In short, at the age of fifteen I was quite oblivious of the fact that Lewis Carroll had written *Alice in Wonderland*, and neither 'Lewis Carroll' nor 'Mr Dodgson' had any associations for me.

When Mr Dodgson stood at the desk in the sixth-form room and prepared to address the class I thought he looked very tall and seemed very serious and rather formidable, beyond that I did not go and, with the ready docility of a schoolgirl of the nineties, I soon settled down to the subject in hand and forgot the lecturer in his own fascinating 'Game of Logic'.

There was a very ingenious diagram marked in squares, and there were red and gray counters, and by placing counters on appropriate squares we were able to try conclusions with such facts and fancies as:

> All cats understand French;
> Some chickens are cats

or:

> All selfish men are unpopular;
> All obliging men are popular.

Mr Dodgson came to school several times and gave us further

* From *Harper's Magazine*, 186 (Feb 1943) 319–23.

elaborations of his most ingenious method, and as he proceeded I think the facts became more fanciful and the fancies more fantastic; nevertheless Logic had them all in hand, and it appeared that skillful manipulation of the little red and gray counters was adequate to any situation. . . .

[Mr Dodgson offered to give me private lessons during the vacation. They] began almost at once, and in those summer holidays I went to and fro to Mr Dodgson's rooms in Christ Church; we worked through the first proofs of the book, and as the subject opened out I found great delight in this my first real experience of the patterned intricacies of abstract thought.

In the beginning my inveterate docility got in the way; I could find nothing to comment on and my response was limited to a repetitive 'Yes, yes . . . yes, I see.' I was ready to accept everything that was put before me. One day after a long series of such feeble affirmatives Mr Dodgson put down his pen and, looking at me with his rather crooked smile, 'You do make the lion and the lamb consort together in your caravanserai, don't you?' he said. I did not understand and thought he was paying me a compliment, so I hastened to say deprecatingly 'Oh! but I'm afraid I don't get on easily with everybody.' He looked at me with his kindest smile and said: 'Well, my dear, let us leave the lamb to fend for itself, and get back to our muttons, shall we?'

His words were Greek to me, but in their very strangeness they lingered in my memory, and much later I understood both his criticism of me and the patience with which he so gently withdrew it in the face of my ignorance.

I did not understand, but I realized that he found my shallow receptivity disappointing. And presently I managed to face the thing more squarely, to halt the flow of passive response, to tell myself and to tell my teacher what I found difficult or obscure in his reasoning. By his own real wish to know what I was thinking Mr Dodgson compelled me to that independence of thought I had never before tried to exercise. I had always learned very easily, and such ready assimilation of all and sundry had filled my mind with a company of somnolent ideas which, awake, must surely have been at odds with one another. Mr Dodgson's protest of the lion and the lamb was indeed justified. But gradually under his stimulating tuition I felt myself able in some measure to judge for myself, to select, and, if need be, to reject.

But while he was urging me to exercise my critical faculties Mr Dodgson at the same time bestowed on me another gift of aspect more gracious. He gave me a sense of my own personal dignity. He was so punctilious, so courteous, so considerate, so scrupulous not to embarrass or offend, that he made me feel that I counted – counted not as much as anyone else, and certainly not more than anyone else, but just in and as myself. There was nothing competitive or precarious in this counting, and thus my own keen awareness of awkwardness, ignorance, and inadequacy could not inhibit this new sense of the freedom of selfhood.

In Mr Dodgson's presence I felt proud and humble, with the pride and humility which are the grace and personality, grace conferred thus upon an ignorant schoolgirl by the magnanimity of a proud and very humble and very great and good man. And then Mr Dodgson gave me his affection – the reflection, in our own particular relation, of his great-hearted concern for all children. He was so patient of all one's limitations, so understanding, so infinitely kind.

By this time Mr Dodgson had got to know the whole family; indeed in my memory there is no gap between the arrival of his first letter to me and his establishment as a friend of us all, of my mother and of us six children. He made a relation with each one, and we were all at home with him.

For myself, a wretchedly shy and tongue-tied schoolgirl, I gave him at once a trust and affection I had rarely bestowed on anyone outside my own family. I accepted and admired him as I admired my own mother, without scrutiny and without analysis or criticism. I never for a moment considered even what he looked like, and I should have much difficulty in calling up a clear picture of him were it not for one special occasion when I saw him for a moment very vividly, not as he *was* but as he *looked*, saw him from a point outside my own relation to him.

I was walking along our little street toward our house when I caught sight of him standing at the door, waiting to be let in: a tall figure in a morning coat, a tall hat, very tall and with a broad, curved brim. He held himself stiffly, one shoulder slightly higher than the other; in his almost overemphasized erectness there was an old-fashioned seriousness, an air of punctiliousness, a breath of the past and of the passing which touched me even then with a quick, sharp pang of apprehension and almost of pity, a breath which now sings itself for me in the age-old song of Thomas Hardy's 'An Ancient to Ancients'.

I had looked at Mr Dodgson once, that first time at school, and now I looked again, and once more I saw him as tall and serious and rather formidable.

It seemed to me as I approached that he dwarfed our house, made the old high doorstep with the big chip out of it look very poor, and I was frightened by a certain incongruity in his presenting himself *at all* at our door, in his coming down our street to see us like this. I was within an ace of turning back and running away, but it was he who turned and saw me, and at once all was well. He held out a hand, and with the words, 'Is your mother at home?' he was inside the low dining room in which we mostly sat.

There he listened to all the news of the family, and then, as on so many other occasions, he entertained us with all sorts of puzzles he had invented, and with quaint *memoria technica*, and he set us problems that had no solution, and told us stories of his own making, preposterous, absurd, wholly fantastic, and half – or perhaps even wholly – true! As I write I see again the one thing I did always see about him, his long upper lip which had a trick of quivering as he spoke, a movement I think connected with a slight stammer that he sometimes had. And I remember his unbroken seriousness, for he never laughed even when he was entertaining us at his most fantastic level. I don't think he ever laughed, though his own particular crooked smile, so whimsical, so tender, so ironic, was in and out all the time, lighting up and, as it were, guiding his narrative.

When he got up to go he proposed that two of us should dine with him in his rooms at Christ Church that evening. Dinner with him in his rooms was to us formal and rather awe-inspiring, with its several courses and the tiny glass of Benedictine with our coffee afterward, but for us, accustomed as we were to a midday dinner and a Sunday joint which we had to make do for most of the week, the plenitude and gracious decorum of this 'late dinner' were both refreshment and initiation. And if we found little to say, well, no matter! – your kind host knew what it meant to us.

In my last term at school Mr Dodgson suggested taking me to London for the day, to see Irving and Ellen Terry in *The Merchant of Venice* at the old Lyceum Theater; and my anticipation of the day and my memories of the day itself are vivid to me still. I had only once before been to a real theater and strangely enough I then saw also *The Merchant of Venice*. But Irving and Ellen Terry were names of magic, and a day in London with Mr Dodgson shone in prospect with all the glitter of a new Wonderland.

I was a little concerned about what I could wear, what would be right for such an occasion, but my mother bought me a new blue coat, an unlined serge coat, double-breasted with big buttons down the front and very nicely cut, as I thought, except for a persistent small crease across the shoulder which I kept trying to smooth out. Then of course I should wear my school hat, the hard white sailor hat with the band of blue and gold, the school colors, round it.

'I think I shall be quite alright', I said to myself, 'like this.'

Nevertheless, in the event, I was nonplussed and bewildered by the many un-looked-for complications of luncheon in a London hotel, and as the day progressed it more and more assumed the character of a strange dream, blissful for the most part but holding also certain nightmare elements for one totally inexperienced.

We sat in the second row of the stalls, in seats which Miss Terry always reserved for Mr Dodgson when he was able to come to see her play, and in these seats we were joined by a young actress, Miss Minna Quin, a cousin, I think, of Mr Dodgson.[2] Before the curtain went up he told us stories of Ellen Terry as a child and as a girl, and of her family, all of whom he knew well, and then at last the play began. I knew the words by heart mostly, and I enjoyed the play enormously, but I remember feeling a little affronted by Irving's very passionate interpretation of the part of Shylock. I thought he overdid it!

We had tea with some of the cast behind the scenes, but by this time I was tired and dazed and my memory is nothing but a hazy dream. Then we took a hansom back to Paddington station, and so back home. . . .

I became a student at the Royal Holloway College in October, 1895, and after that I saw Mr Dodgson very rarely; but I was sure of his friendly interest, and I never felt out of touch with him.

When it was suggested that I should go on from Honors Moderations to work for the Final Honors School Examination in Mathematics at Oxford he was gently concerned and made an urgent protest to my mother on the grounds that the proposed course was altogether unsuitable for a girl, that the work was far too exacting and would impose a strain which might even upset my mental balance! My brother remembers vividly how his distressful apprehensions and vehement opposition reduced my mother to tears. I think he was always very conscious both of the qualities and of the disabilities of women, and perhaps he overemphasized the differences in temperament and in capacity between men and women. But he was never for a moment patronizing to women or to children; he 'consulted' one about this or that and took careful and serious account of any opinion given. He was always completely at ease with women and children, and I fancy he was happier with them than in the company of men.

Throughout my college course he always answered my letters, and he kept me in touch with the work he was doing. . . .

One morning in my third year at college I saw in *The Times* that Mr Dodgson had died. To me the printed words seemed to bear no sense, the fact stated seemed impossible. He had always been so vividly alive to me, and I had never imagined life without him; for days I went on asserting to myself that he *couldn't* be dead, asserting it doggedly but hopelessly against those also strangely insistent paragraphs in the newspapers.

I heard no details of his last illness or of the way of his death, and perhaps the lack of news increased my feeling that it had all happened absolutely irrationally, and simply could not be accepted. It gave me a feeling of forlornness such as I had never known. No one around me was aware of my plight. And there was nothing I could do as an expression of my sorrow – or so it seemed, till finally I hit upon an odd and childish device: I made a large badge out of some black ribbon I had by me, and I fastened this black badge to my petticoat in front just under my shirt blouse. I felt I could not wear the badge outside; people would ask what it was and after all he was no relation; yet I knew I must in some manner 'wear black' for Mr Dodgson.

To me, as I have said, he had always been Mr Dodgson, never Lewis Carroll; I hardly associated him at all with *Alice in Wonderland*, and yet Mr Dodgson, however deeply involved he might be in the composition of Symbolic Logic, was one to the end, I am sure, with the earlier Lewis Carroll.

Both had the faculty of juggling with words and setting them to quaint and unaccustomed uses, both had a power of captivating the imagination, of charming and baffling in the same breath, and they shared the intuitive sympathy and understanding love of children which was the mainspring of the genius both of Lewis Carroll and of Mr Dodgson.

For me, now 'forty years on, and afar and asunder', I think my love for him is as fresh and confident as in the days when I first in my childishness signed myself to him as 'your very loving friend'.

NOTES

1. Ethel Rowell did her logic so well that Dodgson offered to give her extra private tuition during the vacation. 'Heard from Mrs Rowell,' he wrote in his Diaries on 18 April 1894, 'thanking me for my offer. . . . Called, and had tea with her, and (Ethel being away) I arranged to give a lesson to Bessy and Hettie, aged 19 and 14, at Christ Church tomorrow.' The logic lessons progressed, until he could record that Ethel 'can now work syllogisms, by subscripts, quite easily'. The parents of these girls were George Joseph Rowell, a decorator, and his wife, Emily Sarah, born Barrett. Ethel Maud (1877–1951) became Senior Staff Lecturer in Mathematics at the Royal Holloway College; Bessy or Bessie remains a mystery; and Hettie Leonora (1879–1963) became Principal of St Peter's College, Peterborough. Ethel discusses the mathematical import of the *Alice* books in her philosophical memoir *Time and Time Again* (1941) pp. 177–8. For more on Dodgson and the Rowells, see *Letters*, esp. pp. 1019–20.

2. A distant cousin of Dodgson, Elizabeth Menella ('Minna') Quin (1868?–1942) went on the stage, and, although aided by Dodgson and Ellen Terry, did not have a distinguished career. But it was another young friend – not Minna Quin – who made up the party of three at the matinée of *The Merchant of Venice* on 29 June 1895, Mary Agnes Wilson (1875–1927), then a student at St Hugh's, Oxford. Minna met the party at the Royal Academy (*Diaries*, p. 518). For more on that day's outing, see *Letters*, pp. 1062–3, 1065–6.

He Told 'strange and wonderful tales'*

H. L. ROWELL

I knew Mr Dodgson only during the last four years of his life. It was early in 1894 that he first called on my mother and quickly established friendly relations with the whole family, especially with my sister Ethel, whom he had previously met, and whose unusual ability attracted him, so that he soon began to give her lessons in elementary logic in his rooms at Christ Church. It was not, however, until two years had passed that my admiration and awe of him turned to a warmer feeling, and that there thus began a friendship which lasted until his death some eighteen months later.

At this time my sisters were all away, and my brother and I were the only children at home, and gradually it came about that Mr Dodgson would come fairly frequently to have tea with my mother and myself. He always asked to have tea in the dining-room so that, when it was finished, he could spread on the unused half of the table some puzzle or mathematical problem, with or without a solution, or so that we could continue some very elementary work in logic, in connection with the book he was then preparing for the press. This was varied by the telling of strange and wonderful tales or by the repetition of curious rhymes: these after-tea hours were never lesson-hours, but always amusing and stimulating, though at times demanding much concentration on my part.

Then came my first invitation to dinner with him, and, from this time onwards, very occasionally, such invitations would come, always emphasising that his dinner parties were morning dress and adding that he would call for me at $6\frac{1}{4}$ – so he wrote it. I think the happiest of such occasions was in the summer term of 1897. He fetched me, as usual, soon after six o'clock, and, on our way down the Corn Market, we called for one of his old friends, Lady ——, whose name I have forgotten, and who was staying in Oxford for a short visit. On the previous evening the Prince of Wales, afterwards Edward VII, had dined at Christ Church,[1] and Mr Dodgson was seemingly as pleased

* From Hudson, pp. 318–22.

as I was to begin dinner with turtle soup, soup left from the night before – my first experience of tasting such soup. Dinner finished as always with a small glass of Benedictine, and the talk turned for a moment at the end of the evening to *The Hunting of the Snark*,' and finding I did not possess it, he gave me a copy, writing my name in it with his usual flourishes around the date.

On our way back along the Corn Market, I told him what a happy evening it had been for me, and he answered that happiness was nearly always realized only in retrospect, and the thought was not 'I *am* happy now', but rather 'I *was* happy then.' So we talked until I reached home.

I remember, also, a later occasion, when I did *not* go to dinner with him as had been planned. I was then a schoolgirl of seventeen and hoping to enter a university in a year's time. It was discovered, too late, that on the day after that fixed for the dinner, an examination in German for girls going to a university was to be held at school, and that the girl with the highest marks was to recieve a prize of £10 or £20 – I forget which – such money to be spent on books. My mother therefore decided that I should stay at home, work at my German, go to bed early and try to win the £20 prize. As I was rather sadly turning over the pages of some German book in the schoolroom upstairs, the door suddenly opened – it was 6.15 – and Mr Dodgson came into the room, greeted me, and then gave me a German grammar book with my name and the date written in it: whether it was a new book or one he had long possessed, I am unable to say, as I have, alas, lost the book. He was in the room a bare five minutes: I remembered that the walk from Christ Church to our house was just over a mile.

My memory turns to another incident in that summer of 1897. In the following September, the two nieces of Mr Dodgson were coming as pupils to the High School and had, therefore, to live in Oxford during term time. Mr Dodgson had, I think, always had an admiration and respect for my mother and he suggested that his nieces should board with us! He probably thought also that their coming would be of financial help to my mother. I was definitely opposed to the plan, and my mother was hesitant. Our house was old, three-storied and inconvenient: it has long since been pulled down. It was, however, finally agreed that they should come, but the arrangement was soon to be upset. One day, when we were sitting at tea, my brother and his two friends came into the house very noisily from school, and went to the little room opposite the dining-room, used by my brother as his study. My mother turned to Mr Dodgson and made some remark about her son: Mr Dodgson's face fell, and he said, 'I had forgotten your son: it makes all the difference: what are your plans for him?' My mother explained that my brother was hoping to go to Queen's College in a year's time (this he did not do) but to live at home, and that one friend, Cyril Hurcomb, now Lord Hurcomb, was to go to St John's, while the second friend, Jack Drinkwater (he was Jack and not John until he was twenty!) was leaving Oxford that July.[2] Mr Dodgson finished his tea almost in silence and soon left, saying he must reconsider the whole matter. In two days he wrote to my mother saying that he did not think it would be wise to send his nieces to live in a house where undergraduates would be coming in and out, and that he was very sorry indeed that he had forgotten my brother, and neglected to ask what were the plans for his future. This letter closed the incident: it was as though it had never been. I rejoiced at the decision – the schoolroom would still be my very own – and I do not think my mother was sorry.[3]

Looking back to the years when I knew Mr Dodgson I see him first as the celebrated author of *Alice*, quietly conscious of his world-wide fame, but putting on one side the name of Lewis Carroll, and remaining in himself, Mr Dodgson, the friend of children, a kindly, affectionate man, the inventor of many strange and ingenious puzzles, and the teller of many wondrous tales. Then I see him as an Oxford don of the 'eighties, rather than of the 'nineties, moulded and circumscribed by the conventions of the time and place, a moralist and a mathematician. Lastly, there is the lover of beauty, emotional and introspective, lonely in spirit and prone to sadness, a side rather guessed at than known. It is not for me to venture an opinion as to how far these differing elements of his personality made a harmonious whole man. I suggest, however, that, in his later years at least, the Oxford don and the moralist triumphed at times over the lover of beauty, but that the whimsical genius of the man who gave to the world *Alice in Wonderland* and *Alice through the Looking-Glass*, remained dominant to the end, and illumined his whole being. It was a high privilege for me, a schoolgirl, to be numbered among his friends during the last year of his life, and a great honour.

NOTES

1. Dodgson recorded the Prince of Wales's visit to Oxford. On 12 May 1897 he wrote in his *Diaries* (pp. 534–5),

As the Prince of Wales comes this afternoon to open the Town Hall, I went round to the Deanery, etc., to invite them to come through my rooms up on the roof, to see the procession arrive. A party of about twenty were on my roof in the afternoon, including . . . most, if not all, of the children in Christ Church. . . . Dinner in Hall at 8. The Dean had the Prince on his right, and Lord Salisbury on his left. My place was almost *vis-à-vis* with the Prince . . . .

2. Neither Hurcomb nor Drinkwater enters Dodgson's *Diaries*.
3. For Dodgson's letter to Mrs Rowell cancelling the proposed lodging arrangements, see *Letters*, p. 1116.

'At once he caught my idea'*

GERTRUDE ATKINSON[1]

Imagine the sea-side at Sandown in the Isle of Wight where lodgings stretched along the front, each with its balcony on the upper floor and standing in a little garden with steps leading down on to the shore. Imagine a little girl about 8½ absolutely entranced with the lodger next door. To her he seemed quite an old gentleman. In the morning he came out on to his balcony breathing in the sea air as if he could not get enough; and whenever she heard him coming she would rush out on to the balcony to see him. After a few days he spoke to her: 'Little girl, why do you come so fast on to your balcony whenever I come out?' 'To see you sniff', she said. 'It is lovely to see you sniff like this' – she threw up her head and drew in the air.

Thus began a long friendship which ended only with his death.

It was the happiest summer holiday of my childhood that summer of 1875. He was writing *The Hunting of the Snark* at that time, and was also thinking about *Sylvie and Bruno*, which he wrote later, and *Rhyme? and Reason?*. He told me while we sat on the steps or walked up and down on the shore many stories in these, as well as others that he thought of at the time. I would dash off into the sea for a little paddle, but even paddling was often forgotten in the delight of the wonderful stories. I took it as a child does as if it were true and asked sooner or later for some particulars. That was enough as I now see to start a new train of thought; at once he caught my idea, and off he would go into a fresh series of adventures. He was pleased because my mother let me run in and out of the sea in little bathing pants and a fisherman's jersey, a thing quite unheard of in those days. He thought it so sensible and told her not to listen to the mothers who were shocked. He and my mother became very good friends, and after that summer he often invited her to bring me to stay with him in Oxford where he got us lodgings where we could sleep, and we had all our meals with him in his rooms in Christ Church. He also came to stay

* From A. G. Atkinson, 'Memories of Lewis Carroll', *Hampshire Chronicle*, 13 Mar 1948, p. 3.

with us at Rotherwick, not far from Basingstoke, where my father was the Rector.

Now that I am over 81 it is still interesting to take up my copy of *The Hunting of the Snark* and read the charming double acrostic in which it is dedicated to me, then Gertrude Chataway. . . .

His charm to a child was greatly enhanced by the very sympathetic way that he would see the drift of her thoughts and make her feel she was part of the story. He wrote me many letters in the years that followed – lovely nonsense letters. . . .

Many people have said that he liked children only as long as they were really children and did not care about them when they grew up. That was not my experience; we were warm friends always. I think sometimes misunderstandings came from the fact that many girls when grown up do not like to be treated as if they were still 10 years old. Personally I found that habit of his very refreshing. I did not see him often in the last years of his life because I was so much of the time abroad; but the memory of him will always be a very great happiness to me.[2]

NOTES

1. Dodgson records meeting James Chataway (1827–1907), Rector of Rotherwick, Hampshire, on 29 September 1875, and adds that 'Mr and Mrs C., and the 4 [daughters], came in to see photos, etc.' (*Diaries*, p. 343). Soon he was meeting various combinations of Chataways, and on 2 October he 'got Gertrude . . . to come across in her wading attire (blouse and bathing drawers) and made a drawing of her' (p. 344: it is reproduced in Hatch, facing p. 107). The friendship blossomed that autumn and lasted, as Gertrude indicates, for many years. Mrs Chataway was born Elizabeth Ann Drinkwater (1833–93). The Chataways had fifteen children, a governess and six servants. Annie Gertrude (1866–1951) married (1907) Thomas Dinham Atkinson (1864–1948), architect and author.

Fifty years before this reminiscence appeared, Mrs Atkinson recorded some memories of Dodgson in a letter to S. D. Collingwood. Some of the earlier comments embellish the later ones: The stories he told contained

the most lovely nonsense conceivable, and I naturally revelled in it. His vivid imagination would fly from one subject to another, and was never tied down in any way by the probabilities of life. . . . To *me* it was of course all perfect, but it is astonishing that *he* never seemed either tired or to want other society. I spoke to him once of this since I had been grown up, and he told me it was the greatest pleasure he could have to converse freely with a child, and feel the depths of her mind. . . . He used to write to me and I to him after that summer. . . . His letters were one of the greatest joys of my childhood. . . . I don't think that he ever really understood that we, whom he had known as children, could not always remain such. I stayed with him only a few years ago, at Eastbourne, and felt for the time that I was once more a child. He never appeared to realize that I had grown up, except when I reminded him of the fact, and then he only said, 'Never mind: you will always be a child to me, even when your hair is grey.' (*Life and Letters*, pp. 379–80).

2. Almost two dozen of the letters that Dodgson wrote to Gertrude appear in *Letters*, where, facing p. 476, his drawing of her and a photograph of her also appear.

'The most charming and courteous man'*

MAUD FFOOKS[1]

The first time [I saw Lewis Carroll] was as a child quite by accident, in the Forbury Gardens at Reading; he was waiting for a train to Oxford, and we went and sat on the same seat. He began to talk to us, and showed us puzzles and the tiniest of tiny scissors, which fascinated me, I remember, and which he kept in his pocket book. He made us write our names and address and then hurried off to catch his train. A day or two afterwards my sister received a copy of *Alice in Wonderland*, much to her delight. Soon after that he sent me *Through the Looking-Glass*, with a most delightful letter. Twice we were taken to Oxford, where he photographed my sisters and me in his rooms at the House, and once we went to the Chestnuts, Guildford, and had lunch with him and his sisters there. . . . Then I went to school in Berlin for two years, from there to India for about five years, after that to friends in Germany to a most interesting old Schloss . . . and haunted. Then to the Channel Islands. It was there, in Jersey, that we met again, when he came to tea with us, instead of appearing at a large 'At Home', where he was to have been the chief guest. He disliked being lionized, and we were the fortunate ones, for we had him all to ourselves, and he stayed a long time telling us stories. I only wish I could remember some of them. That was the last time I saw him. It was in April 1884, when he got home again; he wrote to me with the purple ink he liked always to use from the Chestnuts, Guildford: 'Among all the pleasure I look back on in my Jersey trip, those conferred by yourself and Isabel are among the highest, and will be long remembered by me. . . .'

He was the most charming and courteous man, very witty and full of fun, and we all loved him. . . .

* From 'Alice in Dorsetland', *The Dorset Yearbook*, 1928, pp. 45–9.

NOTES

1. On 3 September 1869, Dodgson noted that 'the other day, in returning [to Guildford] from Oxford', he was 'delayed for 3 hours in Reading, and went to the

gardens there, where I made the acquaintance with a family of the name of Standen'. On the 17th Dodgson called on the Standens, spent an hour and a half with the children; and on 4 October he photographed Maud and Isabel. Thus a twenty-year friendship was under way (*Diairies*, pp. 283–4). The Standen girls were two of the children who composed what was sometimes referred to as 'the finest family in Southern India'. The father was Douglas Standen (1830–1903), later Lieutenant-General, awarded the Indian Mutiny Medal. His wife was born Annie Aston Liddell (b. 1833). All but one of the children were born in India and sent to England, specifically to Reading, for their education. The daughters whom Dodgson knew best were Henrietta Maud (1857?–1938), who married (1891) Edward Archdall Ffooks (1859–1932), solicitor, Under-Sheriff for Dorset; and Isabel Julia (1859–1941), who married (1911) George Carr Anderson (d. 1930), a tomato-grower in St Peter Port, Guernsey, and secondly (1934) Douglas John Byard (1859–1949), Principal of Halmdorf College, near Adelaide, South Australia, and Schools Examiner at the University, Adelaide. Maud's daughter, Mrs Jean Gordon, wrote (private letter), 'I think Mother chose Russia for a Governess job because Lewis Carroll had been there. They all had to earn their living, as an Army officer with 12 children couldn't manage.' Two dozen letters from Dodgson to the Standen girls appear in *Letters*.

'Your fifteen-minute friend, C. L. Dodgson'*

ISABEL STANDEN

It was a chance meeting in the Forbury Gardens at Reading that was the beginning of my friendship with Mr Dodgson – as I called him – the famous author of *Alice in Wonderland* and other fascinating tales that have delighted children all over the world. We had been taken there by our governess, and he saw us and began to make friends.

Presently he took me on his knee and showed me various puzzles that he always carried about with him to amuse his little friends. I soon felt at home with him, for he was so particularly kind and friendly. One puzzle he showed me was to draw three interlaced squares without taking the pen from the paper or going over the same lines twice.

Another was to make figures of men and women from five dots, which he did most cleverly. Then I was asked to write my name – Isabel – in his pocket-book. When I started with a laborious capital 'I' followed by a small 's' he exclaimed, 'What! is your name Isaac?' Soon our new-found friend had to go and catch his train to Guildford,

From 'Lewis Carroll as I Remember Him', *Queen*, 20 July 1932, p. 14.

so we said good-bye. Next day a quaint little letter arrived for me, which is now one of my most treasured possessions. It was signed 'Your fifteen-minute friend, C. L. Dodgson', and there was a postscript: 'Have you succeeded in drawing the three squares?' In this letter the writer said: 'A friend of mine called Mr Lewis Carroll, tells me he means to send you a book. He is a very dear friend of mine. I have known him all my life – we are the same age and, of course, he was with me in the Gardens yesterday – not a yard off – while I was drawing those puzzles for you. I wonder if you saw him?'

A day or two later the book arrived addressed to me, such a beautiful book, all scarlet and gold, with the most delightful pictures in it, and my name inscribed on the fly-leaf, 'Isabel Standen, from the Author!' I was thrilled, and soon we were all engrossed in the wonderful adventures of the immortal 'Alice'.

Mr Dodgson was as generous as he was kind, and as time went on he duly presented us girls with copies of his charming books as they came out, and there were *eight* of us! Some were translations in German, French, Italian, etc., and the Baby of the family had one in Dutch, but she, thinking it was not a real language but only Double Dutch, did not treat the book with much respect.

Mr Dodgson had a great hobby, and that was photography. He made portraits of many famous people, such as Sir John Millais, Professor Faraday, Lord Salisbury, the Rossettis, Ellen Terry, etc., as well as of his countless childfriends. We were taken first to his home at Guildford and afterwards to his rooms at Christ Church, and 'endured the torture' of being photographed as he afterwards expressed it.

Of one of his little friends, he wrote: 'I have photographed her nearly fifty times from four years old and upwards.' She was a singularly beautiful child and her portrait, taken by himself, used to hang over the mantelpiece in his study at Christ Church.[1]

He used to say that he spent on this hobby of his what other men spent on smoking, a form of pleasure he did not indulge in. . . .

I am proud to think that the friendship formed when I was a child lasted long after I had 'put away childish things'. In a letter he wrote me once (in his favourite purple ink), he said:

'I always feel specially grateful to friends who, like you, have given me a child-friendship and a woman-friendship, too. About nine out of ten, I think, of my child-friendships get shipwrecked at the critical point "where the stream and river meet", and the child-friends, once so affectionate, become uninteresting acquaintances.'

An attractive side to his nature was that he loved to help and encourage young people who were studying – I mean, of course, girls, for boys did not interest him. I remember how he helped me when I was learning singing. An invention called the 'Ammoniaphone' had lately been brought out, and was intended to strengthen the vocal chords by means of inhaling.

It was advertised to produce marvellous results, and famous names were among those who wrote testimonials in its praise, among them the gifted artiste, Miss Leonora Braham of the D'Oyley Carte Company. My kind friend insisted on making me a present of one,[2] and afterwards wrote me the following amusing letter:

'It will be grand for me if this machine fulfils its promise and I see the crowds rushing into Exeter Hall to hear you. I shall walk past at least an inch taller than usual, and friends will say, "either he is walking on pattens, which is improbable, or he has lately grown an inch, which is impossible!" I fancy I hear you muttering to yourself: "Nice complimentary style this! So he means to walk *past*, does he, when *I* am going to sing!" But don't you see, my dear child, the "rush" would be to the five-shilling seats: the unreserved? *I*, having a guinea stall, would simply wait till the "rush" was over and then go in quietly to my place!'

But although so brimful of fun and humour, he was most sympathetic to those who were passing through difficult times, as the following letter will show.

'I can quite understand and much sympathize with what you say of your feeling lonely. I am going to give you a bit of philosophy about that. My own experience is that every new form of life we try is, just at first, irksome rather than pleasant. . . . Our mental nerves seem to be so adjusted that we feel *first* and most keenly the discomforts. . . . But after a bit we get used to them. . . .

'My advice is, don't think about loneliness or happiness or unhappiness for a week or two. Then take stock again and compare your feelings with what they were two weeks previously. You will have had time to realize the enjoyable features of your life which at first you were too much worried to be conscious of. If your feelings have changed, even a little, for the better, you are on the right track.' I feel it was a great privilege to have enjoyed the friendship of such a man for so many years, and the memory will remain while life lasts.

NOTES

1. Alexandra Kitchin. For more on Dodgson and his favourite photographic model, see *Letters*, esp. pp. 192–3; *Lewis Carroll and the Kitchins*, ed. Morton N. Cohen (1980).

2. In early 1884, Robert Carter Moffat (d. 1915), chemist, and Thomas Gilbert Bowick, merchant and manufacturer, patented a solution of water, ammonia, and hydrogen peroxide and a tube, something like a piccolo in size, made of tin or another suitable material. They claimed that their solution, employed as a gargle, in a spray, swallowed, or inhaled through their apparatus would strengthen, enrich, and extend the range of the voice; they also recommended it for 'pulmonary and other affections' (Patent specification 1463, 1884).

He Sent Biscuit Tins*

ALICE STANDEN

Although I cannot claim to be one of Lewis Carroll's 'child friends' –
my elder sisters having had that privilege – I well remember his visit
to our home in the Channel Isles many years ago. It was in the
evening, and I and a small sister were already in bed. But he wanted
to see us, and we came down in our little red flannel nightgowns and
sat on his knee while he 'told us stories'. I was a little shy and I don't
remember now what they were about, but I do remember that a
schoolboy brother hurriedly left the room through the window, as he
had heard Lewis Carroll 'didn't like boys'! . . .

  Shortly after Lewis Carroll's visit to us in Jersey, a large case
arrived. This was full of small biscuit tins, quaintly ornamented with
scenes from *Alice in Wonderland*. . . . There was one for each of us girls,
but I, the youngest, did not at the time share the delight and
enthusiasm of the elders. Childlike, disappointment was my feeling!
. . . The biscuit tins were empty![1]

  * From a letter to *John O'London's Weekly*, 5 Mar 1932, p. 887.

NOTE

  1. Dodgson supervised the manufacture of the *Looking-Glass* Biscuit Tin, produced
in 1892 by Messrs Jacob and Company, biscuit-makers. Characters from *Looking-Glass*
in colour adorn the box. In a letter to the manufacturer dated 26 November 1892,
Dodgson protested vigorously because he discovered that the tins were 'only to be had
by buying *biscuits*. . . . Had I understood,' he wrote, 'when I was asked to let the
pictures . . . be copied . . . I should either have declined altogether, or have stipulated
for the privilege . . . of buying the boxes *ad libitum*, without the necessity of paying for
biscuits . . . .' Two days later the manufacturer replied, 'we can let you have as many
of the boxes empty as you and your friends may wish' (*Letters*, p. 938).

'The Great *Lewis* himself!!!'*

CHARLOTTE RIX[1]

St James's Terrace, London
May 31, 1885

My dearest Mother,
    Yesterday afternoon there were none of your Minchins or Robinsons for *me*! I was content with none less than

The Great *Lewis* himself!!!

I must tell you about it before I answer your letters. I went down to dinner as usual, and was stodging through my meat when the servant put into my hand a Card. I turned pale and read

Rev. C. L. Dodgson
Christ Church, Oxford.

I think I was as much horrified as pleased at first. I had on an old every-day blue dress and a filthy apron. But I tore off that, and made myself as respectable as possible and walked with as much calmness as remained to me, to S. Louisa's room where he was. The first thing he did after shaking hands with me and asking if I was Miss Rix, was to turn me round and look at my back. I wondered what on earth he was doing, but he said that he had been made to expect a tremendous lot of hair, and that he hadn't had the *least* idea what I was like, except that he had a vague vision of *hair*. We sat down and talked for a few minutes, and then he wanted to know if I should be allowed to come out with him, and if we were allowed 'to go forth' with friends. I said we were, so then he said, 'Well then, would you go and ask the lady principal (or dragon, or whatever you call her) if you may come now?' I went and after a little questioning from S. Louisa got leave. He said he was surprised to see that she would let the young ladies go out with any gentleman that called, without even coming to see that

* From *Letters*, pp. 578–80.

they *looked* respectable. He told me that he had business with an artist who would give us some dinner. So we started. And on the way he told me that the artist was that Harry Furniss who draws those splendid parliamentary pictures in *Punch*, and that his business with him was that he was illustrating another book he was writing, which he hoped would be out by next Xmas twelve-month. But he said I was to tell *no one* of it but my family (so mind you don't). He also said I was not to tell anyone who he was as he much preferred being *quite* unknown. So Mother don't tell anybody his real name, because if he ever came to see us everyone would know and he says he doesn't like their knowing and wishes them *not* to know! If they ask you, you can say he wants you not to tell. He said that he had been talked to sometimes about himself; and that once when he was staying in Eastbourne he made friends with a little girl on the sands, and after he had known them a little time, asked her if she knew a little book called *Alice's Adventures in Wonderland*. She hadn't got it so he promised to give it to her. Her Mother said to him 'Ah have you heard about the author of that book? He's gone *mad*!' He said 'Oh really, I had never heard it', and I think he added that he knew something about him. She stuck to it though and said 'Oh yes, it was *quite* true, she could *assure* him. She had had it from a friend at Lincoln who knew it for certain, etc., etc. He had written 3 books, *Alice in Wonderland, Through the Looking-Glass,* and *The Hunting of the Snark*, and now he had gone mad. Two or three days afterwards he sent the little girl the book and put in it,

For So and So
From the Author.

Soon afterwards he met the girl's mother, and when she saw him, she threw up her hands and said 'Oh Mr Dodgson, what *shall* I do? I'll *never* say anything *about* anybody *to* anybody again!' To which he cheerfully replied 'Oh yes Mrs —— you will.'[2] All this time we were walking to Mr Furniss' who lives some way off up St John's Wood Road and we talked and he sent me into fits over one thing and another pretty well all the way, I told him Edie would be awfully jealous (I hope she is) and he said 'yes, *won't* there be a row!' He said he would call some Saturday and take me to see *The Mikado*, but he was afraid that it [would] more than ever 'disturb the domestic peace'. Mr and Mrs Furniss were *very* kind and after dinner I went down with Mr Dodgson and Mr Furniss to his studio. I saw the first drawing for the book; it is most absurd and will come in with a piece of poetry like the Walrus and the Carpenter. Mr Furniss shewed me some drawings he had done for a new children's book that is coming out called *Romps*.[3] They were splendid; and while Mr Dodgson was talking to a Mr Barber[4] (who had come to shew him some photographs and who has a good picture in the Academy this year) I had quite a talk with him. He is very short and has red hair and he had on his working jacket, and I liked him very much. He has three children but I only saw two: a boy and a girl, both rather pretty (about 4 or 5 I should think) and lots of the children in the book are taken from them. We were in the Studio about an hour, and I couldn't help thinking, how six months ago I little thought I should ever find myself in Mr Furniss's studio, with another artist and Lewis Carroll, talking to them just as if they were anybody else, and hearing Lewis Carroll and Mr Furniss discuss his new book! Mr Dodgson said that *Through the Looking-Glass* had taken him 4 years to write and bring out; he [said] that I had found it took a good long time in bringing out my works. Mr Furniss told me he was to get 2*d*. on every volume of *Romps* that was sold, so at that rate he would get enough for a cab fare at every *50*. And he had only to see a gentleman walk out of a shop with 50 volumes of *Romps* under his arm, to be able to say 'Half-a-Crown! My fortune's made.'[5] The whole time I was there I had to keep saying to myself '*That*'s an artist who has a picture in the Academy, *that*'s Mr Furniss and *that*'s Lewis Carroll'! And after saying it over periodically, I could hardly realize it. When we left there we went to call on a Lady, who wasn't home, and then we went to the Grosvenor Gallery. We got there by underground to Baker Street, and then a Cab, and I sacrificed my principles enough to quite *enjoy* it!! He was so absurd and liked the pictures so much himself (at least he criticized them enough) that I liked them too. It is quite absurd how fond he is of children – at least of *girls* (please tell the boys that) and whenever he saw the picture of one he flew to it. He has no end of little girls he has scraped up from all sorts of places, and from what he said, a lot of people that he just writes to like us. He is tall rather, thin, and no beard or moustache and his hair is rather grey; he *looks* eccentric I think and he is deaf with his right ear. He is very fatherly; calls you child, I told him I was glad he hadn't found his heart in his boots, and he said he didn't think he should be quite so frightened of me next time, and he shouldn't wonder that after he had seen me 3 or 4 times he would be able to pluck up courage to call me Lottie. Of course I had observed that he called [me] Miss Rix at present. He had called me Lottie all the time, but no matter – no matter. He brought me back in a cab about 5.30, and he gave me a puzzle that he had made himself I think. It *was* fun, and I felt as if I was dreaming the whole time. . . .[6] I remain

Your *very* loving child,
L. Rix

NOTES

1. In the mid 1880s, when Dodgson's knots of *A Tangled Tale* were appearing in the *Monthly Packet*, Edith Rix sent in a solution to Knot X. Dodgson wrote her a personal letter explaining why her name would not appear among those who sent interesting solutions and sending his observations on her solution. A friendship between them soon developed: they exchanged letters, they met. It was not long before Dodgson became acquainted with Edith's younger sister, who wrote this letter home from school. Edith Mary Rix (1866–1918) was the eldest child of Frederic Shelly Rix (1836–1933), solicitor, and his wife, Jemima Bostock Bradley (1831?–1902); she went to Newnham College, Cambridge, became a 'computer' at the Royal Observatory, Greenwich, and later a cataloguer for the Royal Society. Charlotte Jane ('Lottie', 1867–1952) went on the stage (with help from Ellen Terry, whom she met through Dodgson). For more on Dodgson and the Rixes, see *Letters*, esp. pp. 557–8, 572–3.

2. Dodgson records the incident in his *Diaries* (p. 420).

3. Both *Romps in Town* and *Romps at the Seaside* appeared in 1885; the following year Furniss published *Holiday Romps* and *Romps All the Year Round*.

4. Charles Burton Barber (1845–94), who painted sport, animals, and children, also painted Queen Victoria and her dogs. He exhibited *The New Whip* in the Royal Academy that year. Furniss later wrote an appreciation of him: 'Charles Burton Barber', *The Works of Charles Burton Barber* (1896) pp. 9–14.

5. Lottie's arithmetic leaves something to be desired; Furniss probably said *15* volumes, not *50*.

6. Dodgson does not record an outing to *The Mikado* with Lottie, but he does record his visit with Lottie to Furniss *et al.*:

Spent the day in town, going by the 9 a.m., and returning by the 6.30 p.m. . . . I called . . . on 'Lottie' Rix, at her school in St James's Terrace. I took her with me to Mr Furniss', where we had luncheon and business-talk, and I was introduced to a Mr Barber, a neighbouring artist, who gave me some charming photos of his own doing, 'nude' studies of his children. Then . . . we visited Holman Hunt's picture [*The Triumph of the Innocents* at the Fine Arts Society] and the Grosvenor Gallery. (*Diaries*, p. 436)

'We would climb about him'*

GREVILLE MacDONALD[1]

[I]

[He was] very dear to us. We would climb about him as, with pen and ink, he sketched absurd or romantic or homely incidents, the while telling us their stories with no moral hints to spoil their charm. I clearly remember his urging upon me – and quite in the manner of his *Alice* fun – the advantage to myself if my head were marble; for then it would never suffer from combing its curls and could not be expected to learn lessons. But he drew for me with his pen one possible consequence, namely that such a head might terrify the sculptor Munro, to whom I was sitting as a model for his fountain, *Boy Riding a Dolphin*, still in Hyde Park. Then again he would take us to that old home of delight, the Polytechnic, to see the 'dissolving views' of Christmas Fairy Tales. No pantomime or circus ever gave me the same happiness. There was a toy-shop in Regent Street where he let us choose gifts, one of which will remain my own as long as memory endures. It was an unpainted, wooden horse. I loved it as much as any girl her doll. . . .

[II]

[I]n the summer of 1862 . . . we all had a happy holiday [at our grandfather's house in Hampstead]. . . . Thither Charles L. Dodgson . . . came several times, and took many photographs, remarkable alike in permanence and beauty.

It was about this time . . . that he asked my father's opinion upon a story he had written and named *Alice's Adventures Underground*. . . . My father suggested that an experiment should be made upon his young family. Accordingly my mother read the story to us. When she came

* [I] is from *Reminiscences of a Specialist* (1932) pp. 15–16; [II], from *George MacDonald and his Wife* (1924) pp. 342–3.

to the end I, being aged six, exclaimed that there ought to be sixty thousand volumes of it. Certainly it was our enthusiasm that persuaded our Uncle Dodgson . . . to present the English-speaking world with one of its future classics. . . . How happily could my father laugh over this loving humorist's impromptu drawings, full of the absurdities, mock-maxims and erratic logic so dear to the child-heart, young or old! While Dodgson, the shy, learned mathematician who hated inaccuracy, loved to question the very multiplication-table's veracity, my father, the poet, who hated any touch of irreverence, could laugh till tears ran at his friend's ridicule of smug formalism and copy-book maxims. What with Charles Dodgson [and others] there was plenty of merriment along with sober talk in our home. . . . One annual treat was Uncle Dodgson taking us . . . to go down in the diving bell, or watch the mechanical athlete *Leotard*. There was also the Coliseum in Albany Street, with its storms by land and sea on a wonderful stage, and its great panorama of London. And . . . bath-buns and ginger-beer – all associated in my memory with the adorable writer of *Alice*. . . .

I well remember leaning against him as he drew for me in my copy-book . . . a picture that evoked from us shrieks of delight. In the far distance was a train steaming away from its station to negotiate a humpy railway bridge. In the fore-ground a very stout perspiring gentleman was mopping his head with one hand, while his wife, scraggy and grim, dragged him along by the other, and shouted at him, 'It's puffing away fit to burst itself; we shall lose it John, if you don't run faster!' But out of his mouth soared a balloon of words: 'I can't run no faster, and I won't go no furder!' Also do I remember the frame of a broken hand-mirror into which I pasted notepaper for him to draw reflections upon. A beautiful basket of apples he made under a wonderful tree with my sister Mary, not a bit like her, sitting beside it and the baby Ronald running with another apple to add to the pile.

NOTE

1. The poet and novelist George MacDonald (1824–1905) was an early friend of Dodgson, and his wife and eleven children were particular Dodgson favourites. Dodgson shared with both MacDonald and Mrs MacDonald, born Louisa Powell (1822–1902), a marvellous sense of the ridiculous and a genuine interest in the theatre. Dodgson first met MacDonald in 1859 on a visit to his speech correctionist; they soon discovered that they held similar religious and artistic views, and the friendship established itself. Dodgson first encountered Mary Josephine MacDonald (1853–78) and her brother Greville Matheson (1856–1944) in the summer of 1860 on a visit to the studio of the sculptor Alexander Munro (1825–71), some of whose work Dodgson photographed. Munro was at work on *Boy with the Dolphin*, and Greville was posing. Dodgson noted, 'They were a girl and a boy, about seven and six years old. I claimed their acquaintance, and began at once proving to the boy, Greville, that he had better take the opportunity of having his head changed for a marble one. The effect was that in about two minutes they had entirely forgotten that I was a total stranger, and were earnestly arguing the question as if we were old acquaintances' (*Life and Letters*, pp. 83–

5, quoting the lost *Diaries*). On hearing that a marble head would not have to be brushed and combed, the boy turned to his sister with an air of great relief, saying, 'Do you hear *that*, Mary? I needn't be combed!' Dodgson then replied, 'I have no doubt combing, with his great head of long hair . . ., was *the* misery of his life. His final argument was that a marble head couldn't speak, and as I couldn't convince either that he would be all the better for that, I gave in.' For a sketch by Dodgson of Greville holding a marble head, see Greville's *Reminiscences*, facing p. 16. For more on Dodgson and the MacDonalds, see *Letters*, *passim*; and R. B. Shaberman, 'Lewis Carroll and George MacDonald', *Jabberwocky*, Summer 1976, pp. 67–88.

Their Friendship Survived into her Adolescence*

LAURENCE IRVING[1]

[A]ll trace of the productions by the Christmas Dramatic Wanderers might have vanished with the winter's snow but for the presence of an elderly graduate, as assiduous a playgoer as he was a collector of protégées, one of whom, Edith Lucy,[2] was playing Bianca [in a production of *The Taming of the Shrew* in Oxford during the Christmas season of 1893–4]. Their friendship had begun, as was usual with him, when she was a child; less usually it had survived her transition to adolescence. . . . her friend was the Reverend C. L. Dodgson. . . .

Though Edith Lucy had herself no ambition for the stage, her mentor, in all things a perfectionist, . . . wrote to her a long criticism of her performance. She had made Bianca something of a shrew herself, but he would not accept her excuse that she had done so to please . . . [the director]. . . . Two months later he recorded that Edith Lucy came to tea 'bringing a new friend for me, Miss Dolly Baird.[3] She is very pleasant: she wishes to try the stage.'

. . . as Edith Lucy explained to Dolly, one way and another nobody in Oxford had so many friends at the theatrical court, and already he had helped several girls she knew to start their careers as actresses. If Dolly was determined to go on the stage, he was the man to be consulted.

Dolly's impressions of her host at that tea-party may have been mixed. Others at that time visiting the ageing master of fantastic and precise arts found his ever-green fancifulness a little disconcerting. . . . But she and Edith were his only guests on that occasion. She found

* From *The Successors* (1967) pp. 68–77.

him kind, and so far the only grown-up person she felt she could talk
to frankly who would consider her problems with sympathy and
understanding. She had little difficulty in persuading him to come to
. . . [call at her home] and, with his odd credentials as a man of God
and a friend of the players, to help her mother to see reason when the
issue had to be faced.

The outcome of that meeting was remarkable, less for any practical
help it was to Dolly than for the clear light it threw on Dodgson's
perplexing character. The next day he wrote [a letter to Dolly Baird's
mother in which he reported 'the history of my friend' Ellen Terry,
how she left her husband, lived with another man out of wedlock, and
then, after being divorced from her first husband, married an actor.
Dodgson reports in his account that until she remarried he 'held no
communication with her', but he resumed their friendship after she
remarried and had since then introduced some young friends to her,
but only with the approval of the parents].[4] . . .

It was agreed, however, that as soon as possible he should take . . .
[Dolly] up to London to seek an interview with Ellen Terry.

On 26 May [1894] Dodgson set out for London with Dolly properly
chaperoned by the mother of another of his young friends, with tickets
for them all for the matinée of *Faust* at the Lyceum. . . .

After the second act . . . [Dodgson took Dolly] round to the stage door.
Apparently he had not made an appointment with Miss Terry [but the
manager arranged for them to come back stage]. Ellen Terry greeted her
old, if intermittent friend, and immediately enveloped Dolly in the
warmth of her personality. They chatted away. . . . Dolly managed to
blurt out her misgiving that she was too tall to be an actress. Ellen gaily
suggested that they stood back while Dodgson measured them. They
were exactly the same height. . . .

Dolly returned to Oxford firm in her resolve to become a professional
actress. . . .

NOTES

1. Laurence Henry Forster Irving (b. 1897), grandson of Henry Irving, son of Henry
Brodribb Irving and 'Dolly' Baird, became Director of the Times Publishing Company,
exhibited his pictures at the Royal Academy, designed various stage and film
productions, and wrote a biography of Henry Irving and numerous other works.

2. On 9 June 1887, Dodgson called on Mrs Lucy 'to make friends with Edith, one of
my Logic class' at the High School. 'I brought her down to Christ Church and gave tea
to her', he wrote. 'Edith is very get-on-with-able.' A friendship with the Lucy family
soon developed, and in September Mrs Lucy allowed Edith to accompany Dodgson to
Eastbourne for a seaside holiday. But on the following day Dodgson found Edith 'in
such tribulation at being away from her mother' that he brought her back. Edith
Elizabeth Lucy (1871–1907) was the daughter of William Lucy, an ironfounder, and
his wife, Alice, born Jennings. Edith married (1895) Abel Hendy Jones Greenidge
(1865–1906), Fellow of St John's College, Oxford, and author of books on Roman law.

3. Dorothea ('Dolly') Forster Baird (1875–1933), sixth daughter of John Forster Baird (1824?–82), barrister (Middle Temple), and his wife, Emily Jane (1830–1910), born Brinton. After Dodgson introduced Dolly to Ellen Terry and she was encouraged to try the stage, she joined Ben Greet's touring Shakespeare company. When, on 30 October 1895, she created the part of Trilby opposite Beerbohm Tree's Svengali in the Du Maurier play, her success was assured. She married (1896) Henry Irving's son Henry Brodribb Irving (1870–1919), the actor–manager.

4. For the complete letter and accompanying 'history', see *The Successors*, pp. 72–4; and *Letters*, pp. 1014–16.

'I was not amused'*

EDWARD GORDON CRAIG[1]

We were still living at 33 Longridge Road, Earl's Court. Here ... I saw Lewis Carroll once. He had called to see E[llen] T[erry] at about six o'clock. She was asleep – but about to get up, so as to go to act at the theatre. I can see him now, on one side of the heavy mahogany table – dressed in black, with a face which made no impression on me at all. I on the other side of the heavy mahogany table, and he describing in detail an event in which I had not the slightest interest – 'How five sheep were taken across a river in one boat, two each time – first two, second two – that leaves one yet two must go over' – ah – he did this with matches and a matchbox – I was not amused – so I have forgotten how these sheep did their trick.[2]

* From *Index to the Story of My Days* (1957) p. 32.

NOTES

1. Edward Gordon Craig (1872–1966), actor, producer, designer, theatre critic and historian, was the natural son of Ellen Terry and Edward William Godwin (1833–86), architect.

2. Dodgson was fond of a number of versions of the 'river-crossing' puzzle. One version is 'Four Gentlemen and their Wives' (see *Picture Book*, p. 317); another, 'Missionaries and Cannibals'; another still, 'Fox, Goose, Bag of Corn'. For more on these puzzles and possible solutions, see *Letters*, p. 300; and *The Magic of Lewis Carroll*, ed. John Fisher (1973) pp. 112–13.

'He would talk with us (not *to* us)'*

KATE TERRY GIELGUD[1]

I could read by now, and I owned and treasured an *Alice in Wonderland* with my name written in it by Lewis Carroll himself – moreover Lewis Carroll . . . was a friend of mine. He would come (often to lunch) when the need of some photographic material brought him to London, and would bring us portraits of Mother and her sisters, of family groups he had taken in his rooms at Christ Church, Oxford; he would teach us to do puzzles, and he would talk with us (not *to* us). I was shy with most people, but never with him. One day I went alone with him to the National Gallery and we both wished we might take home with us some of the lovely landscapes by Hobbema and Ruysdael and Constable. He accepted without remonstrance my refusal to look at the ladies and gentlemen 'with no clothes on' and showed me kings and queens instead. He was always kindly and amusing, and never patronizing.

* From *An Autobiography* (1953) pp. 25–6.

NOTE

1. Kate Terry Lewis (1868–1958) was the daughter of Kate Terry and her husband Arthur James Lewis. She married (1893) Francis Henry (Frank) Gielgud (1860–1949), a stockbroker; they were the parents of (Sir) John Gielgud, the actor.

An Abrupt End to a Friendship*

MARGARET DAVIES[1]

It is with a good deal of diffidence that I set down these very personal recollections of such a unique character as Lewis Carroll. There are, I think, two reasons why they may be of interest, the first the rather strange way in which I was fortunate enough to be admitted to the company of Mr Dodgson's child-friends, and the second, my belief that I must have been one of the latest, if not the last, of that company.

I was the youngest of an ordinary Victorian family, an 'after-thought' I always considered myself, my three sisters being respectively seventeen, sixteen and eleven years, and my youngest brother five years older than me. How my three elder sisters became friends with Mr Dodgson I was never told,[2] but I remember my mother telling me the cause of the abrupt ending of that friendship.

It is well known that Mr Dodgson was an ardent amateur photographer. My mother raised no objection to my youngest sister, aged about six or seven, being photographed in the nude, or in very scanty clothing – I cannot now remember which – but when permission was asked to photograph her elder sister, who was probably then about eleven, in a similar state, my mother's strict sense of Victorian propriety was shocked, and she refused the request. Mr Dodgson was offended, and the friendship ceased forthwith.

Being so much the youngest in the family, I might have been rather a lonely child, but for a wealth of young friends and among them, a year or more my senior, a very pretty clever girl, Enid Stevens,[3] who had long been a great friend of Mr Dodgson. In the kindness of her heart, she made up her mind that I should share this privilege with her. So she begged her mother to ask me to tea one day when Mr Dodgson was to be a guest at their house. Now I was very far from being either pretty or clever, and in addition was often very unsuitably dressed, but my friend's manoeuvre succeeded, and during the last two years of his life I spent some unforgettably wonderful hours in Mr

* From Hudson, pp. 322–6.

Dodgson's company. But perhaps before I come to describe the really personal episodes in our friendship, I ought to mention one occasion which could not be termed happy. I must have seen Mr Dodgson out of doors, striding along, head in the air, in semi-clerical dress, his coat of the 'morning' or short-tails style, not the square-cut clerical frock coat; never wearing a 'dog-collar', but always a very low turn-down collar with a white tie, his top-hat well at the back of his head – reminding me of Tenniel's drawing of the Mad Hatter – but the first time I saw him at close quarters, indoors, was on a Sunday afternoon, when our headmistress, the well-known Miss Soulsby,[4] had announced that Mr Dodgson would give an address in the High School Studio. I have no recollection of the subject of the talk, or whether it was announced beforehand, and was suitable for a child of twelve or thirteen, but my mother simply sent me along to hear it with a friend from the country who lived with us in term-time in order to attend the High School.

Now Mr Dodgson suffered from some impediment in his speech, a sort of stutter, and on this occasion he opened his mouth wide enough for his tongue to be seen wagging up and down, and in addition to this, carried away by the theme of his discourse, he became quite emotional, making me afraid that he would break down in tears, I submit that all this was enough to upset a young school-girl's powers of self-control, and I had difficulty in suppressing my giggles, I suppose, on our return home, we gave a truthful account of my behaviour, for I retain the impression that I was made to feel thoroughly ashamed of myself. I began by speaking of this little episode as one that could not be called happy, but I hasten to add that this was the only occasion during our friendship to which the term unhappy could be applied.

Having re-established contact with my family, Mr Dodgson never spoke to me of his earlier friendship with my sisters; but I have discovered that he remembered very clearly its abrupt ending. Through the kindness of Mr Hudson I have been able to read, for the first time, copies of three letters now in the Huntington Library, California, the last of which, addressed to my mother, shows how essentially kind and courteous and punctilious he was, and that he felt he must be careful in dealing with a lady of such strict Victorian principles.[5] The perusal of it touched me very much.

Tea in college with an ordinary undergraduate was quite an exciting event for a school-girl in those days. How much more so was a visit to Mr Dodgson's suite of rooms in the north-west corner of Tom quad, which he told you with pride had been occupied by members of the Royal family, when up at the House.[6]

A very delightful custom of Mr Dodgson's was to commemorate any expedition with him by the gift of one of his books. I was given

Alice Through the Looking-Glass, The Hunting of the Snark and *Sylvie and Bruno*. The first of these expeditions consisted in a walk and prowl round Magdalen College, followed by tea in his rooms, during the summer term of 1896. On this occasion I think there was one other youthful guest. The second was a year later, at the time of Queen Victoria's Jubilee celebrations. With three other guests – the friend to whom I owed so much, and two adults – I was invited to dine in his rooms. Dinner over, we went up on to the flat roof of that part of the College to wait till it was dark enought to sally forth to see the illuminations. We were, I suppose, only about thirty yards away from Tom Tower, and I shall never forget the start I gave when Tom struck the first note of nine o'clock, and how five minutes later we counted the hundred and one notes of the curfew bell. Then on a perfect summer's night followed a walk through the thronged streets, I feeling particularly safe on the arm of Mr Dodgson.

In October of the same year came perhaps the greatest treat, certainly the most intimate and personal, and, as it turned out, the last, namely an invitation to go to a matinée in London on a Saturday. I was provided with a book for the journey to Paddington, and Mr Dodgson even produced a little travelling set of a game which I somehow connect with the name 'Nine Men's Morris'.[7] He told me he knew that girls like driving in hansoms, so in a hansom I was taken to lunch with a friend of his, a Mrs Fuller, and then on to the Royal Court Theatre, Sloane Square, to see Martin-Harvey in a play called *The Children of the King*.[8] We had seats in the middle of the front row of the stalls. Mr Dodgson told me that on one occasion the demand for tickets had been so great that the manager had put some chairs in front of his seats. The man was summoned forthwith, and I of course do not know what passed between them, but Mr Dodgson was promised that if ever such a thing happened again, his tickets would be transferred to the chairs. Back to Paddington, and so home, escorted to the front-door of my home, north of the Parks – and a far cry from Christ Church – by my friend and famous host. I think that must have been the last time that I saw him, for during the following Christmas holidays came the shock of the news of his death following on a sharp attack of influenza.

NOTES

1. Margaret Dorothea Mayhew (1883–1971), who married (1909) James Arthur Davies (1873–1939), barrister, Principal of New College, Madras, was the daughter of Anthony Lawson Mayhew (1842–1917), author and editor, Hebrew Lecturer at Wadham College, Oxford.

2. On 28 November 1878, Dodgson and the Mayhew parents were fellow guests at an Oxford dinner party; on the following day, Dodgson wrote to Mayhew asking whether he was the father of a certain Ruth Mayhew 'whom Mrs [Thomas] Arnold

and other friends have told me I *ought* to photograph'. On the very day that Dodgson wrote, the Mayhews and their daughter Ruth 'came [to Christ Church], and spent an hour or so looking at pictures: but it was too dark to try a photo'. Dodgson's friendship with the Mayhews prospered, and indeed he did photograph Ruth (see *Diaries*, p. 375; *Letters*, pp. 318, 337–41).

3. See pp. 123–8, above.

4. Lucy Helen Muriel Soulsby (1856–1927) was Headmistress of the Oxford High School for Girls for a decade up to 1897.

5. The letters that Dodgson wrote to Mrs Mayhew are divided between the Huntington Library in California and the Rosenbach Library in Philadelphia; they are reproduced in *Letters*, pp. 319–20, 337–9, 341, 342, 342–3 and 1082.

6. Although Dodgson's rooms at Christ Church may very well have been fit for a king (he himself described them as the largest set in the University), I have found no evidence that they had been occupied by 'royalty'. Perhaps Mrs Davies has the Marquis of Bute in mind; he was the previous occupant of Dodgson's spacious Tom Quad rooms.

7. Nine Men's Morris, also known as the Mill of Morelles, is an ancient board-game for two players, each with nine men, not entirely unlike chess.

8. The outing took place on Saturday, 30 October 1897, and Dodgson termed it 'a very pleasant day' (*Diaries*, p. 451). For more on Dodgson and Mrs Fuller, see *Letters*, esp. pp. 134–6.

'He would probably spoil the party'*

RUTH WATERHOUSE[1]

I first met Mr Dodgson in 1892. . . . I was nine years old – nearly ten. We were playing in the garden in an aimless sort of way when Enid Stevens, about my age, told me that perhaps Mr Dodgson was coming. 'He's an old clergyman,' she said, 'but he's really Lewis Carroll.' Now I knew my *Alice*s very well and I knew that Lewis Carroll lived in Christ Church and that that was not his real name, but to be told that he was an old clergyman was rather disconcerting; even if he had written *Alice in Wonderland* he would probably spoil the party. However, in a very short time Mrs Stevens brought Mr Dodgson into the garden, an old clergyman certainly but not at all the decrepit old creature I had so hastily imagined. He stood at the door leading from the house into the garden, a very upright old man with nearly white hair, wearing the long, old-fashioned clerical coat and the turn-down collar and white tie so often worn by old dons in

* From Hudson, pp. 314–18.

orders at that time. He had a pale, clean-shaven face and his thin mouth seemed almost quivering with delight at the prospect of playing with four of five little girls. The party soon became Mr Dodgson's party. We all went indoors to have tea. He talked delightfully, and I remember how exasperating it was to be asked whether I would like another piece of cake when I was trying so hard to hear what he was saying at the other end of the table. After tea he went back into the garden and Mr Dodgson asked us what we would like to do – should we play croquet or would we like him to tell us a story? Now I hated playing croquet and quickly and fervently begged for a story, so we all sat round him on the garden-seat and he recited the nonsense verses and told us stories out of *Sylvie and Bruno*.

Shortly after this party my mother had a letter from Mrs Stevens to say that Mr Dodgson would like to see more of her little girl. If Mr and Mrs Gamlen would like him to make friends with her he suggested that Mrs Gamlen might perhaps like to go for a walk with him so that she might make his acquaintance. I need hardly say that my parents were delighted to fall in with this plan, and my mother and Mr Dodgson went for a walk round the Parks one day to their mutual satisfaction. And so I became one of Mr Dodgson's little girls.

He brought me a present one day soon after this walk, a copy of *Alice's Adventures Under Ground* in facsimile of his handwriting with his own illustrations. I was enchanted. 'How lovely,' I cried, 'and it's my birthday.' 'Oh dear, that won't do at all', said Mr Dodgson. 'I don't approve of birthdays and I never give birthday presents and so I can't give you this book.' I must have looked very disappointed. 'Never mind,' he said, 'you shall have it as an *un*-birthday present and that will make it all right', and that is what he wrote with my name inside the book with his fountain pen, out of which the ink seemed to flow like black cream.

One day I was invited to dine with Mr Dodgson in his rooms. This was a very great treat. He fetched me. We walked to Christ Church. We dined and we talked and at nine we went up on to the roof and waited till Tom rang one hundred and one times[2] and then he took me home. It was a very enjoyable party. Mr Dodgson showed me so many things – so many treasures and contrivances – of which I only remember the tall desk, and the file in which he kept all his menus, so that no little girl dining with him should ever have the same dinner twice. He told me a great many stories about the funny little girls he had met upon the beach at Eastbourne, and after dinner we had a most confidential talk about illustrators, how obstinate and tiresome they were, more especially Holiday who had given him infinite trouble over *The Hunting of the Snark*. And he showed me his rooms – two floors at the N. W. corner of Tom Quad, all except the sitting-room very bare and austere, and the dark room where he had developed his photographs. Another evening we looked at quantities of photographs of his young friends.

Mr Dodgson took me to London one day, and after this he was very anxious that I should spend a few days with him at Eastbourne. He would arrange for me to stay in the house of three old ladies, friends of his, and he would look after me in the day time. My parents were quite firm in not allowing me to go away with him, and I was not at all disappointed. The old ladies sounded formidable, and tho' I liked Mr Dodgson very much I did not want to be with him all day long.

Then there was the episode of the little pantomime actress. You know that Mr Dodgson was very fond of little girls who went on the stage and did not drop them when they grew up. At this time he was much interested in the little Bowman girls, all on the stage, and more especially in Isa, who had been playing in pantomime. He invited Isa to visit him in Oxford and in order that there should be no ill-natured gossip about her visit he arranged for her to stay in the house of an old lady who, my mother said, was gossip's very fountain-head, so associating her with Isa's visit and stopping all chatter at its source. And having invited Isa to Oxford he was very anxious that I should meet her, but of course she was on the stage and he was afraid that my parents might object. You must remember that this was sixty years ago when actresses occupied a very different position to what they do now and that Mr Dodgson was always extremely careful in obeserving social conventions. So in order that my parents might see for themselves what a very nice little girl Isa was he invited them to meet her at dinner. This was a quite unnecessary precaution on Mr Dodgson's part for my parents would have been only too glad that I should know this little friend of his, but of course they were delighted to go. Later my mother said that as a dinner party it had not been a very great success, but she and my father had enjoyed it and been very much amused. You can see it all – Mr Dodgson never very happy in the society of grown-ups, the poor shy little girl of twelve, and my parents (both of them very good company) doing their best to make themselves agreeable. It was a proof of Mr Dodgson's infinite kindness to a child that he should have gone through what must have been a tiresome ordeal on her behalf. After this introduction I was invited to meet Isa Bowman, though Mr Dodgson much disliked entertaining two children at the same time. I must confess that she caused me bitter disappointment. Here was a child who had spent whole weeks flying about in gorgeously beautiful transformation scenes in a pantomime and had nothing whatever to say about her wonderful experiences. She was so shy and silent that she made me feel shy too and I am afraid that the tea-party was no more of a success than the dinner, but I am almost sure that Isa came to tea with me one day and we got on much better.

Now, as presents of books and letters and invitations came from Mr Dodgson, my father, who was an amused on-looker at this friendship, used to say: 'This is all very well while it lasts, but a day will come when he will drop you like a hot potato.' And sure enough it did. I think that a game that Mr Dodgson had invented and that he was anxious that I should play was the beginning of the end, an elaborate game played with pieces on a board. I was not at all a clever little girl and I thought it very dull and tiresome, but other more intelligent children apparently liked it. I can remember no more invitations after this, but one day a parcel containing a book came addressed in Mr Dodgson's handwriting. I tore it open. It was *Symbolic Logic*, a silly book to my young mind, no story but rather like Mr Dodgson's talk only not so amusing. It was a parting present.

NOTES

1. After meeting Ruth at the Stevenses' on 28 May 1892, Dodgson called on Mrs Gamlen (6 June), 'who was *very* pleasant, and gave leave for me to borrow Ruth in the afternoon – and a more delightful companion it would not be easy to find', he wrote in his *Diaries* (p. 491). Florence Ruth Gamlen (1882–1964) was the daughter of William Blagdon Gamlen (1844–1919), Secretary to the Curators of the University Chest and Editor of the University *Calendar*, barrister (Inner Temple); and his wife, Florence Mostyn, born Owen. Ruth married (1907) Amyas Theodore Waterhouse (1872–1956), son of the architect Alfred Waterhouse and brother-in-law of Robert Bridges, himself a physician at the Radcliffe Infirmary.

2. For over three centuries, at 9.05 p.m., Great Tom has been struck 101 times to mark the 100 Students of the 1546 foundation plus the 101st added by benefaction in the 1660s. 'I have never slept in that region myself,' writes the Librarian of Christ Church (private letter), 'and though I'm told one gets used to the din, Dodgson must always have been conscious of it. . . . It is odd, but I can never make myself listen to all the 101 strokes – one just cannot concentrate enough to count them.'

'Here comes Mr Dodgson'*

ETHEL M. ARNOLD[1]

To recall my first meeting with the Reverend Charles Lutwidge Dodgson, or – as he was familiarly known to the world at large – 'Lewis Carroll', I must, I regret to say, go back fifty-nine years. But though I was but a chubby child of five, through one of those odd

* From 'Reminiscences of Lewis Carroll', *Atlantic Monthly*, 143 (June 1929) 782–6; also in *Windsor Magazine*, 71 (Dec 1929) 43–52.

quirks of memory by which certain scenes or episodes of one's childhood are indelibly etched upon one's brain, I remember every detail of that meeting as if it were yesterday.

It was a typical Oxford afternoon in late autumn – damp, foggy, cheerless; the grey towers of the distant Colleges across the 'Parks', as they are called (not because they are more than one, but because Cromwell stationed his parks of artillery on the ground afterwards made into one of the loveliest open spaces in the world), looked greyer than usual in the dim autumnal light. A number of little girls, bursting with youthful spirits, and all agog for mischief, danced along one of the paths, a staid governess bringing up the rear. Presently one of their number spied a tall black clerical figure in the distance, swinging along towards the little group with a characteristic briskness, almost jerkiness, of step. – 'Here comes Mr Dodgson', she cried. 'Let's make a barrier across the path so that he can't pass.' No sooner said than done – the children joined hands and formed a line across the path; the clerical figure, appreciating the situation, advanced at the double and charged the line with his umbrella. The line broke in confusion, and the next moment four of the little band were clinging to such portions of the black-coated figure as they could seize upon. Two little people, however, hung back, being seized with shyness and a sudden consciousness of their audacity, a sudden awe of this tall, dignified gentleman in black broadcloth and white tie. But in a moment he had shaken off the clinging, laughing children, and before the two little strangers had time to realize what had happened, they found themselves trotting along either side of him, a hand of each firmly clasped in the strong, kind hands of Lewis Carroll, and chattering away as if they had known him all their lives. Thus began a lifelong friendship between Lewis Carroll and the younger of these two little girls, myself.[2] . . .

When I first met him in the year 1870 he had already reached the comfortable goal of his career; that is to say, he was what is called a Senior Student of Christ Church and Mathematical Lecturer to the College – a combination of posts which brought him in a comfortable income and gave him lifelong possession of what was perhaps the most spacious and beautiful suite of College rooms to be found in Oxford. . . .

Lewis Carroll was one of the first of the immense family of amateur photographers to take up photography as a hobby – and photography in those days was a very different thing from what it is now. It was no case then of 'Press the button and we do the rest'; you had to do everything yourself, from the coating of your own plates with the old wet silver emulsion to the development and printing. It was no joke photographing or being photographed in those days; and for a nervous child, dressed up as a Heathen Chinee, a beggar-child, or a fisher-maiden, to keep still for forty-five seconds at a time was no mean ordeal. I was an extremely bad subject, I am sorry to say, and Mr Dodgson in consequence only took me when he was afraid my feelings would be hurt by his constant preference for my sister as a sitter. She was, in fact, one of his very best child-subjects, and some of the photographs we still have of her are really beautiful specimens of early photography. Many of the famous men and women of the day posed before Lewis Carroll's camera in the studio he erected on the Christ Church leads; but, with the whimsical contrariness which was characteristic of him, as soon as the wet plate with all its attendant difficulties and messiness went out, and the clean, convenient dry plate came in – as soon, that is, as photography became easy – he abandoned it, and not one photograph did he ever take by the new and infinitely simplified process. But I never catch a whiff of the potent odour of collodion nowadays without instantly being transported on the magic wings of memory to Lewis Carroll's dark-room, where, shrunk to childhood's proportions, I see myself watching, open-mouthed, the mysterious process of coating the plate, or, standing on a box drawn out from under the sink to assist my small dimensions, watching the still more mysterious process of development. And then the stories – the never-ending, never-failing stories he told in answer to our never-ending, never-failing demands! He was indeed a bringer of delight in those dim, far-off days, and I look back upon the hours spent in his dear and much-loved company as oases of brightness in a somewhat grey and melancholy childhood. . . .

I enjoyed the proud distinction of being one of the very few of his child-friends with whom he remained on terms of close friendship after having attained years of discretion. In fact, I believe I was almost the only one of his Oxford child-friends who could claim that distinction. He always used to say that when the time came for him to take off his hat when he met one of his quondam child-friends in the Oxford streets it was time for the friendship to cease. Even *our* friendship was threatened with disruption when I had reached the age of twenty – a situation brought about through the agency of a much-loved Dachshund of mine, the gift of Professor Max Müller.[3] (Oddly enough, both Edward Lear and Lewis Carroll detested dogs, a trait I frankly confess I have always found it difficult to reconcile with the rest of their characters.) My Dachshund, with that unfailing intuition as to their friends and enemies which may almost be said to constitute a sixth sense in the canine race, made, I regret to say, an unprovoked attack upon Mr Dodgson's legs upon the occasion of an afternoon call upon my mother. Nothing would induce him to enter the house after this outrage, though no real injury had been inflicted. Next day came a long letter containing an elaborate diagram of the rent which had been made in his left trouser-leg by Bergmann's teeth, and announcing his determination never again to cross our threshold until the dog had been destroyed. Needless to say, Bergmann was not sacrificed even on the altar of so old and valued a friendship, but Mr Dodgson stuck to his resolution, and ever after that I always had to meet him at a particular spot inside the Park gates when he wished to take me for our regular walks, which ended up in his room for tea and buttered toast. . . .

On the occasion of [my] . . . visit [to The Chestnuts, Guildford], Mr Dodgson read family prayers before breakfast each morning and also the lessons at the Morning Service at the neighbouring church, at which his sisters were regular attendants, and in the churchyard of which he, who brought the priceless gift of common laughter to the civilized world, now sleeps his last most quiet sleep.

The sentence in which he speaks of 'larking about among the theatres', taken in conjunction with his allusions to his sisters' home at Guildford [in a letter he wrote me], brings us up against what was perhaps one of the most curious combinations of what was in some ways an oddly self-contradictory and paradoxical character. What one may call the basic *paste*, both hereditary and individual, of which his personality was composed was a rigid Evangelicalism. His sense of humour, exquisite as it was, failed absolutely when any allusion to the Bible, however innocuous, was involved. The patriarchs, the prophets, major and minor, were as sacrosanct in his eyes as any of the great figures of the New Testament; and a disrespectful allusion to Noah or even to Nebuchadnezzar would have shocked and displeased him quite as much as any implied belittlement of St Paul. Stories of children which even remotely hinged upon Biblical episodes or characters, or even upon any of the hymns in *Hymns Ancient and Modern*,[4] were received always with the severest rebuke to their narrators, and I shall never forget the snub administered to one unfortunate acquaintance unaware of this characteristic of his, who ventured to tell him the familiar story of little Miss Bellairs and her orisons! Taken by itself, this stern Evangelical rigidity of attitude in regard to the Bible and towards any story which, in his opinion, treated religious matters with levity, would not have been in any way unexpected or remarkable in a man of his heredity and upbringing. But what did strike the student of psychology as curious, and to a certain extent as incongruous, was that, side by side with this narrowness of outlook in one direction, was to be found a certain strain of what can only be described as Bohemianism, which showed itself in his love of the theatre, in his enjoyment and pride in the friendship of distinguished theatrical artists such as the Terry sisters, and more particularly perhaps in his love of child actresses. The latter trait showed itself first in the delight he took in dressing up his little girl friends in all sorts of fancy dresses (of which he kept an almost

inexhaustible stock in the great cupboards to be found in his spacious
Christ Church rooms) for the purposes of photography, and found its
full satisfaction and fulfilment in the various dramatic versions of *Alice
in Wonderland* which to his great delight were produced upon the
London stage. . . .

I have had the precious original [of *Alice's Adventures Under Ground*]
in my hand many a time – a slender, leather-bound notebook in which
Lewis Carroll had printed the story in a clear, neat print, and adorned
with his own inimitable illustrations. It was a lifelong regret with him
that he could not draw, and the illustrations are certainly remarkable
for their anatomy, or, rather, lack of it. But at the same time they are
full of the same whimsical humour as marked the text, and anyone
who compares these original drawings in the original text – which was
reproduced in facsimile many years later – will see how many
suggestions Tenniel obtained from them for his own illustrations to
the story in the enlarged form it ultimately assumed for publication. I
remember meeting Mr Dodgson in the street in Oxford one morning,
just after the reproduction of this facsimile had been decided upon,
and the naïve vanity with which he said, 'Well, you see it seemed to
me that the public might like to see the original form of a book of
which over 70,000 copies have been sold in England alone'; and then
he went on to tell me of the precautions that the publishers had had to
take against robbery of the priceless little notebook – of how a
detective had been engaged to sit in the room all the time the pages
were being photographed for reproduction, etc. etc., and all the time
his face beamed with the pleasure the scheme had given him. He was
indeed a curious mixture of harmless vanity and an almost morbid
shrinking from publicity. Nothing annoyed him so much as any
revelation of the identity between Lewis Carroll and the Reverend C.
L. Dodgson, Senior Student of Christ Church, and he used often to
chuckle at the thought of the numerous autographs, presumably his
but which he had persuaded his fellow-College dons to write for him,
which were included in the albums of autograph-hunters all over the
world. . . .

He used always to keep a pencil and piece of paper by his bedside,
for he found that his most absurd ideas generally came to him on the
borderland of dreams, and, as soon as they had assumed form and
shape, he jotted them down. In this way most of the verses scattered
through *Alice Through the Looking-Glass* and *Sylvie and Bruno* were
written, and the story *afterwards* was woven round the poem. He was
often asked what he really meant by *The Hunting of the Snark*, which by
many people was held to contain a profound philosophical thesis, by
others a political allegory, etc. To all such questions he would reply, 'I
meant *nothing at all*. I happened one day to be walking along the sands
at Eastbourne, and the line came into my head: "For the Snark *was* a

boojum, you see" – and the whole poem arose out of that one totally meaningless line!'[5]

NOTES

1. Julia Frances (1862–1908) and Ethel Margaret (1866–1930) were the daughters of the younger Thomas Arnold (1823–1900), nieces of Matthew Arnold, grand-daughters of Dr Thomas Arnold of Rugby, and sisters of Mary Augusta Arnold, who became Mrs Humphry Ward. Julia married Leonard Huxley and was the mother of Julian and Aldous Huxley. As a girl, she was one of Carroll's favourite photographic models, the first to be taken in the glass studio which the Governing Body of Christ Church permitted Dodgson to have built atop his rooms in Tom Quad. Both Julia and Ethel attended the Oxford High School for Girls, both contributed to the school magazine, and both later served as secretary at the school. Julia won a Clockworkers' Scholarship, read English, and took a first at Somerville College. She founded and was Headmistress of Priorsfield School. In a letter that accompanies a copy of *Doublets* that Dodgson gave the two sisters (Pierpont Morgan Library), Ethel recalls how Dodgson invented the game at Christmas 1877 for her and Julia, and, although the account differs from Dodgson's own in the Preface, it is worth noting:

> He had come to pay us a visit one afternoon, as he often did, and found us suffering from an acute form of *tedium vitae*, a state intensely repugnant to his ever active and astonishingly inventive brain, and particularly so in the young! He therefore set to work at once to cure this repulsive state of things and the word-game known afterwards as *Doublets* sprang full-fledged into being then and there. The dedication to 'Julia and Ethel', which he kept a close secret till the publication of the book, was I remember a source of immense pride and gratification to us both.

2. Dodgson gives a different version of his initial meeting with the Arnold girls: 'On Sunday [25 April 1871] I added to my list of friends in Oxford by joining Arnold . . . in the Parks, where he was walking with his children (whom I had met at the Owens' [Sidney James Owen (1827–1912), Tutor and Reader in Law and Modern History at Christ Church]), and going back with him to his house. Of course I arranged to photograph the children, Julia (8) and Ethel (6)' (*Diaries*, p. 296). A biographer of Mrs Humphry Ward summarizes Dodgson's meeting and friendship with the girls:

> Once, playing round their father in the Parks, Ethel and Julia had been introduced to Mr Dodgson, a clergyman in black. . . . Next day he came to their house and photographed them: they had to stand still for forty-five seconds. Later he took them to his rooms in Christ Church. He gave them Chinese clothes, or posed them as beggars with bare arms. The smell of the wet photographic plates haunted Ethel for life. She herself became a skilled photographer. Once Mr Dodgson came to see them act 'The Mad Tea-party' from *Alice in Wonderland* with friends. (It was perhaps the first performance of the sketch which has since been acted by children all over the world.) When they were almost grown up he went to the Town Hall to see them act in *The Merchant of Venice* with the Philothespians (predecessors of the O[xford] U[niversity] D[ramatic] S[ociety]. . . . Ethel never married, and looking back from middle-age she said the hours with Lewis Carroll seemed oases in a 'somewhat grey melancholy childhood'. (Enid Huws Jones, *Mrs Humphry Ward* [1973] p. 50)

3. Frederick Max Müller (1823–1900), orientalist, philologist, Fellow of All Souls and first Professor of Comparative Philology at Oxford. Dodgson was acquainted with Müller and in fact photographed him, his wife and children (see *Diaries*, esp. p. 260).

4. *Hymns Ancient and Modern* first appeared in 1861 and was revised in 1875.

5. The last line of *The Hunting of the Snark* came to Dodgson when he was walking on a hillside at Guildford (see *Diaries*, pp. 334–5, 346).

'Three little girls . . . in a railway carriage'*

Sixty years ago three little girls sat in a railway carriage listening intently to a story which their nurse was telling them to pass away the time during a journey to Sandhurst.

Then the train stopped and the story was interrupted. A gentleman looked into their compartment and decided to get in. He put his bag on the rack, took a seat, and more than once he glanced with interest at the little party.

'Oh, do go on!' the children begged their nurse. 'Do tell us some more of the story!' But the girl had turned self-conscious now that the stranger, who was clean-shaven and wore his hair longer than was the custom, sat opposite. In spite of their entreaties she refused to tell them any more.

The eldest little girl was very indignant. It was a shame! They had been having such a lovely time before this passenger came and spoiled everything.

Then the stranger spoke. In a slightly stammering voice he said: 'I am very sorry to have interrupted the story. But if you will tell me what it is about I will go on with it.' And to the delight of the three little girls he finished the story for them.

Afterwards he took off his grey and black cotton gloves, opened his bag and found inside it three puzzles. He had made them himself, he told them, and he gave one to each of them to find out. When they were tired of this game he produced three little pairs of scissors and paper so that they could cut out patterns. There were many other surprises in that wonderful bag. No journey could ever have passed more quickly. The little girls were disconsolate when the train slowed down and they reached their destination. Before they said good-bye the stranger wrote down their names and address.

'One of these days I will send you a children's book I have written', he said. 'It is called *Alice in Wonderland*.'

* 'Lewis Carroll Interrupts a Story', *Children's Newspaper*, 7 Feb 1931, p. 4.

He did not forget his word. A brown paper parcel arrived one day and in it was a beautiful first edition of this book. On the fly-leaf was written:

MINNIE, ELLA, and EMMIE DRURY
To three puzzled little girls from the Author

Three little maidens weary of the rail,
Three pairs of little ears listening to a tale,
Three little hands held out in readiness
For three little puzzles very hard to guess.
Three pairs of little eyes open wonder-wide
At three little scissors lying side by side.
Three little mouths that thanked an unknown Friend
For one little book he undertook to send.
Though whether they'll remember a friend, or book, or day
For three little weeks is very hard to say.

How delighted the children were! Their mother wrote to the publishers for the real name of Lewis Carroll and for his address. And then they all wrote cordial letters of thanks to their fellow-traveller, whose real name they found was Mr Charles Lutwidge Dodgson.

It was not long before they saw him again, for he came to call on them in their house in London. Needless to say they gave him a big welcome. He invited them all to his home in Guildford.

That was a never-to-be-forgotten day. Their host was tireless in entertaining children. There were not many of his child-friends who did not remember all their lives how his pocket handkerchief would suddenly change into a jumpity mouse or some other animal uncannily alive. They remembered also his wonderful puzzles, especially the favourite one, which was the Fox, the Goose, and the Bag of Corn.[1]

Every hour of this bright August day was filled with lovely things to do. Mr Dodgson took his camera into the garden and photographed Minnie, Ella, and five-years-old Emmie. He had ideas of his own about photography. He could not bear dressed-up children, but liked them to be as natural as possible. He never let them pose for their photographs and it did not matter a bit if their hair was untidy; in fact, it pleased him better.

From that day Lewis Carroll became one of the kindest friends of these three girls. When he was in London he would take them to all kinds of exhibitions, pantomimes, and theatres, and he gave them copies of his books.

One of the most memorable of their treats was their visit to the famous German Reed entertainment. Their immense enjoyment of the three items, Happy Arcadia, All Abroad, and Very Catching, was never forgotten in after-years.[2] Later their friend sent them a copy of *Phantasmagoria*, and inside it he had written:

> Three little maids one winter day,
> When others went to feed,
> To sing, to laugh, to dance, to play,
> More wisely went to *Reed*.
> Others, when lesson-time begun,
> Go half inclined to cry,
> Some in a walk, some in a run;
> But these went in a – Fly.

> I give to other little maids
> A smile, a kiss, a look,
> Presents whose memory quickly fades;
> I give to these – a Book.
> *Happy Arcadia* may blind,
> While *all abroad* their eyes;
> At home this book (I trust) they'll find
> A *very catching* prize.

Only a few weeks ago we reported in the C[*hildren's*] N[*ewspaper*] the death at Guildford of the last surviving sister of Lewis Carroll. Recently the news has come to us of the death in Glasgow of Mrs Emily Wyper, formerly Emmie Drury, the youngest of these three little maids. Lewis Carroll went to her wedding and always took the greatest interest in her. After his death she collected subscriptions and founded a Lewis Carroll Cot at the Western Infirmary in Glasgow. Only a year ago she sold her own edition of *Alice in Wonderland*, which he had given her, for £500.[3]

NOTES

1. For more on the fox–goose–bag-of-corn puzzle, see p. 153n, above.

2. Dodgson was personally acquainted with Thomas German Reed (1817–88), musical director of the Haymarket Theatre, who began, in 1855, to present his 'Entertainments', dramatic performances with music, rather than full-scale theatrical pieces, often in concert halls and designed to present respectable entertainment for an audience that would not ordinarily attend the theatre. On 21 January 1873, Dodgson recorded in his *Diaries* (p. 319) that he 'took Minnie, Ella and Emmie to the German Reeds. *Happy Arcadia* (an opera with words by W. S. Gilbert and music by Frederick Clay) is well written and acted. After taking the Drurys home I dined with Mr Reed at the "Garrick".' *Very Catching*, an operetta by F. C. Burnand and J. L. Molloy, was first performed in 1872; the earliest of three theatre productions entitled *All Aboard*, also an operetta, by Arthur Law, first appeared in 1890.

3. After the encounter on the railway journey, Dodgson and the Drury girls became fast friends, and a friendship ensued that lasted for a quarter of a century. He gave them numerous inscribed books, for their amusement, fabricated a letter that Queen

Victoria might have sent him, took the 'charming trio' on outings, photographed them, and occasionally stayed the night with the family in London (*Diaries*, pp. 278, 283, 289). The parents of the girls were James Samuel Drury (1822–65), physician, and his wife Sophia Louisa, born Bousfield (d. 1886). The daughters were Mary ('Minnie') Frances (1859–1935), who married (1882) Herbert Henry Fuller, land surveyor; Isabella ('Ella') Maude (1862–84), who married (1882) Robert Fischer, of Madras, barrister; and Emily ('Emmie') Henrietta (1864–1930), who married (1883) James Wyper, a Glasgow stationer. After Dodgson's death, Minnie and her daughter Audry Fuller were largely responsible for establishing the *Alice in Wonderland* Cot at Great Ormond Street Hospital in memory of Lewis Carroll.

'You never thought of him as any age in particular'*

MRS H. T. STRETTON[1]

I only knew Lewis Carroll when I was about seventeen. I knew him because he used to spend all his holidays in Eastbourne. My mother had a school there, and until I was married I was there. He used to come up quite a lot to the school. He was awfully good to them. He used to come up to tea and supper, and play Misch-Masch – which was a game he taught you for logic. Then he used to tell the children stories. They were nearly always out of *Sylvie and Bruno*.

One day he told them a story, and I said to him afterwards: 'You made up that story, because I'm quite sure it isn't in *Sylvie and Bruno*.' He laughed, and said: 'Why do you think that?' And I said: 'Well, I know *Sylvie and Bruno* very well, I had it given to me years ago, and I don't remember that story.' About two days later I got *Sylvie and Bruno Concluded* from him, which I didn't know was written, and the story was there.

He was very good with small children. But I think he was rather chastened if they didn't behave quite as politely and properly as they should have done. They used to go to tea, generally in twos and threes, to his rooms in Lushington Road. He would have a very nice tea, and I think they always behaved very nicely. You never thought of him as a middle-aged man: you never thought of him as any age in particular. He was just a friend. Because I think he did become the same age as the children he was talking to. He seemed to be able to draw them out, and they did talk to him very happily.

* 'More Recollections of Lewis Carroll – II', *Listener*, 6 Feb 1958, p. 239.

I have seen him a lot with children, and they liked him. But I think when he got one of these stammering bouts it was rather terrifying. It wasn't exactly a stammer, because there was no noise, he just opened his mouth. But there was a wait, a very nervous wait from everybody's point of view: it was very curious. He didn't always have it, but sometimes he did. When he was in the middle of telling a story about Sylvie and Bruno, he'd suddenly stop and you wondered if you'd done anything wrong. Then you looked at him and you knew that you hadn't, it was all right. You got used to it after a bit. He fought it very wonderfully; I think for him to go and preach was a very plucky thing to do. There are a lot of villages round Eastbourne – Willingdon, and Westham, and Eastdean – and he used to go out there and preach. He liked to take somebody with him and put them in the back seat of the church, and then, walking home, you had to tell him what you remembered of the sermon.

When I was about eighteen he asked me for some books to read. My mother had had Marie Corelli's *Romance of Two Worlds* given her, and I read it: and I told him to take that and read it. I was rather intrigued with it. I've read it since and been horrified. Anyway, he took it and was frightfully upset. He wrote a letter to my mother: I think he was very worried about my religious training.

We used to go up to London and have lunch with a friend, and then he went to a theatre. We loved the theatre. We went afterwards behind and saw Marion Terry: it was nearly always with the Terrys that we went. Whenever I went to a theatre with Mr Dodgson I always had a charming letter afterwards, in which he said: 'I am sending you Marion Terry's photograph which she has signed and written a nice message on, and I suggest that you write and thank her for it': or any other actress – it was always the same. And I went over once by sea with him – rather a rough sea – to Rye, where Marion Terry was living. We went to see her, and spent the day there.

Once we went to the theatre in Eastbourne to see a play called *Broken Melody*. Mr Dodgson thoroughly enjoyed the performance of the leading actor. But he couldn't make up his mind whether he would write and tell him he had enjoyed it or not, because he had a sort of bugbear that people would sell his signature. He was very curious about that: he never signed his name Lewis Carroll, and he generally put in books 'From the Author'. Sometimes he put 'From C. L. Dodgson', but otherwise it was generally 'From the Author'.

Among the children's books he liked was *The Cuckoo Clock* by Mrs Molesworth – he thought that was a very nice story for little girls; and Dickens, of course, especially *A Christmas Carol*, and Kate Greenaway; and also Edward Lear. He liked anything that was nonsense, and any playing with words. I think that was one of his ideas of a sense of humour which should be developed in children.

An old friend of ours, a Mr Ryde,[2] who used to sit next to him at high table at Christ Church, said that he used to keep the hall in fits of laughter the whole time: he was so amusing.

I had copies of *Alice* and *Through the Looking-Glass* given me when I was a very small child, and I had, I'm afraid, mutilated them quite a lot and scribbled in them, but my mother had them both bound together. And Mr Dodgson said would I lend him these two copies to make his alterations on them for a new edition, and then I should have new copies when they got the others out. I lent them to him, and I got them back with his manuscript corrections after he died, from the publisher.

I don't know why, but in some ways he always reminded me of the White Knight, he was so gentle. I always loved the White Knight.

NOTES

1. On 8 October 1894, Dodgson, in Eastbourne, 'called on Mrs Barber, who had a girls' boarding school at West Hill, Mill Road . . . and undertook to go on Thursday to teach her girls something. Saw also her daughter, May, aged 17.' On the appointed Thursday, he spent more than an hour at the school, and on the following day began to give a regular course in daily logic lessons there, which lasted until the 19th, the day before he left Eastbourne. Dodgson became friendly with May, and they met, during the following years, in Oxford, Eastbourne, and London (*Diaries*, pp. 513, 518–20). Students of Mrs Barber's school later helped to endow the Lewis Carroll Cot at the Throat and Ear Hospital, Church Street, Brighton. Mary ('May') Lucy Barber (1877–1962) was the daughter of Edward Coates Massey Barber, physician, and his wife, Charlotte Lucy, born Plume. In 1900, May married Hallyburton Tom Streeton, mining engineer.

2. Walter Cranley Ryde (b. 1857?) was a Junior Student at Christ Church 1875–82. He then went on to become a barrister-at-law (Inner Temple).

A Few Surviving Sussex Friends*

STANLEY GODMAN

For the last 25 years of his life Lewis Carroll spent all his long summer vacations at Eastbourne. This was not, however, his only annual contact with Sussex. He paid equally regular visits in the Christmas holidays to Brighton, where he stayed with his old Christ

* From 'Lewis Carroll at the Seaside', *The Times*, 27 July 1957, p. 6.

Church friend the Rev. Henry Barclay,[1] at 11, Sussex Square and attended the pantomime at the Theatre Royal (where he also saw the stage version of *Alice* in 1887). Brighton has a permanent memorial in the 'Lewis Carroll Cot' in the Throat and Ear Hospital in Church Street, though this was endowed by the girls of Mrs Barber's school in Eastbourne, where he met two of the friends who have provided the occasion for these notes.

Mrs Barber's daughter May, Mrs H. T. Stretton, became one of Dodgson's special favourites. She has a copy of the Golden Treasury edition of Wordsworth's Poems inscribed 'May, with love from Lewis Carroll' – a rare signature in a book, as the author observed when inscribing it. . . .

One of the older pupils at Mrs Barber's school was Miss Amy Perfect,[2] who has two charmingly characteristic letters from Lewis Carroll. . . . She was 18 when Mrs Barber introduced her to Dodgson in 1895. It was, therefore, 'a great privilege', since his interest in young ladies normally ceased once they reached the age of 14. [In August 1896, Dodgson wrote to Amy suggesting that he and his niece (who was visiting him at Eastbourne) visit Amy at Lewes, to] 'renew the pleasure which our brief acquaintance (I think it has lasted 15 or 20 minutes) has given me . . .'. [The visit took place.] After tea the hours passed happily with Dodgson reciting rhymes on the Oxford colleges and showing his favourite games and puzzles.

During his last years Dodgson was a regular worshipper at Christ Church, Eastbourne, and gave several addresses at children's services. The Rev. A. B. Taylor[3] who was curate there at the time, recalls that Dodgson chose the church 'because the prayers were said more slowly there than anywhere else in Eastbourne; he, being deaf, liked to join in the congregational parts at a slow pace and not be left behind'.

He also recalls that 'Dodgson was very nervous before the services and said little to me in the vestry'. Mr Taylor's most characteristic memory is that Dodgson (or, more likely in this case, Lewis Carroll) rented two pews: one for himself and one for his silk hat.

One of the churchwardens at Christ Church, Eastbourne, in Dodgson's time was James Attlee (uncle of Lord Attlee). His daughters remember Dodgson chiefly as 'a very irritable person and the last man to write the amusing nonsense of *Alice*'. In particular they recall the fuss he made about the size of the hassocks in the ordinary pews. Mr Attlee had to have a specially large one made for him. Dodgson's brusqueness with autograph-hunters was notorious, and Miss Elsie Attlee tells a story which confirms this. Her young brother went to Dodgson's rooms with his autograph book, giving his name as 'Mr Attlee'. Dodgson came down expecting to find the churchwarden. When he saw a mere youth at the door he was extremely indignant and promptly dismissed him without an autograph.

On the whole, however, he seems to have left kindlier memories in Sussex. The day after he died a writer in the *Sussex Daily News* recorded that he had seen him not long ago, a 'white-haired, radiant old gentleman, hand in hand with two little girls on the West Pier, Brighton'.

NOTES

1. Henry Alexander Barclay (1833–88) was one of Dodgson's oldest friends. They were fellow-undergraduates at Christ Church, took their BAs together, and then kept in touch after Barclay left Oxford to become a master at Glenalmond and later at Ipswich Grammar School. Later still Barclay took a living at Brighton.

2. When Dodgson went to Mrs Barber's school on 27 July 1895, to see the end-of-term entertainment, he recorded that he saw 'a pretty operetta, *The Rose of Savoy* . . . in which . . . Amy Perfect, who has a delicious voice, sang some solos' (*Diaries*, pp. 518–19). Amy Sophia Perfect (1875–1960) was the daughter of Arthur Pearson Perfect (1838–1910), Rector of St John's Lewes, and his wife, Fanny Maria, born Pemberton.

3. Arthur Bryan Taylor, who took his BA at the University of London in 1892, was Curate of Christ Church, Eastbourne, from 1895 to 1900.

'He . . . gave me the name of "Ducky"'*

EDITH ALICE MAITLAND[1]

I shall never forget when, sitting on a rustic seat with Mr Dodgson under a dear old tree in the Botanical Gardens, I heard for the first time the delightful and ever-entertaining story of Hans Andersen's 'Ugly Duckling'. I was devoted to books, and could read quite well for so small a child, but I cannot explain the delightful way in which Mr Dodgson read and told his stories: as he read, the characters were real flesh and blood – living figures. This particular story made a great impression on me, and, being very sensitive about my ugly little self, it greatly interested me. I remember his impressing upon me that it was better to be good, truthful, and to try not to think of self, than to be a pretty, selfish child, spoilt and disagreeable, and he, from that story, gave me the name of 'Ducky', which name clung to me for many years; in fact, from that day Mary Pearson always called me 'Miss Ducky'.

* From 'Childish Memories of Lewis Carroll' by One of his Alices, *Quiver*, 1899, pp. 407–15.

Many a time has Mr Dodgson said, 'Never mind, little Ducky: perhaps some day you will turn out a swan.'

I always attribute my love for animals to the teaching of Mr Dodgson: his stories of animal life, his knowledge of their lives and histories, his enthusiasm about birds and butterflies, passed many a tiresome hour away. The monkeys in the Botanical Gardens were our special pets, and, oh! the nuts and biscuits we used to give them! He entered into the spirit of the fun as much as 'Ducky' did.

Then there were the mornings spent in the Christ Church and Merton meadows. . . . And how delighted we were to see the well-known figure in his cap and gown coming, so swiftly, with his kind smile ready to welcome the 'Ugly Duckling' sitting in the grass! I knew, as he sat beside me, that a fairy-tale book was hidden in his pocket, or that I should hear something nice – perhaps a new game or a puzzle – and he would gravely accept a tiny daisy bouquet for his coat with as much courtesy as if it had been the finest hot-house *boutonnière*. I was very proud when, between us, we had made a chain of cuckoo-flowers and daisy heads long enough to twine round my hat.

These meadows and the walk along the wall were remarkable then for the quantity of snails of all kinds that, on fine days and damp days, came out to take the air, and to me they were objects of great dislike and horror. Mr Dodgson so gently and patiently showed me how silly I was, how harmless the poor snails were, and told me so much about the shells they carried on their backs, and showed me how wonderfully they were made, that I soon got over the fright and made quite a collection of discarded shells; which collection finally took up its abode in a little crimson-paper trunk that Mr Dodgson found at old Mrs Green's toyshop and bought for me.

About this time also father had added to my nursery literature *Ministering Children, Sandford and Merton*, and *Rosamund; or, The Purple Jar*.[2] All these were shown in great glee to my kind friend, who (as I knew he would) read to me from them.

Two or three times I went fishing with him from the bank, near the Old Mill opposite Addison's Walk (Oxford), and he entered quite into my happiness when a small fish came wriggling up on the end of my crooked pin and line, just ready for the dinner of the little white kitten, 'Lily', he had given me.

In those days Addison's Walk had, in season, its banks covered with pretty periwinkles – white and blue – and there were strict laws not to pick them. I, childlike, could not resist the temptation, and one day, Mary being seated at work near by, 'Ducky', left to play alone, gathered a bunch of the coveted beauties, hid them under her little spencer (a small coat of those days), and trotted by Mary's side, half-frightened, to the lodge of the gruff old porter, who sat reading his paper, glancing always at the passers through his doorway. Nothing escaped his notice. Mary went through and then I, half-trembling, with the periwinkles closely clasped to my side. The street gained, I was safe, but (alas! there is always a 'but'), Mr Dodgson, going to see a friend in the college, came up to me, saying, 'Why so flushed, little Alice? And what is that hanging below your jacket?'

The flowers had not gained anything by their hot pressure under my jacket, and it was a very much ashamed, sad little girl who stood convicted of flower-theft!

'Ducky, come with me': and, taking my unwilling hand, he led me back to the grim old custodian of the cloisters, to whom I had to deliver up the now faded periwinkles, and promise future goodness and 'never to do so any more'. Then Mary took me in hand, and the quiet little 'weep' I indulged in while going home was much enhanced by the sound of Mary's voice telling me: 'Miss Ducky, you are an awful naughty child: you have quite disgusted Mr Dodgson, and you shall go to your bed without supper.' This threat she carried out.

On Sunday afternoons father used to take me for a walk to St John's College gardens, or, perhaps New College gardens, and as they – father and Mr Dodgson – were great friends, he often joined us. And how I enjoyed all the bright sunshine and the shade of the mulberry-trees! And then father, tired from his morning services, snatched a 'forty-winks'. I revelled in stories of small men and maidens, stories so entertaining that I thought I could never read 'line upon line' any more; and then there were the stories of the other little Alice who bore the same initials as myself, and who was so pretty and behaved so well: who sat before the wonderful photographing machine and came out a pretty little beggar girl! I am afraid I was rather envious of this child and a tiny bit jealous, but I took the greatest interest in what she did and said. And I remember all this perfectly.

Before me, as I write, is a likeness of Mr Dodgson; in fact, two photographs. These are just as I remember him. It was his sweet smile and face that endeared him so much to his youthful friends, his never-failing interest in their childlike joys and sorrows. Mr Dodgson was a very quiet, reserved man, and cared little for society, such as large parties and receptions; but to come and go as he liked in the homes of those with whom he was intimate, these visits were some of the pleasures he allowed himself. He also made very welcome the visits of his child-friends, and it was a great treat to go to see him in his rooms in Christ Church.

My dear father (the Rev. E. A. Litton, a very well-known man in the old Oxford days of sixty years ago) was much attached to Mr Dodgson, and they used to meet frequently to discuss points that interested them both. I was always allowed, if I bore a good record in the nursery, to join father when he went to Christ Church, and I knew that, sooner or later during the visit, something good would be for me. The delicious slices of cake and bread-and-butter, the glass of creamy milk: the soft pile of cushions on the sofa if I felt tired, and the glittering little glass balls of his wonderful game of 'Solitaire', for me to play with; the lovely picture-books which I was so careful not to tear or hurt in any way; and then to be allowed to look at the portraits of other little friends who knew and visited him as I did!

Mr Dodgson was a great admirer of photography and he inspired father with a like enthusiasm, and I am the happy possessor of a photograph ... that our dear friend took at Christ Church of father and me. Such a good likeness of father and me, such a lanky, long-legged, shy child, with very short petticoat, low shoes, and a huge flap hat! More than forty years [have passed since this was] ... taken – the two dear friends gone for ever and only the photograph remaining as souvenir of the dear old past – it is almost as fresh as the day it was taken!

Other likenesses were taken, but, though I have hunted about, I cannot find them. Also, to my great sorrow, I have lost several long, illustrated letters written to me with the hope of shaming me out of several bad habits and faults. One in particular was the sucking of my thumb, and this Mr Dodgson always teased me about very much. One day I received a long letter with funny little pictures of a small family of birds who would suck their thumbs (claws). They looked so comical in a row, on a branch, with their claws in their beaks, and the father- and mother-birds below with a pot of bitter aloes, a birch-rod, and long muslin bags to tie up the claws in. The next picture showed the little birds weeping, with their claws in bags, the father and mother enjoying a good repast, and the naughty little birds 'had none'! And so on all the way through this most interesting pictorial letter, till the little birds had no claws left. All sucked away! The story was quite as interesting as the pictures, and I think it did me good, as Mary Pearson always read this letter to me whenever I sucked my thumb more than usual, and protested my thumbs were disappearing as the birds' claws did, and I was terribly frightened; for Mr Dodgson used to say Mary was quite right, and I should be spoken of as 'the little girl without thumbs'.

My hair was a great trouble to me as a child, for it would tangle, and Mary was not over and above patient as I twisted and turned when she wished to dress it. So one day I received a long, blue envelope addressed to myself (letters are always so delightful to children – they raise them almost to the ranks of the 'grown-ups'), and there was a story-letter, all full of drawings, from Mr Dodgson. The first picture was of a little girl – hat off and tumbled hair very much *en evidence* – asleep on a rustic bench under a big tree by the side of a river (supposed to be the dear old seat in the Botanical Gardens), and two birds holding an evidently most important conversation above in the branches, their heads on one side, eyeing the sleeping child. The next picture, the two birds, flying with twigs and straw, preparing to build a nest; the child still sleeping and the birds chirping and twittering with the delight of building their nest in the tangled hair of the child. Next came the awakening. The work complete, the mother-bird on her nest, the father-bird flying round the frightened child. And then, lastly, hundreds of birds – the air thick with them; the child fleeing; small boys with tin trumpets raised to their lips, and Nurse Mary, with a basket of brushes and combs, bringing up the rear! All this, with the well-drawn-out story, cured me of this fault, and Mary, in after-life, told me she 'had no more trouble; just to open the letter and show the unhappy child in the picture, and I was "passive as a lamb"'. Sometimes father would say, patting my head, 'Any more nests to-day, Ducky? Birds would not have a chance now with this smooth little head.'

I have grieved greatly that these picture-stories are no more, and, from several letters which I have seen from other little girls – now grown up and far away in different parts of the world, their letters of a like kind have also gone astray and been lost amidst the movings, changings, and chances of life.

In after years my father often told me another story of Mr Dodgson, which I, being so young, had forgotten. In the very early part of the time in which I knew him, he one day called in Long-Wall Street to fetch father to go with him to 'The Union' to look into some particular subject together. Mr Dodgson was anxious I should go as well, as, perhaps, we might all take a walk, and as I promised to be most obedient and good, I was told to go and get my hat. I trotted along, and, 'The Union' reached, was put in a comfortable chair to wait till they were ready to go on the proposed walk. It was hot, and I was tired, and the crackling of papers turning over and the hum of voices lulled me to sleep. I slept on, oblivious of all, and, I suppose, the two friends, talking intently, forgot my existence and, in earnest conversation, left 'The Union' – and me, sleeping quietly, quite alone.

Mr Dodgson left father in Long-Wall Street, and then went to his rooms in Christ Church. Suddenly, so the story goes, he thought, 'We went out three; we came back two; where is three?'

And then it flashed across him that there had been no 'three' left in Long-Wall Street – only his friend – and so 'three' must have been left somewhere on the road. Though it was just the hour of dinner, this good friend trudged back to 'The Union', intent upon finding the lost lamb, and there I was still asleep, coiled up, as he expressed it, 'like a dormouse'. I was taken home tired and a little cross; it was past supper-time; I was hungry, and quite ready for the white sheets and pillows that lead to dreamland. But, always thoughtful for others, Mr

Dodgson strayed into the ever-famous and delightful shop of Boffins in 'The High', and a sugared Bath-bun and a glass of jelly revived my drooping spirits and raised my courage to meet Mary. I was soon given into her care and my adventures, as told by Mr Dodgson, made me quite a heroine, and I felt myself a person of some importance with a history.

I had a daily governess, a dear old soul, who used to come every morning to instruct my youthful mind. I disliked particularly the large-lettered copies in my writing-book, and, as I confided this to Mr Dodgson, he came and set me some copies himself. I remember two were, 'Patience and water-gruel cure gout.' (I wondered what 'gout' could be.) 'Little girls should be seen and not heard.' (This I thought unkind.) These were written many times over, and I had to present the pages at the end of the week to him without one blot or smudge. . . .

Mr Dodgson and father and myself all went one afternoon to pay . . . [Mr Saul, 'Fellow of Magdalen',[3]] a visit. At that time Mr Saul was very much interested in the study of the big drum, and, with books before him and a much heated face, he was in full practice when we arrived. Nothing would do but that all the party must join in the concert. Father undertook the 'cello. Mr Dodgson took a comb and paper, and, amidst much fun and laughter, the walls echoed with the finished roll, or shake, of the big drum – a roll that was Mr Saul's delight. All this went on till some other Oxford Dons (mutual friends) came in to see 'if everybody had gone suddenly cracked'. I meanwhile, perched amongst the flowers and mirrors, joined in the fun by singing and clapping my hands with delight at the drum, comb, and 'cello. When all had quietened down, a large musical-box was wound up for my edification; such a treat it was for me to listen to the beautiful airs! . . .

Now father had a great friend living near Park Crescent, and one of the bonds of sympathy (and a great one it was) between father, Mr Dodgson, and the little old gentleman, was mathematics. The friend, whose name I have forgotten, lived in one of a row of houses at the top of Park Crescent, and many were the times we all three took this particular walk together to see the old scholar. My delight was resting in the pleasant little parlour of the housekeeper, into whose charge I was always given. She had very beady black eyes, a bunch of keys at her waist, and a most wonderful cap with bouquets of flowers intermixed with lace at each of her ears, and funny little grey curls and combs (like those of the present day) to fasten them back. I always was most polite to her and put on my very best manners. To me she was a most potential personage, and her coltsfoot wine and old-fashioned rock cakes, with which she always regaled me with no sparing hand, were so delicious! Nowhere else did these particular dainties seem to me so good. Perhaps hunger (which is always the best sauce) had something to do with it; but I know I munched the cakes and gazed intently at the swaying grasses and flowers on her head, as she told me that she made all the cakes herself, and also could sometimes make, when little girls were 'extra good', 'almond toffee' of the most appetizing description.

I was always ready to go this walk with father, and I well remember one occasion on which we went. It must have been about July, for it was very hot, and the roses and other flowers were all out. Mr Dodgson and father enjoyed a chat, while I with a mind full of rock cakes, the bright sunshine and all the pretty things of nature in the hedges, and (oh! happy thought!) perhaps the wonderful toffee at the walk's end danced along till the little garden gate was reached and we all passed through. I always shared my goodies with other people when I could, and I had promised to save some rock cakes for father and Mr Dodgson, for upstairs they were always much too intent on conversation to think about 'refreshments of life', and these things of which I am writing happened before 'afternoon teas' of four o'clock were ever thought of.

The toffee was there – rather sticky, owing to the hot weather, but the almonds looked white and cool; and the green plate of cakes and the jug with a dog's face for a spout – all were there just ready for the flushed, tired, little girl. I quite remember the cap that day, for it had bunches of pink May with 'Quaker' grass, and the old lady told me it was her best summer cap and had cost six shillings at Oliver's in Corn Market Street. I thought she must be a very rich woman indeed, and told Mr Dodgson so that afternoon, when we were once more together. I remember his laugh as he said, 'the female mind is full of vanity'. I wondered what a 'female mind' meant, and father said little girls asked too many questions (he often told me this part of the story afterwards, when I was grown up), and that I should not know what it was, even if I were told. Mr Dodgson said, 'Alice, all things come to those who wait; some time, if God spares you to grow up, you will learn many things.'

But the pleasant hour spent with the old housekeeper came to an end, and the bell was rung, which meant that I had to gather myself together and go home. Two small parcels of toffee and cakes were given into my willing, open, little hands; a towel was hastily found to wipe away my general stickiness; and then I went away from his dear little home into 'The Parks' with Mr Dodgson and father, homewards.

It was hot, and I was tired; I am sorry to say that father said I was 'very cross'. My little blue shoes, fastened with straps and tiny pearl buttons, would come undone, and all the brightness and flowery hedges had lost their charm for the now overdone 'Ducky'.

Mr Dodgson lagged behind, and I saw him looking intently in the hedges and all about, as if he were searching for something. This aroused my curiosity. At length, stooping down, he gathered up something in his handkerchief. I could not see what he had found, but I felt very much interested. Holding the tied-up handkerchief above my head, he said, 'This is for my other little Alice; she is a brave girl, and does not cry like a baby at being a wee bit tired. Oh! such a curious, lovely little flower is tied up here!'

At this he waved the handkerchief above my head, and I, so anxious to see what was in it, skipped after him, forgetting the tears and the tired legs. 'Tell me what it is', was my breathless request.

No answer. Mr Dodgson danced on, and I followed, father laughing at the two of us. When we were near dear old Wadham College (not a great distance from Long-Wall Street), Mr Dodgson said to me, with much solemnity, 'Alice, did you ever hear of a "Bella perennis", most wonderfully and beautifully made?'

I was awestruck, and whispered, 'Never. Is that it?'

He nodded, and we went on again till the steps of our house came in view. By this time I was quiet and wondering, and hoping I should be allowed to see inside the handkerchief, and look at this wonderful, mysterious creation.

Inside our hall was an old oaken bench, and there Mr Dodgson sat down; I in front of him, in my favourite attitude, with my long, skinny arms clasped behind my back. I dare not speak as the knots were very, very slowly untied, and oh! only a tiny, withered, half-dead, little daisy appeared to my astonished view! 'Where is the beautiful "Bella something?"' I cried, with a half-sob rising in my throat; I was so bitterly disappointed.

'This is the "Bella perennis", child. See how beautifully and carefully it is made: one of God's fairest small field-flowers'.

I took it in my hand, and, giving Mr Dodgson a big hug, I passed through the baize door, leaving my dear, kind friend with father.

I never forgot that walk! It made a very deep impression on my childish mind, not easily effaced in the long after-years. If people only knew what the sympathy of a 'real, grown-up friend' is to a shy child, what courage it gives to the trembling little heart! How few children would be set down as shy and stupid, and be thoroughly misunderstood (as some are now), if only there were more like Mr Dodgson, who, though one of the cleverest of men, could yet stoop to win the love and confidence and enter into the joys and sorrows of his numerous child friends!

Perhaps I have wearied many who have read this, and it is time I should close these past chapters of my 'childish memories', shut up the book, and lay down the pen; but it has been an inexpressible pleasure to recall, as far as I can, all Mr Dodgson's kindness to me and father. Alas! alas! that life should change; on and on, all the dear, old, familiar places and faces disappear. 'Old Tom' still chimes his daily hours; but the dear footsteps will never more be heard turning in at the door of the old staircase leading to his rooms in Christ Church. Those cheerful rooms, where so many delightful hours were spent, will know him no more. All is gone now: only the memory, and the deep respect and love his child-friends bore him, remain.

Father died on August 27th 1897, and Mr Dodgson on January 14th, 1898; and we, who are left behind, can only hope we may meet them once more in the realms that never change.

NOTES

1. Edith Alice Litton (1849–1919) was the daughter of Edward Arthur Litton (1813–97), Fellow of Oriel, Vice-Principal of St Edmund Hall, Bampton Lecturer (1856), author of theological works. She married John Maitland (1841–1922), advocate.

2. *Ministering Children*, by Maria Louisa Charlesworth, was first published in 1854; *The History of Sandford and Merton*, by Thomas Day, in 1783; and Maria Edgeworth's famous story *Rosamond and the Purple Jar* appeared first in the author's *Parent's Assistant* in 1796.

3. No Mr Saul is recorded as Fellow of Magdalen.

The 'rigid rule of chaperonage was waived'*

EDITH OLIVIER[1]

When I was at Oxford, Lewis Carroll was still living in the rooms in Tom Quad which he had occupied when my father was at Christ Church. He sometimes invited me to dinner. His position in Oxford was such that in his case alone, our rigid rule of chaperonage was waived. If our authorities were sticklers for chaperons, he was equally a stickler for none.

'I only like a tête-à-tête dinner', he said, 'And if you don't come alone, you shan't come at all.'

Miss Moberly[2] gave in, saying with her gay smile: 'Once more, we must make a virtue of necessity.'

Mr Dodgson . . . had instituted a fixed technique for his dinner parties. Dinner was at seven, and at half-past six, he always appeared at St Hugh's to walk with me to Christ Church. The walk took exactly half an hour, and at the end of the evening, my host timed our return to St Hugh's to synchronize with the ringing of the ten-thirty bell in

* From *Without Knowing Mr Walkley* (1938) pp. 176–9.

the passages. He left me at the door precisely at that moment, to show his sincere respect for college rules so long as he approved of what they laid down. He used to say that those walks were the best part of his dinner parties. The food was always the same. Only two courses – first, some very well-cooked mutton chops, and then, meringues. A glass or two of port followed, and, an hour after dinner, we had tea. Mr Dodgson never spoke of *Alice in Wonderland*; but there were three other things in his life of which he seemed really proud. He spoke of them every time we had dinner together. They were his kettle, his logic, and his photographs.

At eight-forty-five in the evening, he always set about boiling the water for our tea, and Lewis Carroll was very like other old people, in that the same thing always reminded him of the same story. He now told the story of his invention. It appeared that he had noticed that most people either burnt their hands on kettles, or used kettle-holders, which were always dirty, and often lost. He had got a blacksmith to attach to his own kettle a long handle like that on a saucepan, and with this he always lifted his kettle off the fire, and filled the teapot. He boasted about this in a most ingenuous manner. Then he was always in the middle of an argument with the university Professor of Logic, and each time I dined in his rooms, he had ready a newly invented problem of his own, which I was asked to solve 'by common sense'. My wild guesses were always lucky enough to agree with Mr Dodgson's own solutions, and to disagree with those of the Professor; so we were both very happy, and congratulated each other a lot. But best of all were his photographs, taken by him in the days before dry plates were invented. The wet plate gives great quality to the prints. Mr Dodgson's were deep, soft, and beautiful. They were mostly portraits in 'carte-de-visite' size, and very unpretentious, but I have seen no photographs which produce so delicately the modelling of the face. They were quite unlike any photographs of to-day, both in this fine portraiture, and in the unaffected realism of their setting. His sitters sat on their chairs and sofas, and round their own tables, conversing in their tall hats and crinolines, and seemingly quite unaware that they were posing for their 'likenesses'. Mr Dodgson was prouder of his sitters than of his art. He had many portraits of King Edward VII as an undergraduate, lots of 'Alice' and the rest of Dean Liddell's family; and there were pages of Rossettis and Terrys, which I always remember.[3]

Mr Dodgson was very fond of little girls, and especially of child actresses, or children who loved plays. At a matinée in Brighton, he once sat in the stalls beside a little girl of about four, and their mutual enjoyment made them quickly friends. After the theatre, he tracked her to her home, and then found out who lived in the house. Though, as I have said, he never appeared very proud of having written *Alice in*

Wonderland, he quite appreciated the value of being the author of that book, when he wanted to make a fresh 'child friend'. He now wrote to the mother of this little girl, saying who he was, and inviting the child to tea. He received a curt and crushing reply. The lady wrote:

'The young lady whom you speak of as my "little girl" is not so very childish after all, and she is not my daughter, but my niece. If she were my own child, I should certainly ask you your intentions before allowing her to accept your invitation, and I must do the same now.'

Mr Dodgson replied that his intentions were honourable, 'though one does not usually have specific "intentions" with regard to a child of four or five'.

By some mistake, the letter had reached the wrong lady, and one who, oddly enough, had been at the same matinée with a niece of nineteen. The episode hurt Mr Dodgson's feelings very much, and he told me that he thought the name of Lewis Carroll might have been allowed to guarantee the safety of a young girl of any age whatever.

And the real little friend of the theatre never knew what a distinguished conquest she had made that afternoon. If any lady who was a child in Brighton in the 'sixties or 'seventies, may happen to read this book, let her search her memory for a swift and intimate friendship which began and ended one afternoon in the theatre there. She captivated Lewis Carroll.

NOTES

1. Edith Maud Olivier (1872–1948) was the daughter of Dacres Olivier (1831–1919), Prebendary of Salisbury, a contemporary of Dodgson at both Rugby and Christ Church. She was also a cousin of Laurence (Lord) Olivier's father. Edith was Susan Esther Wordsworth Scholar at St Hugh's, Oxford, and went on to write novels and books about Wiltshire. She was Mayor of Wilton for several terms.

2. Charlotte Anne Elizabeth Moberly (1846–1937) was the seventh daughter of George Moberly (1803–85), Headmaster of Winchester College and Bishop of Salisbury. Without formal education herself, she became, in 1886, the first Principal of St Hugh's, a post she held for almost thirty years. In later life she became interested in psychic phenomena and was co-author of *An Adventure* (1911), a report of encountering ghosts at Versailles. She and Dodgson were acquainted, and Dodgson gave logic lectures to students at St Hugh's in 1894.

3. Although Dodgson did in fact photograph the Liddells, the Rossettis, and the Terrys, he never achieved Edward VII. As Prince of Wales, he did autograph a photograph of himself taken by another photographer for Dodgson, and he admired Dodgson's photographs. For more on their meeting, see *Letters*, pp. 44–7.

He 'carried her upon his shoulders many a time'*

JOHN MARTIN-HARVEY[1]

Our visit to Eastbourne is memorable, for here I had the privilege of meeting the inimitable author of *Alice in Wonderland*. My wife and he were old friends. Indeed, 'Lewis Carroll' had carried her, as a child, upon his shoulders many a time – even as Yorick had once borne the juvenile Hamlet. Their first meeting was characteristic. When about eight years of age, she had been on holiday with her parents at Sandown, Isle of Wight. Always passionately sympathetic with animals, she had watched with growing anger the way in which Bates, the man who kept the bathing-machines, treated the old horse that drew them up the shore from the water's edge, and suspected that the animal was insufficiently fed. She had also noticed that Bates kept his midday luncheon, carefully wrapped in newspaper, tucked away among the bathing garments in a boat drawn up on the sands. Seeing an opportunity – she snatched the luncheon from its hiding place and fed it to the old horse. Then, armed with a stick, she deliberately smashed the glass in all the little peep-holes of the machines she could reach. This, of course, attracted the outraged holiday-folk upon the shore. The culprit was held up to popular indignation and Bates demanded full recompense for the damage done to his property. Then, from the crowd which had gathered upon the sands a meek little gentleman stepped forward, paid for the damage and, lifting the naughty little girl on to his shoulder, bore her away. 'Lewis Carroll'! Thence ensued a friendship which lasted all through the summer, to be renewed long years after when we visited Eastbourne on our Vacation Tour.

My wife and I paid him a decorous visit at his worn, respectable, Victorian lodgings there. As an amateur photographer he was an enthusiast – if such a burning word can be used to describe anything which the Rev. C. L. Dodgson did. For our entertainment he opened innumerable little boxes filled with '*cartes de visites*' photographs of his friends, of which he seemed modestly proud. We could not induce him

* From *The Autobiography of Sir John Martin-Harvey* (1933) pp. 128–9.

to visit the theatre, for which he had an intense aversion. He was strange and, I thought, quite unreasonable on this subject. Those who have read the preface to *Sylvie and Bruno* may remember what he says.[2]

To 'grown-ups' he seemed just the reticent, chilly, rather shabby Oxford Don, but among children he was one of those innocents of whom is the Kingdom of Heaven; and when he took a pen in hand it dripped a humour and humanity which have made the whole world kin.

NOTES

1. Dodgson's Diaries simply record the fact that he met Nellie de Silva on the beach at Sandown on 6 September 1987, though he does add her birth date (28 August 1865). Angelita Helena de Silva Ferro (d. 1949) married (1889) John Martin-Harvey (1863–1944), actor–manager.

2. Dodgson was a true champion of the theatre – but of highly principled theatrical works that were entertaining, educational, or uplifting morally. He could not abide irreverent, profane, or sacrilegious material, and sought to avoid it completely. 'We go to entertainments, such as the theatre', he wrote in the preface to *Sylvie and Bruno*,

– I say 'we', for *I* also go to the play, whenever I get a chance of seeing a really good one – and keep at arm's length, if possible, the thought that we may not return alive [from the theatre]. . . . I believe this thought, of the possibility of death – if calmly realized, and steadily faced – would be one of the best possible tests as to our going to any scene of amusement being right or wrong. If the thought of sudden death acquires, for *you*, a special horror when imagined as happening in a *theatre*, then be very sure the theatre is harmful for *you*, however harmless it may be for others; and that *you* are incurring a deadly peril in going. Be sure the safest rule is that we should not dare to *live* in any scene in which we dare not *die*.

He Got her the Part of the White Queen*

IRENE VANBRUGH[1]

My first professional London engagement came to me through a college friend of my father's, the Rev. C. L. Dodgson. . . .

As I remember him now, he was very slight, a little under six foot, with a fresh youngish face, white hair and an impression of extreme cleanliness. He had a slight stutter and was rather shy, and resented being recognized or spoken to as Lewis Carroll, the author of *Alice in*

* From *To Tell my Story* (1948) pp. 18–20.

Wonderland. He had a deep love for children, though I am inclined to think not such a great understanding of them. As a child I was his guest for a few days at Eastbourne, where he usually spent his summer, and he came often to our house in London.

Apart from his printed books he was a prolific letter-writer and wrote standing at a desk, which must have been specially built for him. He had ledgers in which he kept records of all letters he wrote, with notes of questions asked and subjects touched on, and it was a great disappointment to him that I never answered his letters in the same precise fashion. In fact, I regret to say I often didn't answer them at all. I wish now that I had kept all his correspondence – so beautifully written and always in violet ink – but with the perverse carelessness of the young I tore them up.

His great delight was to teach me his Game of Logic. Dare I say this made the evening rather long, when the band was playing outside on the parade and the moon shining on the sea? He was kindness and gentleness personified and I only wish I could have appreciated more fully the hours I spent with him. He liked to have photographs of his child-friends, but disliked the way negatives were touched up. So he used to take them to a special photographer at Eastbourne who didn't do this, and he was quite pleased with the result in my case.

The following Christmas a version of *Alice* was to be revived at the old Olympic Theatre in Wych Street of which no trace is now to be found in the fine broad avenues and streets of Aldwych and Kingsway. It was a darling little theatre, and though I am under the impression that it had a very ordinary entrance, something made it look very important and shining in my eyes. Was it sunshine or was it the blaze of illusion?

Lewis Carroll had written to Savile Clarke, who had adapted the play, suggesting me for the White Queen. Violet had just made a great success with Toole[2] in *The Butler* by Herman Merivale, and some of her reflected glory shone on me. Alas! what were my feelings when Savile Clarke, meeting her one evening during rehearsals, told her I was hopeless and he thought he would have to get someone else for the part! I was heart-broken. However, Violet talked to me and went over the part with me and all was well, for I remained in the cast and incidentally met for the first time Edward German[3] who was conducting the orchestra. The glamour of that first engagement, the inexhaustible riches of my salary of a guinea a week!

NOTES

1. Reginald Henry Barnes (1831–89), Prebendary of Exeter Cathedral, had been a fellow undergraduate of Dodgson at Christ Church. In 1887, when Barnes was staying at Oxford, he came round to Dodgson's rooms for a chat. 'He . . . is a friend of Miss E. Terry', Dodgson wrote; 'his eldest daughter, Violet, has gone on the Stage . . . as Miss

Vanbrugh.' Within the month, Dodgson called on the Barneses in Earls Court Road, London, for tea and repeated his call later that month. On 14 May of that year, he saw Violet act in *The Butler* (*Diaries*, pp. 448, 450). Violet (1867–1942) later married Arthur Bourchier (1863–1927), the actor–manager; and Irene (1873–1949), Dion Boucicault the younger (1859–1929).

2. John Lawrence Toole (1830–1906), comedian and toastmaster praised by Dickens and Thackeray, was a favourite of Dodgson's. In 1882 Toole leased the Folly Theatre, renamed it Toole's and produced comedies and burlesques with his own company.

3. (Sir) Edward German (1862–1936) was the musical director of the first revival of *Alice* on the stage. It opened at the Globe Theatre on 26 December 1888, and Irene Vanbrugh played the White Queen and the Knave of Hearts. Elsewhere, Irene recalled that Dodgson 'made himself so entertaining to the children during rehearsal, with his stories and his fun, that more than once he was politely requested to leave the theatre by the worried stage manager'. Edward German remembered that 'the principals, chorus and orchestra seemed like a large family – so happy was everyone' (Reed, p. 73).

An Acquaintance through Letters*

SYDNEY FAIRBROTHER[1]

It was during the run of the *Vagabonds* that I made the acquaintance, though only through letters, of a very interesting author. One night on coming to the theatre I saw a letter under a parcel, which obviously contained a book addressed in a handwriting I did not know. It was a most charming letter from Lewis Carroll written to a child of fourteen or fifteen and addressed to 'dear little Sydney Fairbrother', saying how much he had enjoyed the performance of us two children, that he had been amazed and delighted by our prowess, and that he was sending us each a copy of one of his books in which he had written a little inscription. I fled to Kate's dressing-room and found that she also had received a charming note and present. We felt in a bit of difficulty about our ages, but between us we concocted what we thought was a nice tactful little letter thanking Lewis Carroll for his delightful appreciation, but adding that we could not lay any claim to the heights on which, looking upon us as children, he had placed us, for, though we were neither of us old, we were both very happily married and each the proud mother of a delightful child – mine aged twelve months and Kate's about three years. We added that we would treasure

* From *Through a Stage Door* (1939) pp. 121–3.

our books as we had always loved *Alice in Wonderland* and that we looked forward to the time when we could make our children love it as much as we had done. I got the most adorable answer back with a copy of a *Nursery 'Alice'* for Sydney the second, which was a version made for babies from the bigger book. Time passed and I received three or four letters from Lewis Carroll, always delightful. Then there was a gap of some months. After my young husband died, I eventually went to the Haymarket Theatre and during the run there I received a charming letter saying that the writer was in town and would very much like to meet me on a convenient day and could it be arranged? The writing seemed familiar but I could not place the signature. Something prevented my accepting the invitation, but for some time I continued to receive pleasant chatty letters from the Unknown. The correspondence ceased and we never met. The signature to those letters was C. L. Dodgson, but not being as wise as I am now I did not know that C. L. Dodgson was Lewis Carroll, the creator of Alice.

NOTE

1. On 28 November 1896, Dodgson, in London, went to the matinée at the Princess' Theatre and saw *Two Little Vagabonds* (adapted from the French by G. R. Sims and A. Shirley), which he judged 'a very sensational melodrama, capitally acted. "Dick" and "Wally" were played by Kate Tyndall [d. 1919] and Sydney Fairbrother [1872–1941], whom I guess to be about 15 and 12. Both were excellent, and the latter remarkable for the perfect realism of her acting. There was some beautiful religious dialogue, between "Wally" and a hospital nurse, – most reverently spoken, and reverently received by the audience' (*Diaries*, pp. 530–1). On 17 December, Dodgson added, 'I have given books to "Kate Tyndall" and "Sydney Fairbrother", and have heard from them, and find I was entirely mistaken in taking them for children. Both are married women!'

'He gave one the sense of ... *perfect understanding*'*

ELLA C. F. BICKERSTETH[1]

It is difficult to add anything to what has already been written about Lewis Carroll, but as one of the 'children' whose love for him endured beyond childhood, I should like to tell something of the fascination of his friendship. As a child he gave one the sense of such *perfect*

* From *Picture Book*, pp. 222–9.

understanding, and this knowledge of child nature was the same whether the child was only seven years of age, or in her teens. A 'grown-up' child was his horror. He called one day just after I had 'put my hair up', and I, with girlish pride, was pleased he should be there to see. My satisfaction received a blow when he said, 'I will take you for a walk if you let your hair down your back, but not unless.' What girl could refuse the attraction of a walk with him? I speedily complied with his request, and was rewarded by an hour of happy companionship, mainly occupied as we walked along by playing a game of croquet in our heads. How it was done I cannot recollect, but his clever original brain planned it out by some system of mathematical calculation.

A visit to Mr Dodgson's rooms to be photographed was always full of surprises. Although he had quaint fancies in the way he dressed his little sitters, he could never bear a dressed-up child. A 'natural-child' with ruffled untidy hair suited him far better, and he would place her in some ordinary position of daily life, such as sleeping, or reading, and so produce charming pictures. On one occasion he was anxious to obtain a photograph of me as a child sitting up in bed in a fright, with her hair standing on end as if she had seen a ghost. He tried to get this effect with the aid of my father's ... electrical machine, but it failed, chiefly I fear because I was too young quite to appreciate the current of electricity that had to be passed through me.

In 1873 Lewis Carroll played a practical joke on me which, however, ended quite amicably. I had spent the summer of that year on the Continent, and he had done the same. He called at our house in Oxford early that November, and in the course of conversation promised to lend me the journal of his travels, if I would allow him to have mine. I consented on the condition that he showed it to no one, as the chance of reading his journal was too good to miss.

At the end of a fortnight he returned my journal with ... [an amusing letter, and then a few days later came another letter announcing that he had sent three short chapters of Ella's journal] to be published in the *Monthly Packet*. [After another exchange of letters, Dodgson confessed that it was all a hoax, that he would not have violated Ella's privacy under any circumstances.] I confess to having been rather disappointed [that my journal would not be published], but my love for Mr Dodgson soon led me to his rooms in Christ Church, where we laughed together over the joke; though I told him that I had not forgiven him, and should not have gone to see him, had I not wanted to see his pictures![2]

When I married in 1881, he was then full of his amusing games of Doublets, and wrote in his congratulatory letter to my husband ...:
'Do not make *Ella weep*.'

On his replying that he did not know how to do so, he showed him how to turn the first word into the second in wondrous few changes.[3]

I last saw Mr Dodgson about two years ago, when we had a long talk in the library of the Indian Institute at Oxford, and as he explained to me at length his elaborate scheme for teaching children logic and mathematics, there appeared to me to be no diminution in his physical or mental vigour, or in his love for children. Full of mischievous teasing, as usual, he tried to prove to me – the mother of six sons – how infinitely superior he considered girls to boys. I little thought it would be the last time I should meet the man of so gentle and kindly a nature, whose friendship enriched my childhood.

NOTES

1. Ella Chlora Faithfull Monier-Williams (1859–1954) was the only daughter of (Sir) Monier Monier-Williams, the orientalist. She married (1881) Samuel Bickersteth (1857–1937), Chaplain to George V, Canon of Canterbury. For photographs that Dodgson took of Ella, see Gernsheim, plate 59; and Hatch, facing p. 86.

2. The letters that Dodgson wrote Ella are reproduced in *Picture Book* and in *Letters*. Dodgson's one journey abroad actually occurred in 1867 (see p. 243, below).

3. Complying with Dodgson's rules for the game of Doublets, Denis Crutch (*Bandersnatch*, July 1976) shows how to make *Ella weep*:

> ELLA
> ells
> elms
> alms
> ales
> apes
> aped
> sped
> seed
> weed
> WEEP

'As I sat on his knee'*

WINIFRED HOLIDAY[1]

Unluckily for me, my parents freely lent my *Alice*s, till at last, *Wonderland* came back minus some pages, and the *Looking-Glass* disappeared entirely. Mr Dodgson replaced them for me, but he himself could not

* From two letters to *The Times*, 2 Apr 1928, p. 6, and 30 Jan 1932, p.6.

get first editions. He gave my mother the French translation, beautifully done. Of course, he gave me the *Snark*, with my father's illustrations. Among un-Alice books of his, one of the wittiest is his *Notes of an Oxford Chiel*, and perhaps the best thing in it is his attack on a fearsome erection which apparently for a long time existed at Christ Church – a belfry consisting of a colossal wooden box painted lead-colour and conspicuous from everywhere. 'Originally', he says at one point, 'it was intended that the Belfry should be a reproduction of the Campanile at Venice, but this was subsequently reduced by a series of amendments in committee to a perfect cube.'[2] When he stayed with us he used to steal on the sly into my little room after supper, and tell me strange impromptu stories as I sat on his knee in my nightie. It was very nice to be one of his little girls . . . .

A good deal of play has been made of the difference between the personalities of C. L. Dodgson and Lewis Carroll. To us I feel sure there was no such distinction. It was just as much 'Mr Dodgson' who had written the *Alice*s as it was Mr Dodgson who always took photographs of everyone and had to have a cellar all to himself for a dark room whenever he came to stay; who was my parents' loved friend as well as my adored one, coming to my little room in the evening to tell me wonderful stories, always the same gentle-voiced, quietly happy, and whimsical soul, his faint stammer and slight touch of Oxford dryness of manner only serving to enhance his charm. Certainly he and my father hit each other's moods to perfection. May it not have been because there is always something of the child in the artist? At any rate the dedication in his presentation copy of the *Snark* shows that to his artist-friend 'Dodgson' and 'Carroll' were one and the same. 'Presented to Henry Holiday, most patient of Artists, by Charles L. Dodgson, most exacting but not most ungrateful of Authors.'

NOTES

1. Henry Holiday's only child, Winifred (1865–1949), was a violinist, earned a scholarship to the Royal College of Music, and later was an orchestra conductor. For her father's reminiscences, see pp. 219–21, below.

2. *The New Belfry of Christ Church, Oxford* (1872) is one of the six parts of Dodgson's *Notes by an Oxford Chiel*, essays dealing with Oxford affairs. Here Carroll ridicules the erection of the wooden cube atop the staircase leading to Christ Church Hall, built to house bells moved from the Cathedral tower. The belfry was an eyesore, an ugly protuberance set upon an elegant edifice, and Carroll's choice of 'A thing of beauty is a joy forever' for his epigraph on the title page must have shot home to a good many similarly disapproving members of the University. In 1879 Carroll and his colleagues had the satisfaction of seeing the ugly box covered over with a more appropriate pseudo-Tudor Belfry Tower.

'He discovered her weeping dismally'*

F. E. HANSFORD

Lewis Carroll's friendship with Mary Brown[1] began at Whitby under somewhat curious circumstances. He discovered her weeping dismally as she sat on a gate, and upon inquiring the cause of her grief he learned that she had accidentally torn a stocking and was crying because . . . she thought her mother would be vexed. Mr Dodgson was all sympathy and, much to her relief, he very gallantly offered to take the little girl back to the family hotel and there intercede on her behalf – which indeed he did with unqualified success.

In after years she often smiled as she recalled this incident of her far-away childhood – though at the time it was a very real sorrow to her. Little did she think, on that September morning of 1868, that not once nor twice in the course of her later life she would turn to her old friend for guidance and consolation in days of trial and tribulation.

Her life, indeed, had its full share of trouble and sorrow and tragedy, and perhaps it was this fact that gave to the letters which Carroll addressed to her a more serious tone than that which he employed in writing to his other child friends – though his characteristic whimsicality and playful raillery enliven many of them. She was of a thoughtful and meditative nature, and some of her letters to Lewis Carroll asking for the elucidation of certain 'hard sayings' in the Scripture brought answers so long and full as to resemble sermons. These are the more interesting because they reflected her correspondent's very individual and sincerely-held beliefs. . . .

To be of use to her in her spiritual life was always a happiness to him. But when she told him the miserable history of one very near to her, one whose reckless life proved a terrible trial to her, he wrote even more tenderly. . . .

At times when she encountered religious difficulties, and in days of tragedy, did her old friend strive to bring her help and solace. So, too,

* From 'A Heart of Sympathy: Some Lewis Carroll Letters', *Methodist Recorder*, 22 April 1954, p. 3.

when sorrow darkened her path, he sought to comfort her, and in the deepest sorrow that she ever knew – the death of her mother – he wrote to her in very personal terms, recalling a similar intensity of grief when he had lost his father who, as his nephew . . . has told us, 'had been his ideal of what a Christian gentleman should be'. . . . Of the effect of that severe blow on the son his biographer has written: 'It seemed to him at first as if a cloud had settled on his life which could never be dispelled',[2] and the memory of that cloud doubtless returned to him when he wrote to Mary Brown six months after her own bereavement. She was still groping in the gloom, and God's purpose for her yet remained dark. How strengthening, in those circumstances, must her old friend's words have proved. . . .

NOTES

1. Mary Suter Brown (b. 1861) was the daughter of William Brown junior, manufacturer, and Gideon Scott, born McKenzie. For the letters of religious and spiritual help that Hansford alludes to, see *Letters, passim*. I have not been able to identify Hansford.
2. *Life and Letters*, pp. 131–2.

'We cried when he went away'*

DYMPHNA ELLIS[1]

Lewis Carroll, introduced to my father, I know not how, came to our country home to photograph the children. This was at that time a passion with him. I was the eldest of a little group of five, and I feel sure I was a 'favourite'. He made every child to feel that. He developed the photographs in our cellar, using 'wet plates'. I remember the mess and the mystery of these. The photographs are as fresh as the day they were printed. . . . He came several times. We cried when he went away. . . . His letters were delicious. . . . We were absolutely fearless with him. We felt he was one of us, and on our side against the grown-ups . . . .

* From a letter to *The Times*, 4 April 1928, p. 4.

NOTE

1. Frances Dymphna Harriet (1854–1930) was the daughter of Conyngham Ellis (1817–91), Vicar of Cranbourne, Berkshire, and one of Dodgson's friends-in-photography. When Dodgson visited Ellis in April 1864, he wrote in his *Diaries* (p. 214), 'I went with him to his'house . . . meeting on the way several of Mr Ellis's children . . . and at the house we found the eldest little girl . . . with the extraordinary name of Dymphna.' On 2 December 1867, Dodgson sent Dymphna one of his 'fairy' letters, the entire letter postage-stamp size, the handwriting so miniature as to be almost invisible. He must have written these letters with a fine geographer's pen and meant them to be read with a magnifying glass. Dymphna suggests that this sort of letter was 'one more instance of his imaginative sympathy with the child's mind, and of the trouble he would take to give pleasure to one of them. It was sent with a presentation copy of . . . "Bruno's Revenge" [a short story upon which he later built *Sylvie and Bruno* and *Sylvie and Bruno Concluded* and] . . . purports to have been written by the fairy "Sylvie". . . . I do not think any of us then doubted the reputed authorship, the charm of our friendship with the author being, that he created round himself and us an "atmosphere" which made the things of the imagination even more real than the rice puddings and holland pinafores of the period' – 'An Unpublished Letter of Lewis Carroll', *Strand Magazine*, 52 (Aug 1916) 213. For a photograph of the Ellis children barefoot, see Graham Ovenden and Robert Melville, *Victorian Children* (1972) plate 2. Dymphna's 'fairy' letter appears in facsimile in her *Strand Magazine* reminiscence and in *Letters*, p. 109.

He Rescues a Sodden Child*

HARRY R. MILEHAM

In the summer of about the year 1880, when seven years old and on a visit with relations to Eastbourne, my playmate was a girl cousin of the same age.[1] On one of our low-tide explorations of the chalk-rock pools this cousin slipped and fell full-length in a few inches of water. Refusing to see the funny side of the incident and regarding with dismay her sodden garments, she set up a piercing howl, which no words of mine were able to abate. From the distant crowded parade emerged a black-coated figure of clerical aspect, striding in haste over shingle and sand-flat. Gathering up in his arms the wet mess of my amphibious cousin, he bore her with soothing words to the lodgings where she would be.

It was somehow borne in upon me that I was probably the cause of

* From a letter to *The Times*, 2 Jan 1932, p. 6.

the trouble, and that, anyhow, little boys were of no account, unless conceivably the getting in a mess and making an inordinate fuss should render them of interest to the gentleman who I now learned was the author of *Alice in Wonderland*. Next year my cousin was asked to stay, as one of a number of similar 'Alices', at some sort of holiday-home over which the Rev. Mr Dodgson presided. These visits continued for some years, until the time came when her mother considered that the child's ear for the King's English was suffering through the rather mixed company.

NOTE

1. The wet cousin was Mary ('May') Livock Mileham (1874–1939), the daughter of Charles Henry Money Mileham (1837–1917), artist and architect, and his wife, Mary, born Livock (1850–1914). May married (1905) her father's architecture pupil Courtenay Melville Crickmer (1879–1914).

'So you are another Alice'*

ALICE WILSON FOX[1]

I was, fortunately for me, christened 'Alice', and to that owe a very pleasant acquaintance with Lewis Carroll, which endured for many years. I venture to offer you this anecdote . . . in connexion with his delightful and whimsical personality.

As children we lived in Onslow Square and used to play in the garden behind the houses. Charles Dodgson used to stay with an old uncle there,[2] and walk up and down, his hands behind him, on the strip of lawn. One day, hearing my name, he called me to him, saying, 'So you are another Alice. I'm very fond of Alices. Would you like to come and see something which is rather puzzling?' We followed him into his house, which opened, as ours did, upon the garden, into a room full of furniture with a tall mirror standing across one corner.

'Now,' he said, giving me an orange, 'first tell me which hand you have got that in.' 'The right', I said. 'Now,' he said, 'go and stand before that glass, and tell me which hand the little girl you see there has got the orange in.' After some perplexed contemplation, I said, 'The left hand.' 'Exactly', he said. 'And how do you explain that?' I couldn't explain it, but seeing that some solution was expected, I

* From a letter to *The Times*, 15 Jan 1932, p. 4.

ventured, 'If I was on the *other* side of the glass, wouldn't the orange still be in my right hand?' I can remember his laugh. 'Well done, little Alice', he said. 'The best answer I've had yet.'

I heard no more then, but in after years was told that he said that this had given him his first idea for *Alice through the Looking-Glass*, a copy of which, together with each of his other books, he regularly sent me.

NOTES

1. Alice Theodora Raikes (1862–1945) was actually a cousin of Dodgson, and after he met her in the garden in Onslow Square, Dodgson called on the Raikeses and planted the roots of a long friendship. Alice was the eldest daughter of Henry Cecil Raikes (1838–91), JP, MP, later Postmaster-General, and his wife, Charlotte Blanche, born Trevor-Roper (1836?–1922). Alice married (1889) William Arthur Wilson Fox (1861–1909), Comptroller-General of the Board of Trade. In her own right, she wrote more than a dozen books, lectured, and served as Rural District Councillor for Hatfield.

2. Robert Wilfred Skeffington Lutwidge (1802–73), Dodgson's bachelor uncle on his mother's side, was a barrister and Commissioner in Lunacy. He frequently provided his nephew with London hospitality, shared with him his interest in microscopes, telescopes and gadgets generally, and became the young man's favourite uncle. It was Uncle Skeffington who introduced his nephew to photography.

3. Dodgson's first recorded meeting with the Raikes family occurs in his *Diaries* on 24 June 1871 (p. 300), long after Dodgson had sent the completed manuscript of *Through the Looking-Glass* to the printer. Dodgson may have failed to record an earlier meeting with Alice, and the conjunction of an Alice, a looking-glass, and an orange may, in any case, have inspired additions to his text.

'I alone was invited'*

ROSE L. WOOD[1]

I was staying at Oxford with my parents, and must have been almost 12 years of age. Lewis Carroll, whom I had met as a small child some years previously at Farringford (my father was at that time in command of the Royal Artillery in the Isle of Wight, and lived opposite the Tennysons), sent me an invitation to tea with him in his rooms; this invitation I was delighted to accept, especially as I alone was invited, and neither of my parents. I had a lovely afternoon, and he showed me the proofs of *Alice through the Looking-Glass*, and read a good deal of the story to me. 'Now,' he said, 'I cannot decide what to make the Red Queen turn into.' I said, 'She looks so cross, please turn

* Letter to *The Times*, 15 Feb 1932, p. 6.

her into the Black Kitten.' 'That will do splendidly,' he said, 'and the White Queen shall be the White Kitten.' When *Alice through the Looking-Glass* was published that winter he sent me a much valued copy with my name in it 'from the Author'.

NOTE

1. Rose Lucy Franklin (1857?–1934) married (1883) Frederick John Wood (1834–1913), Vicar of Headingley, Honorary Canon of Ripon. She was the daughter of Charles Trigance Franklin (1822–95), Major-General, and his wife, Lucy Haywood (1828?–1922). For a photograph by Dodgson of Mrs Franklin and Rose, see Gernsheim, plate 44.

Lunch in his Oxford Rooms*

MARGARET L. WOODS[1]

He had formerly been intimate with the family of Dean Liddell, the Head of his college, and the story of Alice had been first told to the Liddell children. When the Alice of his tale had grown into a lovely girl, he asked, in old-world fashion, her father's permission to pay his addresses to her. The Dean might reasonably have refused his permission, on the ground of the girl's youth and inexperience, and the discrepancy in age between her and their friend. But Dean Liddell, whose manner was always haughty, rebuffed Mr Dodgson's appeal in so offensive a way, that all intercourse between them ceased. It is an awkward situation for a Fellow of a College not to be on speaking terms with his Head. Mr Dodgson now took up photography, but here also he found a snag. He invited a very little girl to be photographed, and took her almost unclothed. He mother shrieked at the impropriety of this. No wonder the sensitive man of genius became propriety-stricken. Hence the unsatisfactoriness of my own contacts with him. When I was fifteen he expressed a wish to photograph me, and invited my mother to bring me to lunch in his rooms. Their lunch-time conversation was not amusing and, as manners for school-girls then enjoined, I remained silent. The resulting photograph represents a self-conscious young lady, sitting bolt upright in her chair, with a forced smile on her face. My only tête-à-tête with him,

From 'Oxford in the 'Seventies', *Fortnightly Review*, 150 (1941) 276–82.

about a year later, was still more unfortunate. I met him at Reading station, where I was changing for Oxford. He was seated in a first-class carriage, and found that I was alone, and travelling third-class. This horrified him; not quite so unreasonably as we thought, for there were traps set for young girls on journeys, of which my innocent mother was as ignorant as myself. I got into an empty compartment, and to my embarrassment, Mr Dodgson left his first-class carriage and joined me there. Seating himself at the farthest end to myself, he put arithmetical puzzles to me during the rest of the journey. My education had been neglected, and not being interested in arithmetic, I never learned more than was necessary for keeping accounts. Consequently I could not solve one of his conundrums, and he doubtless concluded me to be a stupid girl, for he took no further notice of me.

NOTE

1. The family of George Granville Bradley (1821–1903), whose reforms as Headmaster at Marlborough made it one of the leading schools in the land, were neighbours of the Tennysons on the Isle of Wight, and Dodgson met them on his visits to the Tennysons. Dodgson and the Bradleys grew closer acquainted when G. C. Bradley left Marlborough in 1870 and became Master of University College, Oxford. One of the Bradleys' daughters, Margaret Louisa ('Daisy', 1856–1945), married Henry George Woods (1842–1915), Fellow and President of Trinity College, Oxford. Mrs Woods established herself as a successful novelist.

'He was one of us'*

BERT COOTE[1]

My sister and I were regular young imps, and nothing delighted us more at parties than to give imitations of some of our grown-up friends, while if we accompanied one of them anywhere a giggling duet was sure to commence presently over some eccentricity, real or imagined, which amused us. It must have been very embarrassing to our adult companion. But we never gave imitations of Lewis Carroll, or shared any joke in which he could not join – he was one of us, and never a grown-up pretending to be a child in order to preach at us, or otherwise instruct us. We saw nothing funny in his eccentricities, perhaps he never was eccentric among children, or may be he had the

* From Reed, p. 95.

brain of a clever and abnormal man with the heart of a normal child. I shall never forget the morning he took my sister and I over the Tower of London and how fascinated we were by the stories he told us about it and its famous prisoners. I suspect now that very few of them were based on strict, historical fact, but that they would have charmed any child there is no question. He was a born story-teller, and if he had not been affected with a slight stutter in the presence of grown-ups would have made a wonderful actor, his sense of the theatre was extraordinary.

NOTE

1. In 1877, Dodgson saw a production of *Goody Two Shoes* that he particularly enjoyed. 'Little Bertie Coote (about 10) was Clown', he wrote in his *Diaries* (p. 359), ' – a wonderfully clever little fellow; and Carrie (about 8) was Columbine, a very pretty graceful little thing – in a few years' time she will be just *the* child to act "Alice", if it is ever dramatized.' After the performance, Dodgson paid his respects backstage, where he had a long chat with the child actors and their mother. Then he walked some way with them and had dinner with them as well. A friendship naturally took root. Albert Coote (1868–1938) was an actor all his life, on the legitimate stage, in music halls, and later in films. His sister Caroline Eva Coote (1870–1907) married (1905) Sir William George Pearce (1961–1907), 2nd Bart, of Cardell House, Renfrewshire, barrister, MP.

Three Girls who Adored Him*

DIANA BANNISTER[1]

My mother was the eldest of three girls all of whom adored 'Lewis Carroll'. According to my mother . . . , Annie (my mother) and Frances had gone to visit him with their father and spent the afternoon 'dressing-up'. They heard him say how much he would like to photograph them in the nude. They promptly hid under the table, which had a cloth nearly reaching the ground and emerged with nothing on, much to the amusement of their father and their host, who promptly took several photographs of them.

Alas, I have lost any trace of the only photograph I ever saw, which had been coloured and rather elaborately framed. The original must have shown my mother lying on the hearth rug reading a book, but in

* From a private letter dated 14 July 1975.

the printed version the hearth rug resembled grass and the back-round vague woodland. . . . Lilian . . . was the much younger sister, and evidently a young lady of very decided views who refused to be photographed in the nude.

I well remember how furious my mother was at the suggestion in some book about Mr Dodgson that there was anything unhealthy in his interest in small girls.

NOTE

1. The writer of this letter is the daughter of Annie Gray Wright Henderson (1871–1951), the eldest daughter of Patrick Arkley Wright Henderson (1841–1922), Fellow of Wadham College, Oxford, author of a life of John Wilkins and editor of the letters of Sir Walter Scott. Annie's mother was Annie Wood Gray (1844?–99), daughter of Major Gray of Carse Gray. The friendship with the Henderson children got under way in late 1878 and became one of the most significant for Dodgson the photographer. When he first started experimenting with photography, he took pictures of adults, landscapes, sculptures, other still life. But his special interest in children drew him to seek them out as sitters, and with them he achieved his greatest success. In time, he sought to take them in their natural state, and the Henderson children were among those who complied, even enjoying the experience themselves. On 18 July 1879, Dodgson recorded (Diaries) that 'Mrs Henderson brought Annie and Frances. I . . . was especially surprised to find they were ready for any amount of undress, and seemed delighted at being allowed to run about naked. It was a great privilege to have such a model as Annie to take: a *very* pretty face, and a good figure: she was worth any number of my [commercial] models of yesterday.' Dodgson photographed Annie and Frances 'in their favourite state of "nothing to wear"' a number of times (*Diaries*, p. 387). Although Mrs Bannister suggests that Lilian would not be photographed, she hardly could be, having been born in the very year that Dodgson gave up photographing. When she was five, Dodgson recorded (Diaries) 'A new experience in Art. Little Lilian Henderson . . . was brought down by Annie and Frances, for me to try some sketches of her, naked, up in my studio. She had a charming little figure, and was a very patient sitter. I made 4 studies of her. . . . To draw the figure from *life* seems to give me quite new powers.' Three photographs of nude children and a watercolour tracing of a fourth survive (Rosenbach Library, Philadelphia). One of the photographs is of Annie and Frances Henderson both standing on a rocky shore. The colourist has covered the girls' loins with cloth and flora and in the background has painted a shipwreck. All four pictures appear in *Lewis Carroll's Photographs of Nude Children* (1978). Annie Henderson married (1900) Arthur Frederic Ruxton (1870–1922), who was associated with a firm of merchant bankers; Hamilton Frances (b. 1872) married James Christopher Delphin Peterson; and Lilian Janet Wright (1880–1966) married (1902) Ernest Theodore Marshall (1865–1935), Major (decorated), East Yorkshire Regiment. Lilian, according to her nephew (private letter), 'was one of the most beautiful women I have ever seen, and this was borne out by those who had known her when a young girl at Oxford'.

'He used a different voice for each fox'*

CONVERSATION WITH DOROTHY BURCH[1]

Miss Burch ... reminisced in private conversation about her friendship with Dodgson. Pouring tea and spreading the honey from her own bee-hives over buttered scones, she recalled his visits to the Burch home in Oxford, how he often shunned adults and walked straight through to the bay window where the children were. There he taught them games and showed them puzzles. Miss Burch remembered one day when Dodgson cut out a circular hole the size of a sixpence in a piece of paper. 'Can you put a ha'penny through it?' he asked. They could not. 'Yes, you can,' he said, 'but you have to know how.' The answer was that you doubled the circle over, and then it would stretch to allow the halfpence through. Another time he produced a French coin, and when he pressed on one of the letters, the coin sprang open revealing itself to be a locket with the portrait of a man inside. Dodgson then said, '*That* man should be the king of France' (presumably the Pretender Louis Philippe Albert, 1838–94, grandson of Louis Philippe). Miss Burch continued: 'I was sitting on his knee at my sister's birthday party, while he told us stories. He used a different voice for each fox when he told "The Three Little Foxes". He was like an actor: you couldn't imagine him having difficulty with speaking.' She went on to comment on Dodgson's interest in how other people's minds work, and recalled a day when he appeared at their home early one morning, an unusual time for him to call, and asked to see her specifically. He had a problem he was putting into a book, and he wanted to see if a child of 5 could do it, whether a child's mind could grasp it. His speech hesitation 'was not exactly a stammer', Miss Burch added, and when he had trouble speaking Mrs Burch told him to 'start again in a whisper'. Miss Burch insists that Dodgson had no difficulty whatever in speaking to children, 'which accounts for his delight in their society'.

* The interview took place in Miss Burch's home near Farnham, Surrey, in August 1974 and is reproduced here from *Letters*, pp. 955–6.

NOTE

1. Dodgson met Mrs Burch and her two daughters in 1893 and, while he became friendly with all three, he apparently saw much more of Mrs Burch than the two girls. Mrs Burch was born Constance Emily Jeffries (1855–1937) and married George James Burch (1852–1914), Professor of Physics, University College, Reading. The elder daughter, whose reminiscences these are, is Violet Dorothy (b. 1889). She went from the Oxford High School for Girls to Girton College, Cambridge, and later became Science and Geography Lecturer at Ripon Training College. Dodgson's records 'telling "Bruno's Picnic" to the little guests at Irene's birthday-party' on 4 May 1896 (*Diaries*, p. 524).

'In his happiest mood'*

ALICE COLLET[1]

My father had been a student of Christ Church, and had known Mr Dodgson. When travelling with my mother and myself, a small girl of about five, he caught sight of Mr Dodgson at a station, and, to our great delight, the author of *Alice in Wonderland* joined us. It was generally a tedious journey for children to where we went every holiday, but this journey was entrancing.

It was Lewis Carroll in his happiest mood, not Mr Dodgson, who took me on his knee and told me stories and drew pictures for me, and the greatest thrill of all was just before he left us, when he produced a minute pair of scissors, about the size of his thumb-nail, and cut off a tiny lock of my hair, which he said he would put in a locket and always keep. I had the luck to be called Alice and to have a quantity of fair hair like his Alice, hence his interest.

* From Reed, p. 66.

NOTE

1. Born Alice Owen, she was perhaps the daughter of James Albert Owen (b. 1842), who took his BA at Christ Church in 1864, was a Junior Student there, 1860–5, and went on to become a Fellow at University College.

He 'looked me gravely up and down'*

NORA McFARLAN[1]

Mother took a house at Eastbourne when we were children, and on the last day of our stay there, everything being packed up, we were allowed to go to the beach for a last paddle. I walked along a breakwater, fell in, and was soaked to the skin! I scrambled out, and was making my way along the beach, dripping, when I came across my sister Mabel, sitting by a strange, elderly gentleman, who was making a pencil sketch of her in his note-book, and stopped to greet her. Mr Dodgson, for it was he, looked me gravely up and down, and then tore a corner of blotting paper from his note-book and said, 'May I offer you this to blot yourself up?'

* From Reed, pp. 66–7.

NOTE

1. Nora Mary Woodhouse (d. 1936) was the daughter of Henry Melville Woodhouse of Brackenhurst, Weybridge, Surrey; she married (1899) Brigadier-General Frederick Alexander McFarlan (b. 1866), mentioned in dispatches during the First World War. On 4 September 1879, Dodgson, on the Parade in Eastbourne, was introduced to Mabel Woodhouse, 'and I at once made friends with ... [her. She] proved to be a quite charming child, and ... [her] elder sister, Nora ... joined us.' On 1 April 1880, Dodgson 'went to Surbiton for afternoon and evening, to the Woodhouses', and took Nora and Mable to call on friends at Summerfield, about a mile away. On 11 October 1880, Dodgson paused in Surbiton on his way from Guildford to London 'to see the Woodhouses, only Nora and Mabel were at home. I taught Nora my new game "Mischmasch"' (*Diaries*, pp. 383, 386, 391).

'I have brought a friend to see you'*

EVELYN S. KARNEY[1]

One of the most vivid recollections of my childhood is of an incident that happened when I was about eight years old.

We were living in Sandown, in the Isle of Wight. I had just had an operation on my knee and was lying on the sofa feeling very lonely. The bright sunshine had tempted my companions away, and the room seemed dull and dreary.

Suddenly the door opened and my father came in with another clergyman. 'I have brought a friend to see you', he said. In two minutes the stranger had drawn a chair to the side of the sofa and, with a ruthless disregard of property, had taken an old-fashioned photograph album that lay on a table near and drawn a fascinating game on either cover. Then he cut out a quantity of paper counters, while I watched with expectant eyes, and in five minutes our heads were close together, deep in wonderful and engrossing games.

That was the beginning of a happy summer friendship. Day by day I was carried on to the sands and my kind friend sat beside me, and drew pictures of the children paddling round.

When he left he gave each of us a copy of his books. I, as the youngest, had *The Hunting of the Snark*. I remember my brother asking: 'Mr Dodgson, what is a snark?' He laughed, and said: 'When you find out tell me.'

To us he was a dear friend, not a great author, and we were a careless happy-go-lucky family of children, so the precious books were read and re-read and learnt by heart, and lent, and were either lost or fell to pieces before we realized what precious souvenirs they were.

They were all first editions, the gift of Lewis Carroll himself, with an inscription and his autograph, and in each he had pasted a charming little Easter letter. 'To every child who loves Alice.' Oh, that I had not been a careless child! How I should treasure my book now!

* Letter to *John O'London's Weekly*, 27 (9 Apr 1932) 58.

NOTE

1. Evelyn was probably the daughter of Gilbert Sparshott Karney, Vicar of Sandown, 1871–81. On 8 August, Dodgson at Sandown 'called on Mr Karney . . . and found him in, and was introduced to Mrs K. and to two quite delightful children, Mary (aged 10) and Evelyn (aged 7): the latter has been laid up for 9 weeks with a bad knee' (Diaries).

'Does your little girl enjoy that book?'*

CHARLES F. N. BOULTON[1]

My grandmother (Mrs Nash) was travelling down to Eastbourne with her small daughter (Edith Mary Nash) by train and my mother was reading one of the *Alice* books. A man travelling in the same carriage turned to my grandmother and said, 'Does your little girl enjoy that book?' My grandmother replied, 'Oh yes – very much – but isn't it sad.' 'What is sad?' replied the stranger. 'Oh, you know that the man who wrote that book is, I am told, completely mad.' The man disclosed the fact that he was Lewis Carroll, and that started a friendship of several years.

* From a private letter dated 1 Oct 1977.

NOTE

1. Charles F. N. Boulton is the son of Edith Mary Nash (1873–1950), the daughter of Isaac Nash, a manufacturer of spades, shovels, forks, blacksmith's anvils, and other metal products; and his wife, born Fanny Ann Foxall. Edith married Frederic James Boulton, a solicitor who became a manager in his father-in-law's metal works. For more on Dodgson and the Nashes, see *Letters*, esp. p. 545.

'Mr Alice in Wonderland'*

LANCELOT ROBSON[1]

When I was a boy it was my good fortune to meet the author of *Alice in Wonderland* frequently, for [he] . . . was a close friend of my father. Both were clergymen and both were mathematicians.

I remember Dodgson as a tall, slim figure, with pale face, dark wavy hair and a peculiar high-pitched voice. His dark blue eyes met a child's with a kindly twinkle. Whatever the weather, he never wore an overcoat over his clerical blacks – but he always wore a tall black hat. And, winter and summer, he invariably wore knitted black woollen gloves. Meeting him in the street you would not have just noticed him, you would have looked twice.

One day we were having a children's party and unexpectedly 'Mr Alice in Wonderland', as we called him, came in to see my father. How delighted we were! He asked us if, at our school, we did sums. A chorus answered, 'Yes.' There was a little pause, then Lewis Carroll said, 'I am afraid you go to a very poor school. I never do sums; I always put the answer down first and set the sum afterwards.'

There was silence.

Then he continued, 'We will do some sums.' He wrote some figures on a piece of paper, and gave it to my stepmother, saying, 'That will be the answer to our sum when we have set it.'

Then he wrote 1,066 on another piece of paper. Choosing a little girl, he let her put down any four figures she liked under his 1,066. Then he put down four figures under hers and a small boy contributed another line. Lewis Carroll added a fifth line, so the column stood:

1,066	Lewis Carroll
3,478	Little Girl
6,521	Lewis Carroll
7,150	Little Boy
2,849	Lewis Carroll

A rather cheeky youngster was allowed to add it up, and he pronounced the answer to be 21,064.

* From 'Give my Love to the Children', *Reader's Digest*, Feb 1953, pp. 35–9.

My stepmother then read the figures on the paper Lewis Carroll had given her: 21,064. There were cries of 'Oh!' from the children.

Actually, it was not so intricate as it first appeared. Whatever figure a child wrote, Carroll each time added a number that made both lines total 9,999. Thus no matter what numbers the children wrote, the total of the five lines would be known to him in advance; it would be 20,000 more, less 2, than the number he originally wrote down at the top of the column.

We begged him for another trick, so he asked a little boy to write the number 12345679. He surveyed it in silence, then said, 'You don't form your figures very clearly, do you? Which of these figures do you think you have made the worst?'

The boy thought his 5 was poorest. Lewis Carroll suggested he should multiply the line by 45. The child laboriously worked it out and to his surprise found the result was 555555555. 'Supposing I had said four, what then?' the boy queried. 'In that case we would have made the answer all fours,' Carroll replied. He would have told the boy to multiply by 36, another multiple of nine. But he did not attempt to explain 'mystic nines' to us. . . .

Of all the stories about Lewis Carroll, I like best one my father used to tell. In Guildford there was a shop called Brett's, where the well-to-do took morning coffee or afternoon tea. The windows were full of luscious cakes and pastries. On a cold winter morning Carroll noticed a group of poor, ill-clad children gazing longingly at the fairy-tale display. He watched the group for a moment, then went up to them and said, 'I think you all ought to have cakes.' And into the shop he led the little band, where all were asked to choose the confections they fancied most.

One of the thousands of playful letters he wrote to his young friends ends charmingly, 'Give my love to any children you happen to meet.' And that is precisely what the shy old mathematician did all his life.

NOTE

1. Lancelot Robson was perhaps a relation of John Henry Robson, Exhibitioner at St John's College, Cambridge; Chaplain, Surrey County Hospital at Guildford; author of books on algebra and geometry. The Rev. J. H. Robson was sometimes Dodgson's companion on a long Sunday walk in Guildford (*Life and Letters*, p. 335).

A Paper Boat*

FREDA BREMER[1]

Our acquaintance began in a somewhat singular manner. We were playing on the Fort at Margate, and a gentleman on a seat near asked us if we could make a paper boat, with a seat at each end, and a basket in the middle for fish! We were, of course, enchanted with the idea, and our new friend – after achieving the feat – gave us his card, which we at once carried to our mother. He asked if he might call where we were staying, and then presented my elder sister with a copy of *Alice in Wonderland,* inscribed 'From the Author'. He kindly organized many little excursions for us – chiefly on the pursuit of knowledge. One memorable visit to a light house is still fresh in our memories.

* From *Life and Letters*, p. 372.

NOTE

1. In 1870, Dodgson and three of his sisters spent five weeks at Margate. On their return to Guildford he wrote in his *Diaries* (pp. 289–90),

At Margate I made very many pleasant acquaintances, chiefly on account of being attracted by their children. . . . Among the younger of my friends were Catherine, Frederika and Florence, children of a Mr Bremer of Tulse Hill. He is in a shipping insurance firm, and the party seem very pleasant acquaintances in every way: I received afterwards an invitation to go and visit them. The day before we left I took Mrs Bremer and the children to see 'the grotto' (a marvellous subterranean chamber, lined with elaborate shell-work, supposed to be three hundred years old, and probably the work of a hermit) and afterwards up the lighthouse, from which a very good view of Margate may be seen.

For Dodgson's double-acrostic verse based on 'Trina' and 'Freda', see *Life and Letters*, pp. 373.

Doling out Cakes*

AN UNIDENTIFIED CHILD FRIEND

My sister and I . . . were spending a day of delightful sightseeing in town with him, on our way to his home at Guildford, where we were going to pass a day or two with him. We were both children, and were much interested when he took us into an American shop where the cakes for sale were cooked by a very rapid process before your eyes, and handed to you straight from the cook's hands. As the preparation of them could easily be seen from outside the window, a small crowd of little ragamuffins naturally assembled there, and I well remember his piling up seven of the cakes on one arm, and himself taking them out and doling them round to the seven hungry little youngsters. The simple kindness of his act impressed its charm on his child-friends inside the shop as much as on his little stranger friends outside.

* From *Life and Letters*, p. 388.

'He used to annoy me'*

MONA M. WALLACE KIDSTON[1]

I also am one of the 'children' who knew Lewis Carroll for many years. . . . He used to annoy me very much by setting me puzzles, and I retaliated by making some paper stars and refusing to show him how they were done. One of his letters is asking me to send him one little star, so that he might find out for himself. I have also two photographs which he took of me in his rooms at Oxford, and of which I did not approve, as I thought they made me uglier than I was. In this I may have been mistaken. I remember him telling me how he had asked a little girl whether she liked *Alice in Wonderland* or

* From a letter to *The Times*, 27 March 1928, p. 12.

Through the Looking-Glass the better: to which she replied, 'I think *Through the Looking-Glass* is even sillier than *Alice in Wonderland*.'

NOTE

1. Mona Margaret Noël Paton (1860–1928), who married (1880) John Wallace Kidston (1851–1926), barrister, Vicar of Upton Grey, Hampshire, was the daughter of Sir Joseph Noël Paton (1821–1901), the popular artist of scenes from fairy tales, mythology, history, and religious tales. Dodgson was attracted to his work and tried to get their mutual friend George MacDonald to induce Noël Paton to illustrate *Through the Looking-Glass*, in vain. When Dodgson was in Scotland in September 1871, he called on the Noël Patons and had a number of delightful hours with them. For an account of that visit, see Dodgson to his sister Mary, *Letters*, pp. 165–6.

Supporter of a Women's University*

ANNIE M. A. H. ROGERS[1]

Another supporter of [a] Women's University was the Rev. C. L. Dodgson, the Lewis Carroll of *Alice in Wonderland*. He anticipated that if residence was recognized it would become compulsory and would bring to Oxford at least 3,000 more young women students. A Women's University would, he maintained, in twenty or thirty years, rival Oxford, not only in numbers but in attainments. Women lecturers and women professors would arise, fully as good as any that the older Universities had produced. Mr Dodgson was somewhat of a recluse and knew nothing about women's education, but had he not written the immortal words:

> I told them once, I told them twice
> They would not listen to advice. . . .

* From *Degrees by Degrees* (1938) pp. 46–7.

NOTE

1. Annie Mary Anne Henley Rogers (1856–1937), a relentless champion of women's education, was the daughter of Dodgson's close friend James Edwin Thorold Rogers (1823–90), author, MP, and Drummond Professor of Political Economy at Oxford. Dodgson's pamphlet *Resident Women Students* appeared in March 1896, during the heated debate surrounding the proposal that women be admitted for BA degrees at Oxford.

Annie Rogers states Dodgson's position fairly: he feared that if the University were suddenly to admit women, its resources would be so strained that all, perhaps most of the women, would suffer, and he sought to petition the Crown to grant a charter of a Women's University, even against the wishes of many champions of women's education: 'Even men very often fail to "desire" what is, after all, the best thing for them to have', he argued. It is a carefully reasoned argument, sensitive to the needs of all parties concerned. For more about Dodgson and the Rogers family, see *Letters*, esp. p. 52; for a photograph of Annie and two of her brothers, taken by Dodgson, see *Letters*, facing pp. 189 and 252; for the photograph of Annie as Queen Eleanor, taken June 1863, see *Illustrated London News*, 14 Apr 1928, p. 616. For more on Dodgson and a women's university, see Morton, N. Cohen, 'Lewis Carroll and the Education of Victorian Women', *Nineteenth-Century Women Writers* . . ., ed. Rhoda B. Nathan (1986) 27–35.

A Typewritten Letter Arrived*

GLADYS BALY HAYES[1]

One of the most cherished childhood memories is my friendship with that unique friend of little girls – Lewis Carroll, or Mr Dodgson, as I always knew him.

I was six years old at the time, and on a visit to Eastbourne, when a letter arrived addressed to me. It bore no postage stamp and it was typewritten, at that time when few people used typewriters. My mother and grandmother were as curious about it as I was, so we all three opened it together. It was an invitation to tea from the gentlemen staying in the rooms above ours – the Rev. C. L. Dodgson.

Next day I was dressed in my best and sent upstairs to my party. I was shy and he teased me about my funny little mannerisms, but all in the kindest way. I was a tiny bit afraid of the tall, thin gentleman, with a halo of greyish hair round a not too handsome face, yet I recollect him best as someone who really understood my feelings when grown-ups told me that I could not, or must not, do certain things.

He took me to my first theater, just he and I together, a wonderful adventure for a little girl of six. We went by train to Brighton to see Wilson Barrett in *The Silver King*. Probably it was this inspiring melodrama and the company of my kind and gallant escort that awakened my love for the theater, for my mother tells me that Lewis Carroll was fond of the theater and was a frequent patron. Two other little girl friends of his came to Eastbourne during my visit and, at his request, they took me for walks. One of them has since become a famous

* 'Recollections of Lewis Carroll', *Christmas Science Monitor*, 24 (23 Feb 1932) 11.

actress; the other has gladdened the hearts of children the world over as Principal Boy in many pantomimes.

Happy, engrossing hours were those I spent with Mr Dodgson, when he showed me tricks and puzzles and taught me how to make a paper pistol that would go off with a bang.

I quite clearly recollect him taking *Alice Through the Looking-Glass* out of a box of new books and giving it to me with his name written inside. He wrote to me many times after I left Eastbourne, althought I never saw him again. In return, I sent him drawings of ships and horses which, at that time, I was fond of making.

In another book that he sent me, he wrote the following verses:

> Girlie to whom in perennial bloom
> Life is all 'Os' and no crosses:
> Artists may take other themes for their skill,
> Dreaming of fairyland just as they will;
> *You* desire nothing but horses.
>
> Sunbeams may glance, happy midges may dance,
> Brooks prattle on in their courses;
> Artists may paint just whatever they please,
> Landscapes and Seascapes and Mountains and Trees;
> *You* are content with horses.[2]

NOTES

1. Gladys Mary Baly (b. 1884) married (1913) Edward Lionel Hayes, a farmer. Dodgson records his meetings with Gladys in his *Diaries* (pp. 486–7). The actress Isa Bowman (see pp. 89–102, above) was Dodgson's house guest at the time, and Dodgson records that he went 'with Isa and little Gladys, to Brighton, to a matinee of [Henry Arthur Jones's] *The Silver King*' on 10 October. No other little actress enters the *Diaries* at the time, but perhaps Gladys came to think that one of Isa Bowman's sisters was at Eastbourne as well.

2. In a letter to *The Times* (2 Apr 1928, p. 6), Gladys recalled that the verse 'hurt my feelings very much at the time: I was only seven – one who took her equine art very seriously and said, "Oh!" very frequently'.

A Visit to Mr Dodgson in Eastbourne*

CATHERINE LUCY[1]

14 June [1887]
Mr Dodgson called to invite Edie to stay with him at Eastbourne in Summer. He stayed to Lunch in the afternoon.

18 September 1887
After leaving Auntie we proceeded on the 3rd of September to Lyndhurst. While there Edie went to stay with Mr Dodgson and came back again the next day. . . . Edie having behaved so very badly to Mr Dodgson when he asked me to go and stay I accepted and so now I am at 7 Lushington Road, Eastbourne, with him. I arrived on Friday evening and on Saturday we went over to Brighton. . . . we went out and looked at the shops. Then we went on to the West Pier and saw Miss Louie Webb's performance, after which . . . Mr Dodgson and I went to tea with his sister. I like her, I think she is like him. We came home in time for dinner and I read for the rest of the evening. [On Sunday, we] went to the church of Christchurch. It was harvest festival in the afternoon. We went for a walk to Beachy Head. There was a very pleasant fresh breeze. We went to church in the evening and I wrote to Mother. . . . Eastbourne is not at all a bad sort of place. I wonder what relation people put Mr Dodgson and myself down as, uncle and niece I shouldn't wonder.

19 September 1887
In the afternoon we went along the Meads Road over the Downs on the land side of Paradise, along a ridge of the Down to Beachy Head, where we had tea at the Hotel, returned to Lushington Road in time for dinner. I read during the evening.

20 September 1887
I went down on the Parade by myself in the morning and in the

---

* These excerpts, from an unpublished diary, appear here in print for the first time with the kind permission of Mrs Christina Colvin.

afternoon we went to Miss Saigman's performance and in the evening we went to the children's performance of *Les Cloches de Corneville*.

21 September 1887
We went for a walk in the afternoon round by old Eastbourne. It was very deliteful but we nearly lost our train for Brighton, where we arrived in time for dinner after which we three repaired to the Dome. Miss Alice Gomes sang very well.[2]

22 September 1887
Started early for London. Arrived Victoria, took a cab to Paddington and disposed of my box. Next we went to the Barneses who live in Earls Court Road.[3] They are very nice indeed. Edith, Irene and I compared experiences. Angela too is very nice. She and Irene are going out to Paris. Mr Dodgson left me there for lunch while he went to see an invalid cousin. Then he took Irene, Angela, and I to the Avenue Theatre to see the Educated Horses and two of the children, Dot and Claris Hethington, who acted in *Alice*. We took them home afterwards. They seem very decent people. Claris is in *The Winter's Tale* now with Miss Anderson. Then he took me to Paddington and I had some tea and then saw me off by the 6.30. . . . All this is written with a stylograph pen which Mr Dodgson gave me; also he gave me *Rhyme? and Reason?* because he said it was ridiculous for me to stay with him and not have a book. Here endeth my holidays for 1887. . . .

15 November 1887
Mr Dodgson called in the afternoon. He is most dreadfully busy.

15 May 1888
Went to call on Mr Dodgson, who told us about his new book on 'parallels' and showed us how the typewriter worked. . . . We had a very fair evening, better than usual. Perhaps our visit to Mr Dodgson improved my temper.

8 June 1888
Mother and Edith went to call on Mr Dodgson. He had expected me but I still think two were enough.

3 April 1891
In the afternoon I went down to Mr Dodgson but he did not feel very vigorous so we did not go for a walk. . . . he showed me [many things]: a chicken, a pair of boats, pair of shoes, box picture frame, a looking-glass, book, and finally a fishing-boat with two seats with backs to them and a basket in the middle for the fish. Then he showed me

some photographs of Hendschell sketches, some of which were lovely. They were mostly children.

9 April 1891
Went out in the morning and found Mr Dodgson had called while we were out, so in the afternoon I started out to go see why. . . . I walked back up St Giles with Mr Dodgson as far as St Giles Church and then back again.

11 April 1891
In the morning I went down and sewed strap on Mr Dodgson's umbrella and then we went down Broad Walk and up the High. He came with me home by the Parks.

29 November 1891
Went to Mr Dodgson's to help him as Secretary.

2 June 1892
I went with Mr Dodgson into Trinity Gardens. . . . Tea at Christ Church. Mr Dodgson walked up St Giles with me.

NOTES

1. Catherine Susanna ('Katie') (1870–1934) was Edith Lucy's elder sister. She married (1894) Albert Frederick Pollard (1870–1948), the historian. Their son, Henry Graham Pollard (1903–76) was the bibliographer who, with John Carter, exposed the T. J. Wise literary forgeries. For more on the Lucys, see p. 152n, above.

2. On 16 September 1887, 'Mrs Lucy brought Katie to meet me at Victoria, and we came to Eastbourne by the 4.30 train', Dodgson wrote in his *Diaries* (p. 455). She stayed five days, and the visit was a success.

3. For more about the Barnes family, see pp. 187–8, above.

PART IV

Artists, Writers, Other Observers

He 'came to see me and my work'*

HENRY HOLIDAY[1]

It was an agreeable surprise when one morning Lewis Carroll ...
came to see me and my work, in company with a friend of his and
mine. We became friends on the spot and continued so till his death.
He was intimate with Dr Kitchin[2] and his family, and shared my
admiration for the beautiful little daughter, of whom he took
photographs at frequent intervals from then till she was grown up. He
made a highly characteristic conundrum about these portraits. The
girl was called Alexandra, after her godmother, Queen Alexandra, but
as this name was long she was called in her family X, or rather Xie.
She was a perfect sitter, and Dodgson asked me if I knew how to
obtain excellence in a photograph. I gave it up. 'Take a lens and put
Xie before it.' I have a collection of these portraits, all good. . . .

We saw a good deal of Mr Dodgson . . . at this time [the early
1870s]. He stayed with us a week or more in 1875 when he spent most
of his time photographing. [During one photography visit] . . . some
of the young Cecils came, the children of the Marquis of Salisbury,
Lady Gwendolen, and two of the sons, I think the present Marquis
and Lord Robert Cecil.[3]

This time . . . he took many of his friends, and gave me a complete
set of prints mounted in a beautifully bound book, with his dedication,
'In memory of a pleasant week.' Among others he photographed Miss
Marion Terry in my chain-mail, and I drew her lying on the lawn in
the same.[4]

Shortly after this he wrote to me asking if I would design three
illustrations to _The Hunting of the Snark_, in three cantos, of which he
sent me the MS. It was a new kind of work and interested me. I began
them at once, and sent him the first sketches, but he had in the
meantime written another canto, and asked for a drawing for it; I sent
this, but meantime he had written a new canto and wanted another
illustration; and this went on till he pulled up at the eighth canto,
making with the frontispiece, nine illustrations.

* From _Reminiscences of my Life_ (1914) pp. 165, 244–6.

We had much correspondence of a friendly character over the drawings. I remember that Dodgson criticized my introduction of the figures of Hope and Care in the scene of 'The Hunting', on the ground that he had intentionally confounded two meanings of the word 'with' in the lines:

They sought it with thimbles, they sought it with care;
They pursued it with forks and hope,

where 'with' is used in the mixed senses of indicating the instrument and the mental attitude, and he thought I had missed this point by personifying Hope and Care. I answered that, on the contrary, I had particularly noted that confusion, and had endeavoured to make confusion worse confounded by laying yet another meaning on the back of poor 'with', – to wit 'in company with'. Dodgson wrote cordially accepting this view, so the ladies were allowed to join the hunt.

NOTES

1. The artist Henry Holiday (1839–1927) enters Dodgson's *Diaries* for the first time on 6 July 1870 (p. 289), but by then the two are already well acquainted. In spite of John Ruskin's opinion that Holiday would not be able to illustrate the *Snark* properly (*Diaries*, pp. 334–5), Dodgson engaged him to do the illustrations and was pleased with the results.

2. George William Kitchin (1827–1912), biographer, historian, Student of Christ Church, Dean of Winchester and Durham, was the father of Dodgson's favourite photographic model (see pp. 142–3, above).

3. Robert Arthur Talbot Gascoyne-Cecil, 3rd Marquess of Salisbury (1830–1903), Prime Minister, was himself educated at Christ Church, and Dodgson met him and his party in June 1870, when the Cecils were in Oxford for Lord Salisbury's installation as Chancellor of the University. Dodgson actually photographed Lord Salisbury alone and with his two sons, James and Robert. He also photographed the two daughters, Maud and Gwendolen. Dodgson became well acquainted with the Cecils, spent time at Hatfield House and met various Cecils in London. He also wrote to Lord Salisbury repeatedly, in an effort to influence the politician's views and urge legislation on various issues. For more on Dodgson and the Cecils, and for a photograph of Lord Salisbury and his two sons, see *Letters*, esp. pp. 211–12, 253.

4. For Dodgson's photograph of Marion Terry, see *Letters*, facing p. 704.

The Illustrations for *The Hunting of the Snark**

HENRY HOLIDAY

In our correspondence about the illustrations, the coherence and consistency of the nonsense on its own nonsensical understanding often became prominent. One of the first three I had to do was the disappearance of the Baker, and I not unnaturally invented a Boojum. Mr Dodgson wrote that it was a delightful monster, but that it was inadmissible. All his descriptions of the Boojum were quite unimaginable, and he wanted the creature to remain so. I assented, of course, though reluctant to dismiss what I am still confident is an accurate representation. I hope that some future Darwin, in a new *Beagle*, will find the beast, or its remains; if he does, I know he will confirm my drawing.[1] . . .

In a copy [of the *Snark*] bound in vellum which he gave me the dedication runs: 'Presented to Henry Holiday, most patient of artists, by Charles L. Dodgson, most exacting, but not most ungrateful of authors, March 29, 1876.'

The above instance will show that though he justly desired to see his meanings preserved, he was not exacting in any unreasonable spirit . . . .

* From 'The Snark's Significance', *Academy*, 29 Jan 1898, pp. 128–9.

NOTE

1. For more on the origin of the *Snark* and its evolution, see *Diaries*, pp. 334–5; Morton N. Cohen, 'Hark the Snark', in *Lewis Carroll Observed*, ed. Edward Guiliano (1976) pp. 92–110; and *Lewis Carroll's 'The Hunting of the Snark'*, ed. James Tanis and John Dooley (1981), where Holiday's drawings of the Boojum are reproduced.

He Examined 'every illustration . . . under a magnifying glass'*

HARRY FURNISS[1]

If ever two men were made by nature to work together, they were Carroll and Tenniel. Tenniel's clear, painstaking finish and irreproachable humour in grotesque figures and humanized animals (his children, Alice in particular, were not successful) were exactly in the spirit of Carroll. . . . Yet the latter informed me in all sincerity that, with the exception of Humpty Dumpty, he did not like Tenniel's drawings! It was as if W. S. Gilbert had said he did not admire Arthur Sullivan's music, or vice versa! But Carroll *did* say so to me, more than once. If Carroll had continued to work with Tenniel . . . there is no doubt that all his books would have been as successful as the two in which they worked together. But, alas! Lewis Carroll the author and the Rev. C. L. Dodgson were two very different persons. Tenniel could not tolerate 'that conceited old Don' any more. Dear, gentle Tenniel was, perhaps, just a wee bit obstinate, and a tiny bit independent; but still there never was anyone easier to work with.

When I told Tenniel that I had been approached by Dodgson to illustrate his books, he said, 'I'll give you a week, old chap; *you* will never put up with that fellow a day longer.'[2]

'You will see', I said. 'If I like the work, I shall manage the author.'

'Not a bit of it; Lewis Carroll is impossible', replied Tenniel; 'you will see that my prophecy will come true.'

It was, therefore in a way, as the acceptance of a challenge that I undertook the work. Carroll and I worked together for seven years, and a kindlier man never lived. I was always hearing of his kindness to others. He was a generous employer, and his gratitude was altogether out of proportion to my efforts.

He presented my wife with beautifully bound copies of both volumes [of the *Sylvie and Bruno* books], with an elaborate inscription of thanks

* From 'Recollections of "Lewis Carroll"', *Strand Magazine*, 5 (Jan 1908) 48–52.

which I need hardly say I do not quote in any egotistical spirit, but merely to show the manner of the kindly author:

Presented to the Wife of
HARRY FURNISS
by
LEWIS CARROLL
in grateful recognition of
the exceptional skill
and the painstaking and patient
labour that have made this book
an artistic treasure.

Christmastide, 1889.

The unconscious humour of the author's ideas for pathetic pictures was a great relief to me in my difficult task of satisfying such a captious critic. Delightful and interesting as Carroll the author was, he, unfortunately, proved less acceptable when in the form of Dodgson the critic. He subjected every illustration, when finished, to a minute examination under a magnifying glass. He would take a square inch of the drawing, count the lines I had made in that space, and compare their number with those on a square inch of illustration made for *Alice* by Tenniel! And in due course I would receive a long essay on the subject from Dodgson the mathematician. Naturally, this led to disagreements, particularly when it came to foreshortening a figure, such as 'Sylvie and the Dead Hare', which is a question for the eye, not for the foot-rule and compass. In fact, over the criticism of one drawing I pretended that I could stand Dodgson the Don no longer, and wrote to Carroll the author declining to complete the work. He replied, pathetically: 'It is a severe disappointment to me to find that, on account of a single square inch of picture as to which we disagree, you decline to carry out your engagement.'

Poor, dear Lewis Carroll, so serious was he that he wrote, in horror of 'Law', to insist on my carrying out his illustrations; and proposed, as an alternative, that we should fight the point out in print. He wrote seemingly delighted at the prospect:

'For a great many years (long before I had the pleasure of knowing you) I have projected a magazine article (or a pamphlet) on the subject of "Authors' Difficulties with Illustrators", but I did not see any way of bringing it out with any *raison d'être*. This you have just given me, and I thank you sincerely for doing so. You shall have your say first, and my paper will come out, most appropriately, as an answer to yours. ... I am sure you will not object to my giving a few mathematical statistics, which my readers can easily verify for themselves, and pointing out that, by actual measurement – I have just done it carefully – the height of Sylvie, with dead hare, is just under *six* diameters of her own head, etc.'[3]

The article was not written. I was a problem solver also, and we worked without further friction to the end of the volume, and through a second volume (*Sylvie and Bruno Concluded*), which occupied some years more.

Lewis Carroll began by illustrating his own writings. . . . But as a draughtsman he was, as he himself admitted, hopeless, although he took himself so seriously as to consult Ruskin. Ruskin's advice, 'that he had not enough talent to make it worth his while to devote much time to sketching, but everyone who saw his photographs admired them', might well apply to many artists today not so modest as Carroll, who wrote to me, when I acknowledged his first sketch – an idea for an illustration – as follows: 'I fear your words' ('I had no idea you were an artist') 'were, to a certain extent, rote sarkastic, which is a shame! I never made any profession of being able to draw, and have only had, as yet, four hours' teaching (from a young friend who is herself an artist, and who insisted on making me try, in black chalk, a foot of a Laocoön! The result was truly ghastly), but I have just sufficient of correct eye to see that every drawing I made – even from life – is altogether wrong anatomically; so that nearly all my attempts go into the fire as soon as they are finished.' . . .

Alice has been invaluable to the political caricaturist. . . . I have been guilty of appropriating [it] . . . for political parody, the last of mine being an adaptation of Lewis Carroll's favourite drawing in his *Alice* – Humpty Dumpty.

NOTES

1. Dodgson first approached Harry Furniss (1854–1925), artist, author, lecturer, and in Dodgson's own words 'a very clever artist in *Punch*', on 1 March 1885, asking 'if he is open to proposals to draw pictures for me' (*Diaries*, p. 432). Dodgson clearly had Furniss in mind to illustrate *Sylvie and Bruno* (1889) and *Sylvie and Bruno Concluded* (1893), a single story in two parts, blending a children's fairy tale and an adult novel, which moves, like the *Alice* books, from prose to verse, from sense to nonsense, and back again. As Furniss indicates, the working relationship moved through stages of cordiality, misunderstanding, disagreement, and even near-disaster, but the books ultimately appeared, author and artist apparently satisfied with the results.

2. In his autobiography Furniss writes, 'Tenniel and other artists declared I would not work with Carroll for seven weeks! I accepted the challenge, but I, for that purpose, adopted quite a new method. No artist is more matter-of-fact or businesslike than myself: to Carroll I was not Hy. F., but someone else, as *he* was someone else. I was wilful and erratic, bordering on insanity. We therefore got on splendidly' – *Confessions of a Caricaturist* (1901) II, 103–4.

3. The ellipses here are Furniss's. 'I not only fully authorise you to print the "5 pages" of my letter,' Dodgson wrote, in part, in the omitted segment, 'which you say would win you "the sympathy of all the Artists", but I call upon you to do so.' For the complete text, see *Letters*, pp. 753–4.

'His egotism'*

HARRY FURNISS

Carroll was as unlike any other man as his books were unlike any other author's books. It was a relief to meet the pure simple, innocent dreamer of children, after the selfish commercial mind of most authors. Carroll was a wit, a gentleman, a bore and an egotist – and, like Hans Andersen, a spoilt child. . . . Carroll was not selfish, but a liberal-minded, liberal-handed philanthropist, but his egotism was all but second childhood.

He informed my wife that she was the most privileged woman in the world, for she knew the man who knew his . . . ideas – that ought to content her. She must not *see* a picture or read a line of the MS.; it was sufficient for her to gaze at me outside of my studio with admiration and respect, as the only man besides Lewis Carroll himself with a knowledge of Lewis Carroll's forthcoming work. Furthermore he sent me an elaborate document to sign committing myself to secrecy. This I indignantly declined to sign. 'My word was as good as my bond', I said, and, striking an attitude, I hinted that I would 'strike', inasmuch as I would not work for years isolated from my wife and friends. I was therefore no doubt looked upon by him as a lunatic. That was what I wanted. I was allowed to show my wife the drawings. . . .

But this egotism carried him still further. He was determined no one should read his MS. but he and I; so in the dead of night (he sometimes wrote up to 4 a.m.) he cut his MS. into horizontal strips of four or five lines, then placed the whole of it in a sack and shook it up; taking out piece by piece, he pasted strips down as they happened to come. The result, in such an MS., dealing with nonsense on one page and theology on another, was audacious in the extreme, if not absolutely profane. . . .

These incongruous strips were elaborately and mysteriously marked with numbers and letters and various hieroglyphics, to decipher which would really have turned my assumed eccentricity into positive madness. I therefore sent the whole MS. back to him, and again threatened to strike! This had the desired effect. I then received MS. I

* From *Confessions of a Caricaturist* (1901) II, 104–12.

could read, although frequently puzzled by its being mixed up with Euclid and problems in abstruse mathematics.

. . . for months we corresponded about the face of the Heroine alone. My difficulty was increased by the fact that the fairy child Sylvie and the Society grown-up Lady Muriel were one and the same person! So I received reams of written descriptions and piles of useless photographs intended to inspire me to draw with a few lines a face embodying his ideal in a space not larger than a threepenny-piece. By one post I would receive a batch of photographs of some young lady Lewis Carroll fancied had one feature, or half a feature, of that ideal he had conjured up in his own mind as his heroine.

He invited me to visit friends of his, and strangers too, from John o'Groats to Land's End, so as to collect fragments of faces. . . . I feel sure that [I would have gone mad] . . . had I attempted to carry out Lewis Carroll's instructions. I therefore worked on my own lines with success. . . . Still he was enthusiastic in his praise, and absurdly generous in his thanks. He was jealous that I would not disclose to him who my model was for Sylvie. When dining with us many a smile played over the features of my children when he cross-questioned me on this point. Repeatedly he wrote to me: 'How old is your model for Sylvie? And may I have her name and address?' 'My friend Miss E. G. Thompson, an artist great in "fairies", would be glad to know of her, I'm sure', and so on.

The fairy Sylvie was my own daughter! All the children in his books I illustrated were my own children; yet this fact never struck him!

. . . one picture in *Sylvie and Bruno* (vol. i., p. 134) . . . brings back to me the only sorrowful hour I had in connection with the otherwise enjoyable work. My wife was very ill – so ill it was a question of life and death. Expert opinion was called in, and the afternoon I had to make that drawing – with my own children as models – the 'consultation' was being held in my wife's room. Carroll was on his way from Oxford to see the work, and I was drawing against time. It's the old story of the clown with the sick wife. Caricaturists are after all but clowns of the pencil. They must raise a laugh whatever their state of mind may be. For a long time I never would show Lewis Carroll my work, for the simple reason I did not do it. He thought I was at work, but I was not. That's where my acting eccentricity came in. I knew that I would have to draw the subjects 'right off', not one a month or one in six months. Correspondence for three months, as a rule, led to work for one week. Isolated verse I did let him have the illustrations for, but not the body of the book. This was my only chance, and I arrived at this secrecy by the following bold stroke.

Lewis Carroll came from Oxford one evening, early in the history of the work, to dine, and afterwards to see a batch of work. He ate little, drank little, but enjoyed a few glasses of sherry, his favourite wine.

'Now,' he said, 'for the studio!' I rose and led the way. My wife sat in astonishment. She knew I had nothing to show. Through the drawing-room, down the steps of the conservatory to the door of my studio. My hand is on the handle. Through excitement Lewis Carroll stammers worse than ever. Now to see the work for his great book! I pause, turn my back to the closed door, and thus address the astonished Don: 'Mr Dodgson, I am *very* eccentric – I cannot help it! Let me explain to you clearly, before you enter my studio, that my eccentricity sometimes takes a violent form. If I, in showing my work, discover in your face the slightest sign that you are not *absolutely* satisfied with any particle of this work in progress, the *whole* of it goes into the fire! It is a risk: will you accept it, or will you wait till I have the drawings *quite* finished and send them to Oxford?'

'I-I-I ap-appreciate your feelings – I-I-should feel the same myself. I am off to Oxford!' and he went.

I sent him drawings as they were finished, and each parcel brought back a budget of letter-writing, each page being carefully numbered. . . . To meet him and to work for him was to me a great treat. I put up with his eccentricities – real ones, not sham like mine. – I put up with a great deal of boredom, for he was a bore at times, and I worked over seven years with his illustrations, in which the actual working hours would not have occupied me more than seven weeks, purely out of respect for his genius. I treated him as a problem, and I solved him, and had he lived I would probably have still worked with him. He remunerated me liberally for my work; still, he actually proposed that in addition I should partake of the profits; his gratitude was overwhelming. 'I am grateful; and I feel sure that if *pictures* could sell a book *Sylvie and Bruno* would sell like wildfire.'[1]

NOTE

1. Elsewhere Harry Furniss writes more graciously of his association with Dodgson:

I have illustrated stories of most of our leading authors, and I can safely say that Lewis Carroll was the only one who cared to understand the illustrations to his own book. He was the W. S. Gilbert for children, and, like Gilbert producing one of his operas, Lewis Carroll took infinite pains to study every detail in producing his extraordinary and delightful books. . . . This, of course, led to a great deal of work and trouble, and made the illustrating of his books more a matter of artistic interest than of professional profit. I was *seven years* illustrating his last work, and during that time I had the pleasure of many an interesting meeting with the fascinating author, and I was quite repaid for the trouble I took, not only by his generous appreciation of my efforts, but by the liberal remuneration he gave for the work, and also by the charm of having intercourse with the interesting, if somewhat erratic genius.' (*Life and Letters*, pp. 319–20)

'My beloved friend'*

E. GERTRUDE THOMSON[1]

In trying to sketch this outline of my beloved friend – one of the most unique and charming personalities of our time – my own shadow, so to speak, must perforce, to my regret, sometimes fall across the picture. I shall not attempt to give any of his incomparable humour, all the world knows that through his immortal books, but I want to show that little known view of him – that 'other side of the moon' – visible only to those who knew him best.

It was at the end of December, 1878, that a letter, written in a singularly legible and rather boyish-looking hand, came to me from Christ Church, Oxford, and signed 'C. L. Dodgson'. The writer said that he had come across some fairy designs of mine, and he should like to see some more of my work. By the same post came a note from my London publisher (who had supplied my address) telling me that the 'Rev. C. L. Dodgson' was 'Lewis Carroll'.

Alice in Wonderland had long been one of my pet books, and as one regards a favourite author as almost a personal friend, I felt less restraint than one usually feels in writing to a stranger, though I carefully concealed my knowledge of his identity as he had not chosen to reveal it.

This was the beginning of a frequent and delightful correspondence, and as I confessed to a great love for fairy lore of every description, he asked me if I would accept a child's fairy-tale book he had written called *Alice in Wonderland*. I replied that I knew it nearly all off by heart, but that I should greatly prize a copy given to me by himself. By return came *Alice*, and *Through the Looking-Glass*, bound most luxuriously in white calf and gold.

And this is the graceful and kindly note that came with them – 'I am now sending you *Alice* and the *Looking Glass* as well. There is an incompleteness about giving only one, and besides the one you bought was probably in red and would not match these. If you are at all in doubt as to what to do with the (now) superfluous copy, let me

---

* From 'Lewis Carroll: A Sketch by an Artist-Friend', *Gentlewoman*, 16 (29 Jan and 5 Feb 1898) 147, 166–7.

suggest your giving it to some poor sick child. I have been distributing copies to all the hospitals and convalescent homes I can hear of, where there are sick children capable of reading them, and though, of course, one takes some pleasure in the popularity of the books elsewhere, it is not nearly so pleasant a thought to me as that they may be a comfort and relief to children in hours of pain and weariness. Still, no recipient *can* be more appropriate than one who seems to have been in fairyland herself, and to have seen, like the "weary mariners" of old –

> Between the green brink and the running foam
> White limbs unrobed in a crystal air,
> Sweet faces, rounded arms, and bosoms prest
> To little harps of gold.'[2]

'Do you ever come to London?' he asked in another letter; 'if so, will you allow me to call upon you?'

Early in the summer I came up to study, and I sent him word that I was in town. One night coming into my room after a long day spent at the British Museum, in the half-light I saw a card lying on the table. 'Rev. C. L. Dodgson.' Bitter, indeed, was my disappointment at having missed him, but just as I was laying it sadly down I spied a small T.O. in the corner. On the back I read that he couldn't get up to my rooms early or late enought to find me, so would I arrange to meet him at some museum or gallery the day but one following? I fixed on South Kensington Museum[3] by the 'Schliemann' collection, at twelve o'clock.

A little before twelve I was at the rendezvous, and then the humour of the situation suddenly struck me, that *I* had not the ghost of an idea what *he* was like, nor would *he* have any better chance of discovering *me*! The room was fairly full of all sorts and conditions as usual, and I glanced at each masculine figure in turn, only to reject it as a possibility of the one I sought. Just as the big clock had clanged out twelve, I heard the high vivacious voices and laughter of children sounding down the corridor.

At that moment a gentleman entered, two little girls clinging to his hands, and as I caught sight of the tall, slim figure, with the clean-shaven, delicate, refined face, I said to myself, '*That's* Lewis Carroll.' He stood for a moment, head erect, glancing swiftly over the room, then bending down, whispered something to one of the children; she, after a moment's pause, pointed straight at me.

Dropping their hands he came forward, and with that winning smile of his that utterly banished the oppressive sense of the Oxford don, said simply, 'I am Mr Dodgson; I was to meet you, I think?' To which I as frankly smiled and said, 'How did you know me so soon?'

'My little friend found you. I told her I had come to meet a young lady who knew fairies, and she fixed on you at once. But, I knew you before she spoke.'

Thus began that close and happy friendship which gladdened and enriched my life for eighteen years, and ended only when *his* beautiful life drew to its close, scarcely a week ago.

Soon after our meeting in London he wrote from Oxford: 'Are you sufficiently unconventional (I *think* you are) to defy Mrs Grundy, and come down to spend the day with me at Oxford? Write and ask permission of your father.' Needless to say the permission was given, and the visit arranged.

'What would you like to eat?' he wrote. 'Choose your own lunch, and, whether possible or impossible, it shall be got!' I went down by an early train, and he met me at the station with two more little girls. Always little girls! We did the lions in Oxford. Glorious of course. Then the children were taken home, and we returned to his beautiful rooms at Christ Church.

Lewis Carroll was not only an admirable amateur photographer, but an enthusiastic sketcher of children, especially when they were 'dressed in nothing', as he called it, and, *apropos* of this, he once told me an amusing remark of one of Sir Noël Paton's children. They were very beautiful, and served their father as models in those two exquisite illustrations for Kingsley's *Water Babies*. In the design of the fairies floating through the water the front view figure is an absolute portrait of one little daughter. One day a friend in looking at it said to the child, 'Why, that's *you*.' 'Yes,' was the reply, 'it's *me* but I don't *often* dress like that!'

I consider that he naturally had a decided gift for drawing, but he was entirely untrained, so that his sketches, though they had a certain feeling for beauty, were, of course, very crude. He had a singularly correct eye for form, so much so that he would instantly detect slight flaws in drawing in some of the work I did for him, which had escaped my more practised eye. Complimenting him one day on his ability as art critic, he said, 'I can't draw in the least myself – that's the first qualification for an Art Critic. One approaches a subject in such a delightfully open and unbiased manner if you are entirely ignorant of it!'

Writing to me once on this subject he said: 'I *love* the effort to draw; but I fail utterly to please even my own eye. But I have no time now left for such things. In the next life, I do hope that we shall not only *see* lovely forms, such as this world does not contain, but shall also be able to *draw* them.'

He was always anxious that whatever work I did for him should be drawn from life. 'I do want you to do my fairy-drawings from *life*', he wrote. 'They would be very pretty, no doubt, done out of your own head, but they will be ten times more valuable if done from life. Mr Tenniel is the only artist who has drawn for me who resolutely refused to use a model, and declared he no more needed one that *I* should need the multiplication table to work out a mathematical problem!'

Soon there followed another day at Oxford.

'Come and photograph human fairies', he wrote. . . .

[In his photographic studio, we] would group together on the floor, Lewis Carroll, the fairies, the beasts and myself, and gay indeed were the hours we spent. How his laugh would ring out like a child's!

And the exquisite nonsense he talked! It was like pages out of the *Alice*s, only more delightful, for there was his own voice and smile to give the true charm to it all. I used to try to recall and record it. It was impossible – as impossible as to catch the gleam of colour on sunlit water, or grasp a drifting rainbow. It was a mystic, intangible, gossamer-like thing, that, to chain it down in the words with which we should have translated it, would have been to crush out all life and grace – to destroy it altogether.

His love for children was not merely for the amusement they afforded him; it was deeper far than that. It was their purity and innocence that appealed to him; and if ever a child showed by word or look any unlovely feeling, the change in his face was startling; all the light would die out of it, and his tender reproof was inexpressibly touching.

To show his sensitiveness of conscience and dread of evil for children, I will quote a passage from one of his letters. I had a little girl model, about eight years of age, whose lovely head I had sketched and sent to him, and as I was at the time working at some fairy designs for him, in which all the little figures were to be 'dressed in nothing', I wrote, 'I mean to ask Edie to sit to me as a "fairy" – that is, if she doesn't mind.'

I must quote from memory, for the letter is mislaid. He wrote to say that if Edie showed the slightest shrinking from this, that he must implore me not to try to overcome it. If she had such a feeling, it would be a crime in the sight of God to persuade her to consent.

One day he came to my studio to sketch a very charming child whom I had engaged specially for him. She had travelled some little distance from the North of London to come to us, and I expressed some surprise that her mother had allowed her to come alone, but the child said she was 'used to it'.

On his return to Oxford he wrote to me:

'I don't quite like the idea of that small and pretty child going all that way alone on my account. If she got lost or stolen I should feel an awful responsibility in having caused her to run the risk. I fear such beauty, among the very poor, is a very dangerous possession.'

For many years there was a delightful interchange of visits. I would go down to Oxford for the day to photograph or draw portraits of his child-friends for him. The children would return home, sometimes before, sometimes after lunch; in the afternoon Mr Dodgson and I would each bury ourselves in a luxurious armchair and talk, or look over sketches I had brought for him to see, or go through part of his vast collection of photographs of famous people taken long years before. Many of Gabriel Rossetti and his sister Christina, Ruskin, the Millais children, the Terry family.

I remember one of Ellen Terry, taken when she was about eighteen; she happened to laugh at the moment, and she looked one of the loveliest young creatures imaginable.

Then he would make the afternoon tea himself, all in his deft and dainty fashion, and this would bring the happy visit to its close.

A lady friend of Mr Dodgson's – a good woman, eminently practical and steeped to the lips in convention – once took me to task.

We had spent the morning at her house sketching her children; at least, I sketched while she talked *Alice*.

He left before lunch, and after this meal was over she sent the children away, and, taking up her sewing, sat down in front of me.

'I hear that you spent the other day in Oxford, with Mr Dodgson?'

'Yes, it was a most delightful day.'

'It's a very unconventional thing to do.'

'We are both very unconventional.'

'Mr Dodgson is not at all a ladies' man.'

'He wouldn't be my friend if he were.'

'He is a confirmed bachelor.'

'So am I; and, what is more, he is old enough to be my father.'

She steadily regarded me for a moment, and then said, 'I tell you what it is. Mr Dodgson doesn't think of you as a "young lady" or anything of that kind, he looks upon you as a sort of "old child"'.

I laughed delightedly. 'I don't mind if Mr Dodgson looks upon me as a sort of old grandmother if only he will ask me down to Oxford.'

But I was deeply offended. Our pure and beautiful friendship seemed hurt somehow by this coarse handling.

Sometimes he would come up to town for the day. We would meet, lunch together, and go off to a matinée, sometimes coming back to my rooms for tea. Once I had a ghastly experience.

I have an artist-friend, a rare genius, as unique in his way, perhaps, as Lewis Carroll, but as opposite as the poles. Rugged, full of angles, charming in private life, gauche in the presence of strangers. I call him Solomon Eagle, from his striking resemblance to that picturesque person, and for his holy horror of the world, the flesh, and the devil, particularly as displayed in theatrical performances.

I had spoken of this friend to Lewis Carroll, and shown him autotypes of his work which greatly impressed him.

One day Lewis Carroll had been up in town and had taken me to a matinée at Wilson Barrett's theatre. We had just returned to my rooms for tea when my artist-friend was announced. I asked permission to introduce him. 'Very pleased', was his reply, and Solomon Eagle was ushered in.

Instantly my blood began to curdle, for I saw at a flash what I'd never dreamed of before, that they were denizens of different planets, so to speak.

At the sight of a 'grown-up', the 'Lewis Carroll' dropped from off my Oxford friend like the petals of a rudely shaken flower, leaving only the dry stalk. He stood, an aristocrat to his finger tips, the cold, serene, dignified Mr Dodgson, the Don. Solomon Eagle, nervous, gauche, spasmodic.

The greeting passed off well enough. If only it had ended there! Feeling at a loss for the next remark my artist-friend approached the chimney-piece, against which, at either end, Mr Dodgson and I were leaning. He caught sight of a photograph, which I had propped up against the clock, of the principal actress in the play we had seen that afternoon.

'What on earth possesses you to put a thing like that up there? It will ruin your taste!'

Before I could reply Mr Dodgson quickly remarked: 'Our friend kindly accepted that from me. It is a portrait of the chief actress in Mr Wilson Barrett's theatre.'

The fat was now fully in the fire, and I drew in my breath and braced myself for the inevitable frizzle.

'The theatre is the mouth of Hell!' shrieked Solomon Eagle, and he flashed his brilliant eyes upon me.

There was no help for it, so I meekly replied: 'Yes, we've both been there this afternoon.'

Like a mad bull he turned to rend another rag, and glared again at the hapless photograph.

'Photography and Ruskin have done more to destroy English art than –.'

'Mr Ruskin is one of my dearest friends, and I am proud of it. Photography is my hobby, and I am not inclined to apologize even for that!' Thus the Don.

I prayed that the earth might open and swallow me up, or that a fiery chariot would descend and whirl away Solomon Eagle on the spot; but Providence didn't see fit to interfere.

Solomon brought to his senses by this cold douche, instantly apologized, and suddenly remembering a pressing engagement, abruptly wished me 'Good-night.'

The bows that were exchanged between the artist and the Don were studies in deportment. If I hadn't been so utterly wretched I should have laughed.

I took the ruffled Eagle downstairs to see him safe off the premises, and his language was more picturesque than polite.

'Bloodless fossil!' were the words he hurled into the quiet street as he left the door.

In justice to him I ought to say that he had not the faintest idea beforehand of Mr Dodgson's views on any subject.

It was entirely my fault in bringing ice and fire together.

On re-entering the room I found that Mr Dodgson, the don, had disappeared, and 'Lewis Carroll' was standing on the hearthrug, smiling.

'I don't like your friend', he remarked airily.

'Neither do I,' I groaned, dropping into a chair like a limp rag 'at present.'

Oddly enough they collided on my door-step a day or two later, and after a few minutes' chat, Mr Dodgson came up to my room.

'I met your friend,' he said, 'and I was mistaken – I think now that I rather do like him.' . . .

I remember once – having offered me his rooms at Eastbourne for a week or two, as he was detained in Oxford – his writing: 'If you have any overworked, tired friend who needs a holiday, take her down with you to occupy that other room, and please allow me to pay all her expenses.' In small things as well as greater, his kindly courtesy and consideration were unfailing.

'While you are doing so much for my pleasure' – (I was designing some fairies for him) – he wrote once, 'it were churlish not to do something for yours, so, though I am writing *Logic* about six hours a day, I have spared time to write out these two little acrostic poems for you.'

'I wish you a very Happy Christmas,' began another letter, 'but my wishes will come a little late, as, to spare the overworked letter carrier, I shall leave this to be posted after Christmas.'

The most distinguishing features about him were his delicate reserve and dignified modesty; he shrank with painful over-sensitiveness from being 'lionized' in any way. To be pointed out as the '*Alice* man' was to him abhorrent.

'I can't imagine what people saw in *Alice*', he once remarked to me. 'I believe its popularity has more to do with Tenniel's lovely drawings, than with any nonsense of *mine*!'

'I never read criticisms of my work', he said to me only the other day. 'If they praise one it makes one vain; if they abuse one it makes one angry, and both states of mind are bad.'

I always had a mysterious feeling, when looking at him and hearing him speak, that he was not exactly an ordinary human being of flesh and blood. Rather did he seem as some delicate, ethereal spirit, enveloped for the moment in a semblance of common humanity.

His head was small, and beautifully formed; the brow rather low, broad, white, and finely modelled. Dreamy grey eyes, a sensitive mouth, slightly compressed when in repose, but softening into the most beautiful smile when he spoke. He had a slight hesitancy sometimes, when speaking, that reminded one of dear Charles Lamb's immortal stammer; but though Mr Dodgson deplored it himself, it added a certain piquancy, especially if he was uttering any whimsicality.

It is just two months to-day since we spent our last day together.

He had written asking me if I would go with him to the matinée of *The Little Minister*, and I had suggested that he should come to my studio in the morning for an hour's sketching.

I secured a lovely little girl as model, and he promptly appeared at 11 o'clock.

He was charmed with the child, and they made friends at once. In the 'resting' intervals he sat with her on his knee drawing comic pictures to amuse her, and warming her little hands, for the morning was chilly.

We were to lunch with some friends of his in Lowndes Square, and being rather behindhand, we hailed a hansom. Something frightened the horse and it bolted with us.

'Well,' observed Lewis Carroll serenely, 'if we are alive when we reach Lowndes Square, we certainly shall not be late!'

He was exceptionally brilliant that day at lunch, full of repartee and anecdote. He looked extremely well, and as if many years of work still lay before him. As we were driving to the theatre he confessed to me that he had been working very hard lately, sitting up till 5 o'clock in the morning. When I ventured to gently remonstrate, he smiled.

'It suits me', he said; 'I feel very well.'

Then suddenly turning to me, he said, while a wistful look grew in his eyes, 'My time is so short. I have so much to do before I go, and the call might come any day.'

Little did I dream that before two months were over the call *would* have come.

He was charmed with *The Little Minister*.

Miss Winifred Emery, by her enchanting personation, won his warmest admiration.

The part of the boy was played by a young actress with whom he had just become acquainted.

While in the theatre he scribbled a note. 'May we come round and see you?' and handed it to one of the officials to send it to her.

Presently back came a note; he glanced at the superscription, and on his lips played the old whimsical smile.

'This is evidently intended for *you*', he said quietly. 'Will you allow me to open it?'

It was addressed, 'Mrs Dodgson'!

How we laughed.

'That "we" was misleading', he remarked. 'Well, we are certainly labelled *now*!'

After the play he asked, 'Have you anything special to do? If not, come and have tea with me at Paddington, and see me off.'

All too swiftly the last half-hour glided away, and I went with him to take his seat.

At the door of the compartment he turned to shake hands. 'Good-bye, I've had such a happy day', he said simply. 'I hope you have.'

Just before Christmas he wrote, 'Write to me at "The Chestnuts", Guildford, where I shall stay until the middle of January.'

The middle of January is here.

But the hand that wrote those words has laid down the magic pen for ever: and he, who called forth the purest, gayest laughter the world has ever heard, has passed into that silent land of shadows where no voice can reach, nor footsteps follow!

A grey January day, calm, and without a sound, full of the peace of God which passeth all understanding.

A steep, stony, country road, with hedges close on either side, fast quickening with the breath of the premature spring. Between the withered leaves of the dead summer a pure white daisy here and there shone out like a little star.

A few mourners slowly climbed the hill in silence, while borne before them on a simple hand-bier was the coffin, half hid in flowers.

Under an old yew, round whose gnarled trunk the green ivy twined, in the pure white chalk earth his body was laid to rest, while the slow bell tolled the passing –

> Of the sweetest soul
> That ever looked with human eye.[4]

NOTES

1. Emily Gertrude Thomson (1850–1929) was the daughter of Alexander Thomson (1815–95), Professor of Greek and Hebrew at Lancashire Independent College. She

studied at the Manchester School of Art, won a number of Queen's Prizes, and became a member of the Royal Society of Miniature Painters. At various stages in her career she painted portraits, illustrated books, created greeting cards, and designed stained-glass windows. She exhibited in Manchester, Liverpool, Brussels, and Canada. Works by her are in the permanent collections of the Manchester Art Gallery and the Victoria and Albert Museum; her stained-glass windows can be seen at Cheltenham College and at the Church of St John the Divine, Brooklands, Cheshire. She designed the covers for *The Nursery 'Alice'* and illustrated Dodgson's last book, *Three Sunsets and Other Poems*. A photograph of her appears in *Life and Letters*, p. 194; Thomson's miniature portrait of Dodgson appears as the frontispiece in *Catalogue of an Exhibition at Columbia University to Commemorate the One Hundredth Anniversary of the Birth of Lewis Carroll* (1932); and a pencil drawing by her of Dodgson is the frontispiece of vol. II of *Letters*.

2. Tennyson's 'The Sea-Fairies', II. 2–4.

3. Now the Victoria and Albert Museum.

4. Tennyson's *In Memoriam*, LVII, 11–12.

He Photographs the Rossettis*

WILLIAM MICHAEL ROSSETTI[1]

[I]

One of the earliest [of the authors that I met in my brother's house in Cheyne Walk] . . . was the Reverend C. L. Dodgson. . . . He was a skillful amateur photographer, and he took some few photographs of Dante Rossetti, and of other members of the family. He continued keeping up some little acquaintance with Christina till the close of her life, sending her successive publications. . . . He impressed me mainly as belonging to the type of 'the University Man': a certain externalism of polite propriety, verging towards the conventional. I do not think he said in my presence anything 'funny' or quaint.

[II]

Ford Madox Hueffer (Ford) wrote that, if his grandfather Ford Madox Brown may be believed, 'the wombat of Rossetti was the

* [I] is from *Some Reminiscences of William Michael Rossetti* (1906) pp. 328–9; [II] is compiled by the editor from Ford Madox Hueffer, *Ford Madox Brown* (1896) p. 261; Frances Winwar, *Poor Splendid Wings* (1933) p. 306; Mackenzie Bell, *Christina Rossetti* (1898) p. 149; Marya Zaturenska, *Christina Rossetti* (1949) pp. 186–7.

prototype of the dormouse in *Alice in Wonderland*'. 'Perhaps', writes
Frances Winwar, 'sensing a timid soul in Dodgson . . . [Christina]
chatted of how she and William Michael had disovered the furry
wombat at the zoo, of how they had introduced the delightful creature
to Gabriel, and of how he made of it a pet and a fad – yes, the little
round wombat that slept all day long in the epergne of the dining-
room table and ate expensive cigars. . . . She may have thought of the
wombat and of . . . [Dodgson's] visits when she chuckled over the
misadventures of a certain sleepy dormouse in a presentation copy of
Lewis Carroll's fairy tale of Alice.' Christina herself recalled that, with
all the animals that Dante Gabriel collected, his house and its grounds
'became a sort of wonderland; and once the author of *Wonderland*
photographed us in the garden. It was our aim to appear in the full
family group of five; but whilst various others succeeded, that
particular negative was spoilt by a shower, and I possess a solitary
print taken from it in which we appear as if splashed by ink.'
According to Marya Zaturenska, 'Dodgson's photographs and
conversation delighted Christina. Unworldly, humorous, erudite, and
not unedifying, his conversation was the kind she liked best, though to
Dante Gabriel he was merely one of the quaint personages he liked to
collect, as he collected the wombat and other odd animals. William
Michael, who was becoming more and more serious as he became
interested in socialism, found Dr Dodgson's quaintness tiresome and
too whimsical for his taste. But to Christina and her mother he had a
special value; he too was a devout and orthodox churchman, and
Christina, like Dr Johnson, felt that the priests of her church should
be treated with honor, respect, and no criticism.'

NOTE

1. On 30 September 1863, the sculptor Alexander Munro introduced Dodgson to
D. G. Rossetti (*Diaries*, p. 201) at the artist's home and studio in Cheyne Walk. '. . . saw
some very lovely pictures,' Dodgson recorded, 'most of them only half finished: he was
most hospitable in the offers of the use of house and garden for picture-taking, and I
arranged to take my camera there on Monday . . . and on Wednesday take him and his
mother and sister.' On 6 October he took his camera to the Rossetti house and noted
that while he was unpacking his equipment

Miss [Christina] Rossetti arrived and Mr Rossetti introduced me to her. She seemed
a little shy at first, and I had a very little time for conversation with her, but I much
liked the little I saw of her. She sat for two pictures, Mr Rossetti for one. . . . I
afterwards looked through a huge volume of drawings, some of which I am to
photograph – a great treat, as I had never seen such exquisite drawing before. I
dined with Mr Rossetti, and spent some of the evening there. . . . A memorable
day.   (*Diaries*, pp. 203–4)

On successive visits, he photographed the entire family and some Rossetti drawings.
Christina Rossetti's children's book *Speaking Likenesses* (1874) owes an obvious debt to

Alice. When Tennyson died, Dodgson hoped that Christina Rossetti would be made Poet Laureate (see Dodgson to Mrs C. F. Moberly Bell, *Letters*, p. 986). Dodgson's photographs of the Rossettis have been reproduced; see, for instance, Gernsheim, plates 21, 23, 24; *Letters*, facing pp. 125, 640.

'I beg . . . you not to put me in *Vanity Fair*'*

MRS E. M. WARD[1]

We knew 'Lewis Carroll' . . . very well indeed; he was so exceptionally modest that if anyone mentioned *Alice in Wonderland* or any other of his works he would frown, fidget, and disappear as soon as he could. His great hobby was children. Little girls were special favourites, and he carried on a correspondence with numbers of children, keeping an album in which he wrote the ages of all his juvenile friends. He often sent me word that he was coming to town, and would be glad if I would give lunch to himself and some little friend he was taking to the theatre. He would turn up for lunch with one and sometimes two children. The entertainments he enjoyed as much as his little friends.

Lewis Carroll was once asked by my son if he might do a cartoon of him for *Vanity Fair*. In reply he wrote: 'As a friend of your father and mother I beg and implore you not to put me in *Vanity Fair*, or any other paper. I would rather anything than that.' A compromise was finally made that Lewis Carroll was to be let off on condition that he wrote something for *Vanity Fair*; to this he reluctantly agreed.

Towards the end of his life he only came to town on rare occasions. . . . He used to send me his books directly they were published, and *Sylvie and Bruno* arrived one day in manuscript, to see if I could suggest any improvements. He never would allow me to say anything in praise of his work, for in his own opinion he was a nonentity. I never knew anyone less conceited.

Lewis Carroll was a delightful creature, and though very odd, always felt at home with us; one day he arrived with three tea-cannisters, decorated with pictures from *Alice in Wonderland*. My daughters and I preserve them still. I recollect his telling me once that the success *Alice in Wonderland* had achieved was due 'entirely to its

* From *Memories of Ninety Years* [*c*. 1923] pp. 56–8.

beautiful illustrations'. I smiled, as I knew it was nonsense for him to say so, but did not venture to contradict him.

NOTE

1. Dodgson admired Mrs Ward's painting at the Royal Academy as early as 1857. Introduced by a mutual acquaintance, he called on the Wards in 1866, thought them all very pleasant, and stayed 'a long while'. A friendship grew easily. On 8 February 1876, the Wards' son, Leslie (1851–1922), the famous 'Spy', called on Dodgson and wanted to do a caricature of him for *Vanity Fair*. Dodgson did write for *Vanity Fair*: his *Doublets* appeared there in 1879. Edward Matthew Ward (1816–79), the father, was the historical painter who did corridor frescoes in the Houses of Parliament. His wife, Henrietta Mary Ada Ward (1832–1924), was a distinguished artist also who painted and instructed the Royal Family.

'One of my earliest friends among literary folk'*

ELLEN TERRY[1]

Mr Dodgson . . . once brought a little girl to see me in *Faust*. He wrote and told me that she had said (where Margaret begins to undress): 'Where is it going to stop?' and that perhaps, in consideration of the fact that it could affect a mere child disagreeably, I ought to alter my business!

I had known dear Mr Dodgson for years and years. He was as fond of me as he could be of any one over the age of ten, but I was *furious*. 'I thought you only knew *nice* children', was all the answer I gave him. 'It would have seemed awful for a *child* to see harm where harm is; how much more so when she sees it where harm is not.'

But I felt ashamed and shy whenever I played that scene. . . .

Mr Dodgson was one of my earliest friends among literary folk. I can't remember a time when I didn't know him. He saw Kate and me act as children, and gave us a copy of *Alice in Wonderland*. . . . The *Alice* ceremony was gone through with every member of the Terry family, and in later years with their children.

Mr Dodgson was an ardent playgoer. He took the keenest interest in all the Lyceum productions, frequently writing to me to point out

* From *Ellen Terry's Memoirs*, ed. Edith Craig and Christopher St John (1933) pp. 141–3.

slips in the dramatist's logic which only he would ever have noticed! He did not even spare Shakespeare. I think he wrote these letters for fun, as some people make puzzles, anagrams, or Limericks! . . .

Mr Dodgson's kindness to children was wonderful. He *really* loved them and put himself out for them. The children he knew who wanted to go on the stage were those who came under my observation, and nothing could have been more touching than his ceaseless industry on their behalf.

NOTE

1. During his early photographing days, Dodgson was determined to get the Terry family to sit before his camera. On 20 August 1864, after at least one earlier unsuccessful attempt, Dodgson succeeded in breaking the barrier with the help of an introduction from his friend the dramatist Tom Taylor. When he presented himself at the Terry home, Mrs Terry invited him in, but Dodgson found that most of the luminary Terrys were out. He returned the same day to show his photographs and arranged to photograph the entire family in the following October. But he did not meet Ellen Terry until December, when he called on his way to Guildford for Christmas. He finally got a four-day photography session with the Terrys in July of the following year. A friendship took root, and thereafter Dodgson was always welcome. The father of the family was Benjamin Terry (1818–96), actor; the mother, Sarah Ballard (1817–92). The two daughters mentioned here were (Dame) Ellen Terry (1847–1928) and Eliza Murray Kate Terry (1842–1924), also an actress until she married. For more on Dodgson and Ellen Terry, see Morton N. Cohen, 'The Actress and the Don: Ellen Terry and Lewis Carroll', in *Lewis Carroll: A Celebration*, ed. Edward Guiliano (1982) pp. 1–14. For some of Dodgson's photographs of the Terrys, see *Letters*, facing pp. 156, 704.

The Stage as an Elevating Influence*

A. W. DUBOURG[1]

I gathered from my intercourse with Lewis Carroll that, subject to rigid limits as to the normal character of the play, he had considerable sympathy with the drama, believing that within those limits the stage might have a valuable and elevating influence upon all classes of playgoers and upon the public generally; but with regard to the slightest transgression of those limits he was greatly sensitive, perhaps super-sensitive to the mind of a layman, and I have known him leave a

* From *Picture Book*, pp. 161–3.

theatre in the midst of a performance for a very small deviation from the line he had marked out.

He was particularly sensitive as to the use of oaths on the stage – he strongly protested against it, and I know that he once entered into a serious controversy with a leading manager on the subject. The stage will always be a potent factor in social life, and the support accorded by seriously minded persons like Lewis Carroll will always tend to wholesomeness and moral elevation, because this support will make *good* things *pay*, and managers must look for profit from what they give to the public.

Lewis Carroll took a kindly interest in child-life on the stage. I always think that any little girl of ten or twelve was potentially an 'Alice' in his eyes; and I know that many a kind and generous act has he done for those stage-children and their parents – persons oftentimes greatly in want of substantial assistance.

In conclusion, I should like to say these few words about my personal intercourse with Lewis Carroll.

I knew well and greatly valued Charles Dodgson in the friendly intercourse of life; but the friend of the fireside and the family dinner-table was totally unlike the Lewis Carroll that popular imagination would picture – a quiet retiring, scholarlike person, full of interesting and pleasant conversation, oftentimes with an undercurrent of humour, and certainly with a sense of great sensitiveness with regard to the serious side of life. The very thought of being lionized was utterly distasteful and abhorrent, and I never heard him utter in conversation a single telling sentence on the lines of *Alice* or the *Snark*. I may truthfully say that throughout much friendly intercourse with Charles Dodgson, the remembrance of which I value greatly, I never met that exquisite humorist, Lewis Carroll.

NOTE

1. Dodgson first met Augustus William Dubourg (1830–1910), Clerk in the House of Lords and a dramatist, on 11 January 1869, at a 'gay and striking' garden party, and he became friendly with him and his family. Dubourg tried to help Dodgson to get *Alice* put on the stage (*Diaries*, p. 281).

A Journey to Russia*

HENRY PARRY LIDDON[1]

[In 1867, Dodgson made his first and only journey abroad, accompanying his friend and fellow Student at Christ Church, Henry Parry Liddon, to Russia. Both Dodgson and Liddon kept a journal of their travels. The following excerpts are from Liddon's journal.]

12 July (Friday)
. . . Dodgson arrived [at the Lord Warden Hotel, Dover,] at 10.30 p.m. . . .

13 July (Saturday)
. . . Between Lille and Tournay, a Belgian father and mother and two little children got into our carriage. The youngest girl greatly interested Dodgson; who drew her.[2]

15 July (Monday)
Brussels–Cologne. . . . Great difficulty in saving the train at Verviers owing to Dodgson's delay about the tickets. . . . Dodgson was overcome by the beauty of Cologne Cathedral. I found him leaning against the rails of the Choir and sobbing like a child. When the verger came to show us over the chapels behind the Choir, he got out of the way: he said that he could not bear the harsh voice of the man in the presence of so much beauty.[3]

16 July (Tuesday)
Cologne–Berlin. . . . Dodgson went to the Apostelkirche to see a marriage.

18 July (Thursday)
Berlin. . . . Spent the greatest part of the morning in going about to shops for photographs for Dodgson. . . . We walked out a little after 8 after deciding on our plans for the future.

* From *The Russian Journal – II: A Record Kept by Henry Parry Liddon of a Tour Taken with C. L. Dodgson in the Summer of 1867*, ed. Morton N. Cohen (1979).

19 July (Friday)
... In the late evening Dodgson insisted on our going out in quest of the New Jews Synagogue which we found. ... A discussion with him on our way home as to the duty of maintaining the rule of saying the Daily Morning and Evening Service.

20 July (Saturday)
Berlin–Potsdam. After breakfast went with Dodgson to the Jews Synagogue.

22 July (Monday)
Dantzig. ... After breakfast we went to see the Cathedral of Marienkirche: and spent 3 hours within it and one hour on the Top of the Spires.

23 July (Tuesday)
Dantzig–Königsberg. ... Bad stomach-ache and diarrhoea at going to bed. ... At 12.30 Dodgson sent for a Dr Wohlgemuth – so severe were my spasms. He put on a piece of blotting paper soaked in spirits of mustard, and gave me some morphia powder, and quantities of camomile tea.

24 July (Wednesday)
Königsberg. ... I went with Dodgson to see the Börse-Garten where there was military music.

25 July (Thursday)
Königsberg. ... Dodgson went to the Theatre.[4]

28 July (Sunday)
St Petersburg. ... After church a long argument with Dodgson.[5]

31 July (Wednesday)
St Petersburg. ... Dodgson not well during the night.

7 August (Wednesday)
Nijni Novgorod. ... Dodgson ... to the Russian theatre, where ... [he] saw a burlesque of Aladdin and his lamp.[6]

9 August (Friday)
Moscow. ... wrote [a letter] ... and did accounts during the morning, while Dodgson went to the Bank. ... Dodgson ... went to the Theatre.

11 August (Sunday)

Moscow. Dodgson did not get up until 9.30 so we went after breakfast to the English Church where I preached. . . .

13 August (Tuesday)

Moscow. . . . A great argument with Dodgson on the character of Russian religion – he thought it too external, etc. After dinner we went to the zoological Gardens. Spent some time in looking at the animals before we discovered where some Tyrolese were singing whom Dodgson much wished to hear.

14 August (Wednesday)

Moscow. Our whole morning was lost. Dodgson did not get up until 9.30. . . . After dinner . . . I had a warm argument with Dodgson about Prayers for the Departed: he appealed as usual to the general practice of the actual church of England.

15 August (Thursday)

. . . Up at 6 and left by the 8 o'clock train . . . for Kriokovo. . . . Thence drove to . . . [a] village . . . where we saw a Russian cottage inside as well as out. Dodgson drew it: but in this was lost $\frac{3}{4}$ of an hour. . . .

17 August (Saturday)

Troitska. . . . Dodgson bought some toys. . . .

26 August (Monday)

St Petersburg–Warsaw. . . . A good view of Jupiter through Dodgson's telescope.

1 September (Sunday)

Dresden. . . . Some discussion with Dodgson in the Evening. He thought the Roman Catholic Church like a Concert-room – and went out. Disliked the name Catholic because it connected us with Rome.

9 September (Monday)

Paris. . . . Dined with . . . Dodgson at the Café Européen. . . . [He] went to the Theatre.[8]

10 September (Tuesday)

Paris. . . . Dined at the Café Européen with Dodgson: went to 2 shops and with Dodgson heard some open air music in the Champs Elysées.

NOTES

1. Henry Parry Liddon (1829–90) was Student of Christ Church, Canon and Chancellor of St Paul's Cathedral, a distinguished theologian and gifted preacher. Dodgson's journal was privately printed as *Tour of 1867* (1928) and published in *The Russian Journal and Other Selections* . . . , ed. John Francis McDermott (1935).

2. Dodgson also records the incident: 'From Lille to Tournay we had the company of a family-party, the 2 children being about 6 and 4, and the younger one hardly ceased talking a moment the whole way. I made a drawing of the little creature, which was inspected by the family, and freely (and I think favorably) criticized by the original. She was sent back again by her mother, as they were leaving the carriage, to bid us "Bon soir" and to be kissed' (*The Russian Journal*, p. 74).

3. 'We spent about an hour in the cathedral,' Dodgson records (ibid., p. 76), 'which I will not attempt to describe further than by saying it was the most beautiful of all churches I have ever seen, or can imagine. If one could imagine the spirit of devotion embodied in any material form, it would be in such a building.'

4. Liddon did not share Dodgson's enthusiasm for the theatre; on the contrary, he wrote that he believed 'that the influence of the theatre . . . lies in the *direction* of sin' – John Octavius Johnston, *Life and Letters of Henry Parry Liddon* (1904) p. 284.

5. Dodgson does not record the 'argument', which must have been on some point of religion. For more on Liddon's and Dodgson's differing views of religion, see the Introduction to *The Russian Journal – II*.

6. 'In the evening I went . . . to the Nijni Theatre', Dodgson wrote (*The Russian Journal*, p. 97),

which was the plainest I ever saw – the only decoration inside being white wash. It was very large, and not more than a tenth full, so that it was remarkably cool and comfortable. The performance, being entirely in Russian, was a little beyond us, but by working away diligently at the play bill, with a pocket dictionary, at all intervals, we got a tolerable idea of what it was all about. The first and best piece was *Aladdin and the Wonderful Lamp*, a burlesque that contained some really first-rate acting, and very fair singing and dancing. I have never seen actors who attended more thoroughly to the drama and the other actors, and looked less at the audience. . . . The other pieces were *Cochin China, The Hussar's Daughter*.

7. ' . . . to the "Little Theatre" of Moscow', Dodgson wrote (ibid., p. 98), ' – really a large handsome building. There was a very good audience, and the pieces, *The Burgomaster's Wedding* and *A Woman's Secret*, won great applause, but neither pleased me so much as *Aladdin*. It was all in Russian.'

8. '. . . visited the "Theatre Vaudeville" in the evening to see *La Famille Benviton*, a capitally-acted play. . . . "Fanfan" was played by one of the cleverest children I ever saw . . . who could not have been more than 6 years old' (ibid., pp. 119–20).

An Unexpected Guest*

M. E. MANNERS[1]

'Mr Dobson wants to see you, miss.'

I was in the kitchen looking after the dinner, and did not feel that I particularly wished to see anybody.

'He wants a vote, or he is an agent for a special kind of tea', thought I. 'I don't know him; ask him to send a message.'

Presently the maid returned. –

'He says he is Mr Dodgson, of Oxford.'

'Lewis Carroll!' I exclaimed; and somebody else had to superintend the cooking that day.

My apologies were soon made and cheerfully accepted. I believe I was unconventional enough to tell the exact truth concerning my occupation, and matters were soon on a friendly footing. Indeed I may say at once that the stately college don we have heard so much about never made his appearance during our intercourse with him.

He did not talk *Alice*, of course; authors don't generally *talk* their books, I imagine; but it was undoubtedly Lewis Carroll who was present with us.

A portrait of Ellen Terry on the wall had attracted his attention, and one of the first questions he asked was, 'Do you ever go to the theatre?' I explained that such things were done, occasionally, even among Quakers, but they were not considered quite orthodox.

'Oh, well, then you will not be shocked, and I may venture to produce my photographs.' And out into the hall he went, and soon returned with a little black bag containing character-portraits of his child-friends, Isa and Nellie Bowman.

'Isa used to be Alice until she grew too big', he said. 'Nellie was one of the oyster-fairies, and Emsie, the tiny one of all, was the Dormouse.'

'When *Alice* was first dramatized,' he said, 'the poem of the "Walrus and the Carpenter" fell rather flat, for people did not know when it was finished, and did not clap in the right place; so I had to write a song for the ghosts of the oysters to sing, which made it all right.'

He was then on his way to London, to fetch Isa to stay with him at Eastbourne. She was evidently a great favourite, and had visited him

* From *Life and Letters*, pp. 399–402.

before. Of that earlier time he said: – 'When people ask me why I have never married, I tell them I have never met the young lady whom I could endure for a fortnight – but Isa and I got on so well together that I said I should keep her a month, the length of the honeymoon, and we didn't get tired of each other.'

Nellie afterwards joined her sister 'for a few days', but the days spread to some weeks, for the poor little dormouse developed scarlet fever, and the elder children had to be kept out of harm's way until fear of infection was over.

Of Emsie he had a funny little story to tell. He had taken her to the Aquarium, and they had been watching the seals coming up dripping out of the water. With a very pitiful look she turned to him and said, 'Don't they give them any towels?' [The same little girl commiserated the bear, because it had got no tail.]²

Asked to stay to dinner, he assured us that he never took anything in the middle of the day but a glass of wine and a biscuit; but he would be happy to sit down with us, which he accordingly did and kindly volunteered to carve for us. His offer was gladly accepted, but the appearance of a rather diminutive piece of neck of mutton was somewhat of a puzzle to him. He had evidently never seen such a joint in his life before, and had frankly to confess that he did not know how to set about carving it. Directions only made things worse, and he bravely cut it to pieces in entirely the wrong fashion, relating meanwhile the story of a shy young woman who had been asked to carve a fowl, the joints of which had been carefully wired together beforehand by his too attentive friends.

The task and the story both finished, our visitor gazed on the mangled remains, and remarked quaintly: 'I think it is just as well I don't want anything, for I don't know where I should find it.'

At least one member of the party felt she could have managed matters better; but that was a point of very little consequence.

A day or two after the first call came a note saying that he would be taking Isa home before long, and if we would like to see her he would stop on the way again.

Of course we were only too delighted to have the opportunity, and, though the visit was postponed more than once, it did take place early in August, when he brought both Isa and Nellie up to town to see a performance of *Sweet Lavender*. It is needless to remark that we took care, this time, to be provided with something at once substantial and carvable.

The children were bright, healthy, happy and childlike little maidens, quite devoted to their good friend, whom they called 'Uncle'; and very interesting it was to see them together.

But he did not allow any undue liberties either, as a little incident showed.

He had been describing a particular kind of collapsible tumbler, which you put in your pocket and carried with you for use on a railway journey.

'There now,' he continued, turning to the children, 'I forgot to bring it with me after all.'

'Oh Goosie,' broke in Isa; 'you've been talking about that tumbler for days, and now you have forgotten it.'

He pulled himself up, and looked at her steadily with an air of grave reproof.

Much abashed, she hastily substituted a very subdued 'Uncle' for the objectionable 'Goosie', and the matter dropped.

The principal anecdote on this occasion was about a dog which had been sent into the sea after sticks. He brought them back very properly for some time, and then there appeared to be a little difficulty, and he returned swimming in a very curious manner. On closer inspection it appeared that he had caught hold of his own tail by mistake, and was bringing it to land in triumph.

This was told with the utmost gravity, and though we had been requested beforehand not to mention 'Lewis Carroll's' books, the temptation was too strong. I could not help saying to the child next to me –

'That was like the Whiting, wasn't it?'

Our visitor, however, took up the remark, and seemed quite willing to talk about it.

'When I wrote that,' he said, 'I believed that whiting really did have their tails in their mouths, but I have since been told that fishmongers put the tail through the eye, not in the mouth at all.'[3]

NOTES

1. 'Wonderland', a poem in eleven traditional stanzas by 'One Who Loves "Alice"', appeared in the Christmas number 1885 of *Sylvia's Home Journal*. It was the first poem by Mary Emmeline Manners (1858–1941) to appear in print. On 4 December 1885, Dodgson recorded in his *Diaries* (p. 439) that he 'received a cutting from *Sylvia's Home Journal* with a very pretty poem on "Wonderland"'; and on the following day, he wrote to Miss Manners (*Letters*, p. 607) thanking her for 'the very sweet verses'. A friendship grew up between the two, and Miss Manners was responsible for procuring Dodgson's agreement for her brother's manufacturing firm to produce the *Looking-Glass* Biscuit Tin. Miss Manners went on to write more verse, later collected in Mary E. Manners, *The Bishop and the Caterpillar and Other Verses* (1943). 'Wonderland' is reprinted in *Life and Letters*, pp. 247–50.

2. Bracketed sentence is by S. D. Collingwood.

3. On 17 July 1889, Dodgson wrote in his *Diaries* (p. 472), 'Fetched Isa from London on a visit. Pause at Croydon to make acquaintance with Miss M. E. Manners, whom I have only known by correspondence as yet.' On 10 August he recorded (p. 473), 'I took Isa and Nellie ... to town, to see [Pinero's] *Sweet Lavender*, and ... we paused on the way to lunch with Miss Manners.' Dodgson 'was not a very good carver', S. D. Collingwood writes (*Life and Letters*, p. 403), 'for Miss Bremer also describes a little difficulty he had – this time with the pastry: "An amusing incident occurred when he

was at lunch with us. He was requested to serve some pastry, and, using a knife, as it was evidently rather hard, the knife penetrated the d'oyley beneath – and his consternation was extreme when he saw the slice of linen and lace he served as an addition to the tart!"'

He 'sorely tried the patience of his publisher'*

CHARLES MORGAN[1]

[T]he Rev. Charles Lutwidge Dodgson, a mathematical don at Christ Church, made arrangement with the Clarendon Press to produce *Alice* at his expense, and the first references to it in the Macmillan files are on the subject of binding. There was never an author more elaborately careful than Lewis Carroll for the details of production or one that can have more sorely tried the patience of his publisher. The beginning was harmless enough. He wanted *Alice* to be a table-book and thought that red would be most pleasing to childish eyes; the edges were to be cut smooth but to be ungilded – though he afterwards liked the gilding used on a new impression. He was anxious, he said, to have fifty of the two thousand copies as soon as possible, as his young friends were all growing out of their childhood so fast, and one copy was to be bound in white vellum for Alice Liddell. The edition, an octavo, was peacefully printed by the end of June 1865, but, when forty-eight copies had been given away, a storm broke. The author, dissatisfied with the printing of the text and of the Tenniel illustrations, recalled them, cancelled the whole edition, and shipped off the 1952 unbound sheets to Messrs Appleton of New York.[2] Some of the presentation copies were not returned and have since made fantastic prices at auction, with the result that a year seldom passes even now in which no one sends to the Macmillans a copy plainly marked '86th thousand' and an offer to part with it for a few hundred pounds. There have been bibliographers, too, who have maintained as contrary to human nature that a man so sensitive to the appearance of his book should have allowed the defective sheets to go to New York, but it was by no means contrary to Dodgson's nature. The correspondence is full of evidence that supplies which did not come up to his standard were considered by him quite good enough for Americans, of whose

* From *The House of Macmillan* (1944) pp. 79–81, 107–14.

taste his opinion was low. This opinion was confirmed in 1888. The coloured pictures in the first printing of *The Nursery 'Alice'* were condemned by him as too gaudy. No copy, he said, was to be sold in England; all were to be offered to America. They were offered, and declined as not being gaudy enough.

When the 1952 of the first printing were safely out of sight, Richard Clay prepared another edition, dated 1866. The sales were not rapid. Dodgson was nervous of printing another three thousand copies in the same year, and thought it would be some time before he again indulged in paper and print; nevertheless, he had 'a floating idea' for a sequel. Next year, the other half of him produced *An Elementary Treatise on Determinants and their Application to Simultaneous Linear Equations and Algebraical Geometry* – 'for the use of beginners'. While they were beginning, *Alice* loitered in her tenth thousand, and the author was pleased to find that he had made in two years a profit of £250 on his original outlay of £350, which had included the illustrations. Not that he greatly cared how many copies were sold; it mattered to him only that each copy should be flawless. He was fully prepared to miss the Christmas market rather than hurry an edition, and yet for all his care mistakes crept in. They became an obsession; he felt them as an old lady feels draughts. Uneven inking, cropped margins, irregular levels of opposite pages – he missed nothing. Genuinely faulty copies, with pages in the wrong order, found their way to him as they do to all authors, and it struck him as exceedingly odd that these defects had a habit of appearing in his specially bound copies. It was less surprising than he supposed. The binders were called upon to produce at the same time a large ordinary impression and fifty copies in red, twenty in blue, twenty in green, two in vellum, one with edges uncut, one with primrose edges, and one with a piece of mirror on the cover – and the binders' heads span. The publishers' also: 'Have you done any more with coloured inks and papers?' 'Have you ever considered the effect of *gold* type?' and when, in 1869, he produced his book of verses, *Phantasmagoria*, he wanted one edition, containing an Oxford squib, to be sold for 5s. 6d., and another, without it, for sixpence less.

. . . with Dodgson you were never safe, his genius for the discovery of error was infinitely retrospective, and in 1878 he observed, in a copy of the forty-second thousand, that both the Kings had vanished from the chess-diagram. This was present calamity – but how far back did it go? A slip must at once be inserted, and if the Kings were found to have escaped long ago the fact must be advertised. When they had been caught again he turned his attention, moral and mathematical, to the conditions of the trade. His trouble was, first, that booksellers had the lion's share of what the public paid for a book, and, secondly, that their system of underselling one another was preposterous, as indeed it was. He calculated that, from the sale of a 6s. copy of *Alice*, the author received 1s. 2d., the publisher 10d. and the bookseller 2s. His view was that the author should have 2s. 2d., the publisher still 10d., and the bookseller be content with 1s. The suggestion that booksellers might, in these circumstances, refuse to stock his books did not intimidate him. In that case, he proposed to notify the public that they could obtain his works carriage free from the publisher. As a skirmish in the attack on the old discount system which Frederick Macmillan was to carry through to the Net Book Agreement, this outburst of Lewis Carroll's has its historical place. It has to be remembered that his books were, by his own wish, published 'on commission' – that is to say at his own and not the publisher's risk.[3] 'A former pupil of mine', he said in one of his letters to the firm, 'wants you to publish a book for him. He seems to be suffering from a nervous fear, not uncommon to authors, that publishers are an inscrutable race, who make money vanish as if by magic, and never render up any profit to their victims. What *other* publishers may do I know not: but I gave him full assurance that he was in good hands.' What Lewis Carroll understood, though few others do so, is that in persuading a great house to publish for him on commission he was rarely fortunate. . . .

Lewis Carroll was not only in good hands; he was, while his books prospered, the most fortunate of men, for he appears to have delighted in the detail of production from which other writers wish to be exempt. As a boy he had provided earthworms with weapons in order that they might fight the more intelligently, and throughout his life he had, with an intense shyness, a passion for little changes, little inventions, oddities of all kinds. For *The Hunting of the Snark* (1876) he made a suggestion more practical than most of his. Plain white paper wrappers had hitherto been put upon his books. Now he asked that the title used lengthways on the spine of the book itself be repeated on the wrapper in sloping letters which might be easily read when the book stood upright on a shelf. This plan, which may claim a share in the ancestry of the elaborate wrapper now called a 'jacket', made up most of the satisfaction that Carroll had out of *The Snark*, for reviewers were hard on it and buyers reluctant. But the author was undeterred. Books, ingenuities and trouble poured from him. When he wished to go to a theatre, Macmillan's were asked to buy the tickets – on the extreme right, if possible, because he was deaf in the right ear, and at all costs not in the centre of the first rows because, from there, his line of sight was interrupted by waving conductors. When he sent his watches to be mended, his publishers were asked to retrieve, and did retrieve them, by what he called 'a trusty and resolute messenger'. And he knew better than anyone else how to tie up parcels. He supplied a diagram, which long hung in the post-room at Bedford Street, showing how the string on all parcels should be, and how the string on all his parcels must be, knotted. This queer love of telling a lion how to roar and a cat how to lap milk grew upon him. *Doublets*, a word-puzzle of 1879, was to be priced at 'Five Groats' and *Euclid and his Modern Rivals* ought, he thought, to have a few words added to its title to indicate that it was not a funny book. Dodgson and Carroll were becoming a little entangled. The binders, perhaps undesignedly, had their own back when, upon his asking for a dummy copy of *Doublets* (for he wished to invent more puzzles on its blank sheets), they filled the binding with pages from assorted works on religion – an incongruity that touched Dodgson–Carroll on the quick. For *Lawn Tennis Tournaments. The True Method of Assigning Prizes, with a proof of the Fallacy of the Present Method* (1883, price sixpence), he used his own name – 'my usual course with *mathematical* books' – and mathematical it was indeed.

Having gone so far with this strange man – in many respects so likable and yet, with his itch for interference, so sharp an irritant – it is, perhaps, worth while to break chronological sequence and go with him to the end. *A Tangled Tale*, written at the request of Miss Yonge, was slashed by the reviewers and never accepted by the public as part of the canon.[4] A reproduction of the manuscript book, *Alice's Adventures Under Ground*, upon which the first *Alice* had been based, contained the author's own illustrations, but had little success. Carroll blamed the uneven printing. *The Game of Logic* – a game with cards and counters – led him into corresponding distress: here it was the Oxford production that was at fault, and there had to be a reprint by Clay. Next he undertook a children's book, grimly named *Bumble-bee Bogo's Budget*, written by 'a Retired Judge' – a friend of his named Synge.[5] He gave as much attention to it as to his own work – writing one morning to say that the author was anxious to have the book out and the next morning to explain that he would not have his trouble brought to nothing by Macmillan's hurrying to save a few days. When Carroll and Dodgson took in a partner and so could speak with three voices simultaneously, life in Bedford Street could not be tranquil. Worse was to come. In thousands of copies of his books he had inserted at the end of his list of works a 'Caution' in which he had disavowed authorship of a story, *The Land of Idleness*, published in a magazine over his signature. He had not written it, the 'Caution' explained; he had done no more than forward it to the editor on behalf of a foreign lady, whose name he gave. Now, when it was too late, he found he had given the name of the wrong lady. There was no remedy but to insert thousands of erratum slips. Gradually, as the years pass, one begins to think that to Carroll erratum slips were a form of pleasurable vice.

Two hundred and fifty copies of *Curiosa Mathematica* appear to have come through unscathed, but *The Nursery 'Alice'* was a disaster. The first printing was doomed to America for the reason already mentioned – that the colours were too bright; America refused them; nevertheless another ten thousand must be done. Then the covers were wrong: the thickness of the book had not been allowed for and the March Hare was out of centre. When all this had been put right, still the early copies were returned. They cracked when he opened them; their leaves curled obstinately.

Of all this Carroll, not without protest, bore the cost, but he was not a little perturbed. His books were not selling. Neither *Sylvie and Bruno* nor *Sylvie and Bruno Concluded* fluttered the nurseries, and their author thought that the position might be saved if only a good morning paper could be induced to fold a leaflet about the book inside each copy of a day's issue. By June 1890, he felt that somehow he must have a larger share of the proceeds of his work. The whole problem was complicated by his having kept to his own special terms of sale to booksellers, though by this time the firm were applying the Net System to other publications. There was nothing for it – Dodgson had to amend the terms of sale printed in all his works.

It is pleasant to recall that, though he was never again to enjoy success comparable with that of *Alice*, and though, with the possible exception of his *Euclid*, none of his mathematical works was of much value to mathematicians, his devotion to logic brought him in the end some reward. *Symbolic Logic, Part I*, was a development of the *Game of Logic*. It appealed to people who had what would now be called a cross-word mind, and had much greater success than might have been expected. This was in 1896. Part Two was never published.[6] The last work produced by the firm for Lewis Carroll was 'a tale for tiny boys', *The Lost Plum Cake*, by E. G. Wilcox (his cousin, Mrs Egerton Allen).[7] In January 1898, he died. To study the record of his publishing adventures is to be persuaded that he would have been better – on all grounds except, possibly, those of enjoyment – to have held firm to authorship. He wasted his own and everyone else's time by his detailed wilfulness. He wrote so many letters about printing and binding and prices that he had little time left to write the books themselves. A publisher might have saved it for him. But not even a Scottish publisher could have cared as desperately as he – and desperately is the word – to give the public perfection. This was his theme-song, and his justification.

Nor must it be forgotten that he made, or intended to make, noble amends to his publishers, for Collingwood's *Life* quotes the following passage from a pamphlet explaining his trade terms entitled *The Profits of Authorship*: 'The publisher contributes about as much as the bookseller in time and bodily labour, but in mental toil and trouble a great deal more. I speak with some personal knowledge of the matter, having myself, for some twenty years, inflicted on that most patient and painstaking firm, Messrs Macmillan & Co., about as much wear and worry as ever publishers have lived through. The day when they undertake a book for me is a *dies nefastus* for them. From that day till the book is out – an interval of some two or three years on an average – there is no pause in "the pelting of the pitiless storm"[8] of directions and questions on every conceivable detail. To say that every question gets a courteous and thoughtful reply – that they are still outside a lunatic asylum – and that they still regard me with some degree of charity – is to speak volumes in praise of their good temper and of their health, bodily and mental.'

It is very much in the tradition of the Snark that, although the *Life* mentions this pamphlet as having been published by Macmillan's in 1884, the bibliographers who faithfully include it in their lists are also compelled to add that no copy of it has ever been found.[9]

NOTES

1. Charles Morgan (1894–1958), novelist and drama critic for *The Times*, worked for and advised the firm of Macmillan and wrote the official history of the house. The members of the house that Dodgson dealt with primarily were: the co-founder Alexander Macmillan (1818–96), George Lillie Craik (1837–1905), a partner, and Alexander's nephew, (Sir) Frederick Orridge Macmillan (1851–1936).

2. The myth that Dodgson was dissatisfied with the printing of the first edition of *Alice* was exploded long ago. It was Tenniel – not Dodgson – who was dissatisfied and demanded the reprinting. Dodgson capitulated. For the details, see Harry Morgan Ayres, *Carroll's Alice* (1936); W. H. Bond, 'The Publication of *Alice's Adventures in Wonderland*', *Harvard Library Bulletin*, 10 (1956) 306–24; and Warren Weaver, 'The First Edition of *Alice's Adventures in Wonderland*: A Census', *Papers of the Bibliographical Society of America*, 65 (First Quarter, 1971) 1–40. Tenniel himself later wrote to one of the Dalziels, 'I protested so strongly against the disgraceful printing that . . . [Dodgson] *cancelled the edition*' (MS, Huntington Library, California).

3. We have no evidence that Macmillan published Dodgson on commission 'by his own wish'. The extensive correspondence between the author and the publisher reveals no discontent about the original agreement through the long relationship. Macmillan published 'on commission' from the very start of the firm's existence, and it may just as easily have been Alexander Macmillan's wish not to risk too much on an unknown author that brought the commission agreement into being.

4. Dodgson admired both the novels and children's stories by Charlotte Mary Yonge (1823–1901) and was delighted to meet her on 3 May 1866, at a luncheon party in Oxford (*Diaries*, p. 243). On the following day he photographed Miss Yonge and her mother (Gernsheim, plates 56, 57). 'Romantic Problems: A Tangled Tale', the early title of *A Tangled Tale*, consisting of ten 'knots', appeared in the *Monthly Packet* between April 1880 and March 1885 and as a book in late 1885. 'The writer's intention was to embody in each Knot (like the medicine so dextrously, but ineffectually, concealed in the jam of our early childhood) one or more mathematical questions . . . for the amusement, and possible edification, of the fair readers of . . . [the *Monthly Packet*]', Dodgson wrote in the Preface. On 27 March 1886 Dodgson wrote to Macmillan, 'Many thanks . . . for a long series of notices, condemnatory of *Tangled Tale*. . . . Spite of this chorus of blame, it is selling pretty well, don't you think?' – *Lewis Carroll and the House of Macmillan*, ed. Morton N. Cohen and Anita Gandolfo (1987) p. 199.

5. William Webb Follett Synge (1826–91), diplomat, author, was a neighbour of the

Dodgsons in Guildford; his friendship with Dodgson flourished at Guildford and at Eastbourne after the Synges moved to the seaside in the eighties. Synge's health was in decline when Dodgson undertook to see his children's book through the press, and both were eager to see the book published while Synge was still alive. It appeared in 1887. For more on Dodgson and Synge, see *Letters*, esp. p. 175.

6. *Symbolic Logic, Part II*, was already in printer's proof when Dodgson died. John Cook Wilson (1849–1915), Fellow of Oriel, Wykeham Professor of Logic, and a distinguished Oxford teacher, in a lecture he gave shortly after Dodgson's death, referred to the unpublished second part of *Symbolic Logic*, of which Dodgson, 'with his usual kindness, sent me the most important of the proof sheets'. These proofs of the book, together with other proof sheets at Christ Church, Dodgson's diagrams and logic workbooks at Princeton and Texas, form the basis of *Lewis Carroll's Symbolic Logic, Part I and Part II*, ed. W. W. Bartley III (1977), a work that has brought about a favourable reassessment of Dodgson's contribution to logical studies.

7. Dodgson's wrote the introduction to his cousin's story: he dated it Christmas 1897, and it was the last of his writings to appear in print in his lifetime. Dodgson's book of verse *Three Sunsets and Other Poems*, with twelve 'fairy-fancies' by E. Gertrude Thomson, appeared posthumously in 1898, but also published by Macmillan.

8. *King Lear*, III.iv.25.

9. For a more detailed account of the Dodgson–Macmillan saga (and one hopes, a more objective and more accurate one), see Morton N. Cohen, 'Lewis Carroll and the House of Macmillan', *Browning Institute Studies*, 7 (1979) 31–70. For the actual correspondence between author and publisher, see *Lewis Carroll and the House of Macmillan*.

'Sir, I never do that for any one'*

HOWARD HOPLEY[1]

In the autumn of 1895 the Vicar of Eastbourne was to have preached my Harvest Sermon at Westham, a village five miles away; but something or other intervened, and in the middle of the week I learned he could not come. A mutual friend suggested my asking Mr Dodgson, who was then in Eastbourne, to help me, and I went with him to his rooms. I was quite a stranger to Mr Dodgson; but knowing from hearsay how reluctant he usually was to preach, I apologized and explained my position – with Sunday so near at hand. After a moment's hesitation he consented, and in a most genial manner made me feel quite at ease as to the abruptness of my petition. On the morrow he came over to my vicarage, and made friends with my daughters,

* From *Life and Letters*, pp. 327–9.

teaching them some new manner of playing croquet, and writing out for them puzzles and anagrams that he had composed. . . .

On Sunday our grand old church was crowded, and, although our villagers are mostly agricultural labourers, yet they breathlessly listened to a sermon forty minutes long, and apparently took in every word of it. It was quite extempore, in very simple words, and illustrated by some delightful and most touching stories of children. I only wish there had been a shorthand-writer there.

In the vestry after service, while he was signing his name in the Preachers' Book, a church officer handed him a bit of paper. 'Mr Dodgson, would you very kindly write your name on that?' 'Sir!' drawing himself up sternly – 'Sir, I never do that for any one' – and then, more kindly, 'You see, if I did it for one, I must do it for all.'

NOTE

1. Dodgson met Howard Hopley (1828?–1922), Vicar of Westham, Hastings, and author of *Under Egyptian Palms* (1869), through his friends the Schusters, whose children he had been teaching logic in Eastbourne. On 25 September 1895, he journeyed to Westham to arrange with Hopley 'about the sermon I have undertaken'. On the 29th he went over to Westham to preach. 'Winnie Schuster came with me. We went by train in the afternoon. I took as text Psalms 116. 11' (*Diaries*, p. 519).

'The stillest and shyest full-grown man'*

MARK TWAIN[1]

We met a great many other interesting people, among them Lewis Carroll, author of the immortal *Alice* – but he was only interesting to look at, for he was the stillest and shyest full-grown man I have ever met except 'Uncle Remus'. Doctor [George] MacDonald and several other lively talkers were present, and the talk went briskly on for a couple of hours, but Carroll sat still all the while except that now and then he answered a question. His answers were brief. I do not remember that he elaborated any of them.

* *Mark Twain's Autobiography* (1924) II, 232–3.

NOTE

1. On 26 July 1879 Dodgson wrote in his *Diaries* (p. 382), 'Called on the MacDonalds.
. . . Met Mr Clemens (Mark Twain), with whom I was pleased and interested.'

'I heard mysterious noises under the table'*

GEORGE BADEN-POWELL[1]

My first introduction to the author of *Through the Looking-Glass* was about the year 1870 or 1871, and under appropriate conditions! I was then coaching at Oxford with the well-known Rev. E. Hatch, and was on friendly terms with his bright and pretty children. Entering his house one day, and facing the dining-room, I heard mysterious noises under the table, and saw the cloth move as if some one was hiding. Children's legs revealed it as no burglar, and there was nothing for it but to crawl upon them, roaring as a lion. Bursting in upon them in their stronghold under the table, I was met by the staid but amused gaze of a reverend gentleman. Frequently afterwards did I see and hear 'Lewis Carroll' entertaining the youngsters in his inimitable way.

We became friends, and greatly did I enjoy intercourse with him over various Oxford matters. In later years, at one time I saw much of him, in quite another *rôle* – namely that of ardent sympathy with the, as he thought, ill-treated and deserted islanders of Tristan da Cunha. His brother, it will be remembered, had voluntarily been left at the island with a view to ministering to the spiritual and educational needs of the few settlers, and sent home such graphic accounts and urgent demands for aid, 'Lewis Carroll' spared no pains to organize assistance and relief. At his insistence I brought the matter before Government and the House of Commons, and from that day to this frequent communication has been held with the islanders, and material assistance has been rendered them – thanks to the warm heart of 'Lewis Carroll'.

* From *Life and Letters*, pp. 344–5.

NOTE

1. When in 1883 Dodgson was earnestly seeking aid for Tristan da Cunha, he personally approached one public figure after another. No one was more helpful than

Sir George Smyth Baden-Powell (1847–98), MP and Joint-Commissioner to inquire into the administration of the West Indian Colonies.

'They were listening to him open-mouthed'*

MRS J. N. BENNIE[1]

Mrs Bennie . . . gives a charming account of a meeting with Lewis Carroll at Whitby in 1870. At the hotel breakfast table, before her children and their nurse had come down, Mrs Bennie had encountered a grave and distinguished-looking stranger who had passed the compliments of the day but, otherwise, had seemed shy and reserved. Mrs Bennie writes,

Next morning, nurse took our little twin daughters in front of the sea. I went out a short time afterwards and found them with my friend of the table, who was seated between them, with his knees covered with minute toys. They were listening to him open-mouthed, and, seeing their great delight, I motioned to him to go on. A most charming story he told them, about sea urchins and ammonites. When it was over I said, 'You must be the author of *Alice in Wonderland*?' He laughed and replied, 'My dear madam, my name is Dodgson and *Alice's Adventures* was written by Lewis Carroll.' I replied, 'Then you must have borrowed the name, for only he could have told the story as you have done.' After some sparring he admitted the fact.

* From Langford Reed, 'The Droll and the Don', *Listener*, 3 Feb 1932, p. 171.

NOTE

1. On 4 September 1868, Dodgson in Whitby 'took a stroll with a gentleman I had first met at the table d'hôte . . . and who turns out to be a Mr Bennie. . . . He has two very attractive looking children here, twins (Mary and Elizabeth, alias Minnie and Doe), and I proposed presenting them with a copy of *Alice* but found they had it already.' On the following day he took the Bennies to the local photographer and supervised their being photographed. On 15 January 1870, Dodgson records, he went to Leicester for his third visit with the Bennies. 'Our brief acquaintance at Whitby', he writes, 'was resumed at a point considerably further on than where we left off. Minnie and Doe, [born] August 17, 1856, are (though as yet indistinguishable to me)

wonderfully beautiful.' On the 18th, still with the Bennies, he writes, 'I have at last learned to see some shadowy points of difference between the faces of my lovely little friends.' On 12 September 1877, Dodgson received a visit from Mr and Mrs Bennie in Eastbourne; and during the following August the Bennies came again to Eastbourne: 'the twins not so much alike as in the olden times'. Just over three years before he died, on 18 September 1895, Dodgson recorded that 'Mr Bennie, Minnie, and Doe came to tea' (*Diaries*, pp. 274, 286, 372). The father of the twins was James Noble Bennie (1832?–99), Vicar of St Mary's, Leicester.

Extracts from Letters to the Family upon Dodgson's Death*

From G. E. Jelf[1]

It is quite a shock to me to see in the paper to-day the death of your dear, good brother, to whom we owe so much of the brightening of our lives with pure, innocent fun. Personally I feel his loss very much indeed. We were together in old Christ Church days from 1852 onwards; and he was always such a loyal, faithful friend to me. I rejoice to think of the *serious* talks we had together – of the grand, brave way in which he used the opportunities he had as a man of humour, to reach the consciences of a host of readers – of his love for children – his simplicity of heart – of his care for servants – his spiritual care for them. Who can doubt that he was fully prepared for a change however sudden – for the one clear call which took him away from us? Yet the world seems darker for his going; we can only get back our brightness by realizing Who gave him all his talent, all his mirth of heart – the One who never leaves us.

From Frederick Harrison[2]

The occasional visits that I received from your late brother showed me a side of his nature which to my mind was more interesting and more worthy of remembrance even than his wonderful and delightful

* From *Life and Letters*, pp. 351–4.

humour – I mean his intense sympathy with all who suffer and are in need.

He came to see me several times on sundry errands of mercy, and it has been a lesson to me through life to remember his zeal to help others in difficulty, his boundless generosity, and his inexhaustible patience with folly and error.

My young daughter, like all young people in civilized countries, was brought up on his beautiful fancies and humours. But for my part I remember him mainly as a sort of missionary to all in need. We all alike grieve, and offer you our heartfelt sympathy.

From Bartholomew Price[3]

I feel his removal from among us as the loss of an old and dear friend and pupil, to whom I have been most warmly attached ever since he was with me at Whitby, reading mathematics, in, I think, 1853–44 years ago! And 44 years of uninterrupted friendship. . . . I was pleased to read yesterday in *The Times* newspaper the kindly obituary notice: perfectly just and true; appreciative, as it should be, as to the unusual combination of deep mathematical ability and taste with the genius that led to the writing of *Alice's Adventures*.

From an unidentified Oxford friend

Mr Dodgson was ever the kindest and gentlest of friends, bringing sunshine into the house with him. We shall mourn his loss deeply, and my two girls are quite overcome with grief. All day memories of countless acts of kindness shown to me, and to people I have known, have crowded my mind, and I feel it almost impossible to realize that he has passed beyond the reach of our gratitude and affection.

Extracts from some of his child-friends, 'now grown up', also unidentified

[i] How beautiful to think of the track of light and love he has left behind him, and the amount of happiness he brought into the lives of all those he came in contact with! I shall never forget all his kindness to us, from the time he first met us as little mites in the railway train, and one feels glad to have had the privilege of knowing him.

[ii] He was to me a dear and true friend, and it has been my great privilege to see a good deal of him ever since I was a tiny child, and especially during the last two years. I cannot tell you how much we

shall miss him here. Christ Church without Mr Dodgson will be a strange place, and it is difficult to realize it even while we listen to the special solemn anthems of hymns to his memory in our cathedral.

[iii] It must be quite sixteen years now since he first made friends with my sister and myself as children on the beach at Eastbourne, and since then his friendship has been and must always be one of my valued possessions. It culminated, I think, in the summer of 1892 – the year when he brought me to spend a very happy Sunday at Guildford. I had not seen him before, that year, for some time; and it was then, I think, that the childish delight in his kindness, and pride in his friendship, changed into higher love and reverence, when in our long walks over the downs I saw more and more into the great tenderness and gentleness of his nature.

NOTES

1. George Edward Jelf (1834–1908), who in 1857 took over from Dodgson as Sub-Librarian of Christ Church, later became Canon of Rochester and Master of Charterhouse.

2. On 24 December 1883, Dodgson spent a number of hours 'sending to my friends about 180 copies of a letter (printed) about the Dymeses' (*Diaries*, p. 422). In this printed circular, Dodgson refers to Thomas Jamieson Dymes (1830?–1913), Oxford graduate, classical scholar, author, schoolmaster, as 'a friend of mine who is in great distress'. The letter goes on to say that Dymes, having lost his post as under-master at a boys' school, has fallen heavily in debt in his efforts to support his wife and eight children, and 'found himself, a few months ago, in a state of insolvency'. The circular seeks employment for Dymes and other members of his family. Frederic Harrison (1831–1923), the author and positivist, was another friend of Dymes who came forward to help, and in that connection Dodgson and Harrison met and joined efforts. The difficulty that beset Dymes must have been resolved: Dodgson records, before long, that he called on the Dymes family, comfortably established in London, and dined with them (Diaries, p. 437).

3. Bartholomew Price (1818–98) was Sedleian Professor of Natural Philosophy, later Master of Pembroke College. He was the author of treatises on differential and infinitesimal calculus. He was Dodgson's tutor at Christ Church and coached him through his first in mathematics. He later became a close friend and adviser.

Index

Numbers in bold type represent main biographical entries. See *Works* under *Dodgson, Charles Lutwidge*, for all titles published under both C. L. Dodgson and Lewis Carroll.